What they said about
Rule No. 5: No Sex on the Bus

Hilarious observations about European travel . . .
  Travel & Leisure (USA)

(Thacker) takes readers along for a jolly ride.
  USA Today

Thacker's relentless sense of humour and eye for the
ridiculous win the reader over.
  Australian Bookseller and Publisher

I laughed my guts out.
  Andrew Caldwell

Love your book. I bought it yesterday then took the rest
of the day off to read it.
  Amy Rouse

It's the best roll-around-the-floor-laughing book I have
EVER read!
  Alison Goodall

Thanks for letting me relive the best time of my life.
  Colleen Roth

I picked up *Rule No. 5* at Sydney airport for some in-flight
reading and laughed so hard passengers were turning around
in their seats to make sure I wasn't having a fit.
  Sam McPherson

It took me a week to get past the first chapter because
I was splitting my sides so much.
  Reg Quelch

My kids kept telling me to stop laughing because they
couldn't hear the telly.
  David Leikhold

PLANES, TRAINS
& ELEPHANTS

BRIAN THACKER

ALLEN&UNWIN

First published in 2002

Allen & Unwin
83 Alexander Street
Crows Nest NSW 2065
Australia
Phone: (61 2) 8425 0100
Fax: (61 2) 9906 2218
Email: info@allenandunwin.com
Web: www.allenandunwin.com

National Library of Australia
Cataloguing-in-Publication entry:

Thacker, Brian, 1962- .
    Planes, trains and elephants.
    ISBN 1 86508 884 6
    1. Thacker, Brian, 1962 – Journeys.
    2. Travel – Anecdotes.
    I. Title.
    910.4

Cover and text design by Brian Thacker
Typeset by Pauline Haas
Printed by McPherson's Printing Group

10 9 8 7 6 5 4 3 2

To Jasmine Grace Thacker

Donkeys, Ferries & Toboggans

Whether you're setting out as an explorer or a tourist, the journey often proves to be more exciting than the place you wind up in. Not to mention more alarming, entertaining, spectacular, dangerous or farcical. All of which is pretty closely connected to your chosen mode of transport—from pottering along on a stubborn donkey to hurtling down a hill totally out of control on what seemed such a cute, wooden toboggan.

I've always liked the journey. Ever since I travelled down the Ovens River in the Victorian Alps on a rubber inner tube as a skinny ten-year-old, I've been on the lookout for different ways to get around. Once I stepped onto a plane for the obligatory Big Trip OS, my lively interest in travelling became a hopeless addiction.

I jumped into travelling feet first by hitchhiking around the European continent for seven months. After two years spent working in London, it was only the dodgy weather and my craving for Cherry Ripes that brought me back to Australia. I lasted two years before my very itchy feet coaxed me onto a plane again and back to Europe—this time as a tour leader for busloads of drunk Aussies and Kiwis.* For me this was perfect. I was now getting *paid* to travel (albeit only from one bar to the next). In between the summer tours I even managed to talk my way into a job as a ski guide in the Swiss Alps. My battered liver forced me to retreat to Australia again, but it didn't take long before I was poring over maps planning my next journey—should I go to Fiji this year or to Mongolia?

I haven't included all my journeys in this book—the ten-minute tuk tuk trip from my hotel in Bangkok to the local market (read: ten minutes of car horns and pollution after ten minutes of haggling over the price) didn't quite warrant an entire chapter. The journeys I'm going to tell you about are all special in different ways: some are seriously spectacular, others pretty funny, and a few very scary. For all sorts of reasons, these are journeys I'll never forget.

* See *Rule No 5: No Sex on the Bus*

Rowboat

Bright, Australia
January 1976

My oldest brother, Mick, was a gifted thief. There was no doubt about it. He was a joy to watch. I'd seen him walk out of a hobby shop with the biggest model aeroplane box on the shelf under his arm, looking calm and totally relaxed. He was good. But this was no plastic model. He wanted to steal a 1:1 scale aluminium rowboat. I was terrified. I was only thirteen. I didn't want to spend the rest of my life in jail. Or, worse, face the wrath of my father and his dreaded—and painfully effective—knuckle-bash to the top of the head. We'd already been in big trouble the week before. Well, we should have been, at least. I'd taken us all on a rather long journey down the river on our old car innertubes.

'How far do you reckon we could go down the river?' I'd asked Colin.

'Not too far, we've got Bruce.'

Bruce was the youngest brother. He had only just turned ten. I glanced down the river to the first set of rapids, 'I reckon we go all the way to Porepunkah and hitch back.'

Colin sighed, 'Dad will kill us.'

'I'll be all right,' Bruce chipped in.

'See,' I said, 'Anyway, we won't be away long.'

Try seven hours. I escaped the knuckle-bash to the head though. I blamed it all on Bruce.

So, here we were, promoting ourselves to a real boat. 'We're only borrowing it,' Mick said. He also promised we would return the boat when we had finished with it. That, however, turned out to be a little difficult.

My four brothers—Mick, Colin, Malcolm, Bruce—and I could barely fit into the small boat. There wasn't much need for the oars—or oarsmen, for that matter. Mick thought it was a good idea to steer the boat down the rapids.

It seemed like a smashing idea to begin with. We floated merrily down the Ovens River for half an hour. When I asked Mick how we would return the boat, he said we would row it back. 'It'll be easy,' he said. He was my older brother, so I didn't point out how ridiculous that was. Not because I respected his seniority, but because I didn't want a vicious whack on the back of the head.

There was another flaw in Mick's plan. Five boys turned out to be a bit too much for the little boat and it started to take on water. The river also became quite shallow and the boat made a horrible this-is-not-good-for-the-hull noise as it dragged along the bottom. Then Mick had a brilliant idea. My four brothers jumped out and left me (being lighter than my porky siblings) to try and steer a now very waterlogged rowboat through a shallow and fast-moving stretch of the river, while they barked conflicting orders from the bank.

I soon lost control, and the boat careered into a mess of thick branches that hung over the water. 'Push it out sideways,' Mick bellowed. 'Use the oar,' Colin screamed. 'Do something!' Malcolm shrieked. I was doing something, all right. I was getting tangled up in the branches while the empty boat continued its journey down the river. Then the boat marooned itself on top of a large rock twenty metres from me. 'Shit! The boat!' my brothers chorused. As they tried in vain to retrieve the boat, I fought my way out of the bushes and crawled up the bank. I was covered in scratches. My brothers did what all brothers around the world would do. They laughed at me.

We left the boat where it was (funny that) and traipsed back to our camp.

Two days later we hiked past the spot we had 'borrowed' the boat from and there it was, floating near the bank, with a dad and his kid sitting in it. 'Stop staring,' Mick said, 'and don't look so guilty.'

I was never good at the stealing caper. In the years that followed I tried to follow in my brother's illustrious footsteps, but got caught too often

Mick is no longer a thief. Mind you, he does have an incredible collection of computer paraphernalia. And there is that new car that just appeared out of nowhere . . .

Hitchhike

Melbourne to Mooloolaba
December 1983

Our driver wasn't quite sure of his name or where he was from. When I asked him his name he said, 'Er ... um ... Paul'. He lived in 'er ... um ... Altona'. Still, he seemed nice enough and his car was virtually brand new. He must have been doing all right. He only looked about eighteen. The car was a Nissan something-or-other and still had the plastic covering on the back seat. Best of all, though, we'd only had to wait ten minutes for our first lift.

We were hitchhiking 1700 kilometres from Melbourne to Mooloolaba. I was travelling with my friend 'Mad Dog' Morgan, so-called because he looked like a murderous bushranger (in a nice friendly sort of way). He was also nicknamed 'The Oldest Man in the World' because, at 34, he was the oldest student I had known at college. It wasn't because he was very slow, I hasten to add, it was because he decided at 31 he didn't like the job he was doing and went back to study.

Besides my parents I didn't know anyone else that old.

We were going to be staying at another college friend's place for a month or so. He was nicknamed 'The Tallest Man in the World'. This was our big End of College Trip before we had to go into the Real World and get a Job. We had four days to get to Mooloolaba in time for New Year's Eve. 'Bloody easy,' Mad Dog had said. He was an experienced hitchhiker. This was my first time.

After what is about to unfold, you'd think I'd never hitchhike again. The thing is, I took it up with gusto. I have hitchhiked over 20 000 kilometres in my travels through seventeen different countries. That may seem like a lot but it's nothing compared to Stephen Schlei of Germany. Since 1972, he has hitched 807 000 kilometres. That's around the world 25 times. An average of 415 kilometres every single week for the last 30 years.

When you have the time, hitching is a great way to see a country. You might get picked up by the odd fruitcake, and sometimes you end up standing in the middle of a motorway for three hours in the pouring rain, but there isn't a better way to meet the locals.

Er-um-Paul was driving to the Gold Coast. It was only a few hours drive from there to Mooloolaba. Mad Dog was right. This was bloody easy. The only annoying thing was, Mad Dog had the front seat. I was sticking to the plastic seat covering in the back. I was regretting wearing shorts. I wasn't looking forward to stopping. I didn't think I'd be able to get unstuck.

Er-um-Paul kept turning around to talk to me (the 'Old Man' had already dozed off to sleep). He'd drive for a long stretch without looking at the road. He also managed to use 'fuck' every third word. It was very impressive. You try it. It's really hard.

Er-um-Paul stopped at a dodgy-looking pub in the back streets of Albury. He really did have trouble with his name. I said, 'Paul, would you like a drink?' three times before he finally responded, 'Oh, fuckin' sorry, yes please.' And like a drink he certainly did. He had five pots in

40 minutes. The food was traditional Australian pub fare. I went for the old pub standard, Chicken Parma. It was the size of the table (and tasted only slightly better). Mad Dog had the calamari. There is always calamari on a pub menu. Even if the pub is a thousand kilometres from the sea there is always calamari. And, as Mad Dog should have known, it's always rubbery. These ones we could have used as spare fan belts.

'I know a fuckin' short cut,' Er-um-Paul said. We were heading inland. 'It saves us fuckin' goin' through fuckin' Sydney,' he added. It seemed odd to me. But what did I know? The short cut involved a lot of very dark and very narrow country roads. Mad Dog naturally dozed off to sleep again. He was in the back now. His cheek was stuck to the plastic on the back seat.

Just as I was close to dozing off myself, the car shuddered to a noisy and sudden stop. Er-um-Paul had missed a turn-off and driven up an embankment. Mad Dog woke with a fright. 'Stupid fuckin' roads,' Er-um-Paul moaned as he stepped out of the car. The car looked all right. It was just stuck on the embankment. A bit of steam was coming out from under the bonnet. Er-um-Paul tried to start the car, but it just made a sick groaning noise like someone dying. All three of us looked at the engine. All three of us had no idea which bit to look at. Er-um-Paul twiddled a few things. It didn't start. Mad Dog twiddled a few more things. It still wouldn't start. All the while they were saying things like, 'Oh, it must be the carby', or 'I think the points need tuning'. 'It might be the diff', I said (I didn't even know where the diff was, but I felt left out).

Er-um-Paul pulled a large spanner from his bag and started doing what every good mechanic does: tapping random parts of the engine. It still wouldn't start. Astonishingly, he then began to bash the engine with the spanner. 'Fuckin' thing!' he screamed angrily. In disbelief, I watched as he started bashing the side of his car, leaving huge dents. Christ, I thought, that's his new car!

Then he dropped the big clanger. 'Fuck it. Leave it here. I'll get another one!' Another one? What did he mean by another one? Click!

He'd stolen the car. I looked at Mad Dog. He looked as shocked as I felt. Ah, so that was why Er-um-Paul wasn't sure about his name or where he lived. He'd made it up. It would also help to explain why we stopped at a backstreet pub in Albury and why we were taking the very long 'short cut' to Queensland. It was funny that I didn't notice some of the other things though. Like that he didn't have a key, for example.

Meanwhile, Er-um-Paul had given it one more go and got the car started. What should we do? We had no idea where we were. It was also one o'clock in the morning. I whispered to Mad Dog, 'We'll stay till the morning, then clear off'. He shrugged and jumped in the back. Er-um-Paul must have known we knew, but he didn't say anything or even seem to care. Maybe he was going to kill us, anyway.

As every set of headlights approached us I tightly clenched my fist. I was sure each car was the police. What could we say? 'Oh, we're just hitchhikers, officer,' as he threw us into jail. Years later, I had a similar scary experience. I was hitching from Amsterdam to Paris and was picked up by a young English guy in his dad's French consulate car (he'd driven it to Amsterdam for the weekend without his parents' permission). At the Belgian–French border we were stopped and the car was searched (they even went through my dirty underwear!). Ten kilometres after the border he pulled over and opened the boot. 'Put your hand here,' he said. I shoved my hand down behind the back wheel. 'That's where the police put their hand,' he said. 'Now put your hand up.' I twisted my wrist slightly and put my hand up. I felt something plastic and dragged out a plastic bag with twelve giant blocks of hash in it. If he'd been busted, I would have been too. 'But officer …' I'd say, as he put his fingers up my rectum.

Two months after that, I was sure it was going to happen again. I was in Ireland this time, and was picked up by two Germans who'd driven all the way from Dusseldorf in a tiny Fiat. Driving into Dingle on the south-west coast, a police car pulled us up. Here we go again, I thought. What did the Germans have stashed in the boot? Heroin?

AK47s? Dead bodies? The policeman leaned into the window, 'Where are yez orf to?'

'Dingle,' Herbert had said nervously.

'Ah, so will ya be drinkin' t'noit?'

'Um . . . maybe vun or two,' Herbert stammered.

'Well, Oi'll tell ya a great poob t'go to,' the policeman said with a huge beaming smile. 'It's called O'Flatterys and Oi'd love to buy ya a drink. Oi carn't believe you've driven all this way from Germany.'

The police were the last people I wanted to mention to Er-um-Paul. In fact, for once in my life I couldn't think of anything at all to talk about. Mad Dog was already asleep in the back (or pretending to be at least). What could I say? 'So, have you stolen any cars lately?' 'Do you prefer the coathanger or the old smashed window technique?' Was he escaping from somewhere? Prison? His parole officer? A murder? Maybe I could tell him how I broke into the school tuckshop one night and stole 20 boxes of lollies? That would impress him. He was driving like a madman (maybe because he was one?). It was pitch-black and the road went up and down and round and round like a roller-coaster. He was doing 130 km/h. (I suppose wear and tear on the engine wasn't a real concern for him.) I've only ever been frightened like this once since. I was picked up by drunk man in a bad suit driving a very expensive BMW on the autobahn outside Frankfurt. He would get the car up to 270 km/h then, as he approached a slower car in front (they were only doing 200!), he would slam on the brakes just before we ploughed into the back of it. It was a pity, really. If he hadn't been so drunk, it would have been like a very scary amusement park ride. Instead, I spent most of the trip with my eyes closed, clutching the armrest till my fingers went numb.

Er-um-Paul suddenly swung the steering wheel. There was another horrible noise. Oh, here we go again. The car lurched to one side and stopped on the edge of the road. Oh, good. A blown tyre. The car was sitting on the edge of a steep hill. A farmhouse with a light on sat fifty metres below us. Er-um-Paul stood outside for a minute. 'We'll have to take out the fuckin' back seat,' he moaned. Of course, he didn't have a key to the boot. He tore out the middle seat in the back and got me, being the smallest, to climb in and fetch the tyre and the jack. When Er-um-Paul finished changing the tyre, he pointed the discarded one down the hill towards the farmhouse and let it go. It went tumbling at great speed straight towards Farmer John's bedroom window. He was going to get quite a shock when a tyre smashed through and joined him and his wife for an unexpected threesome.

We all jumped in and Er-um-Paul quickly sped off.

Just after sunrise we stopped at a shop for a drink. 'We'll get out here,' Mad Dog said, 'we're in no rush. We'd like to take our time.' No rush, all right. No rush to go to jail. Er-um-Paul grunted, then sped off, spitting gravel all over us.

We had no idea where we were. We had no map and we couldn't see a sign anywhere. We were surrounded by rolling hills covered in dry grass and sheep. We could have been anywhere in Australia. We waited three hours for a lift. Finally, a slow-talking farmer picked us up. 'I'm not garn far,' he drawled. 'That's OK,' I said, 'every lift helps.' He dropped us off three kilometres down the road. From where he dropped us off we could almost see where he'd picked us up. We did find out where we were, though. But it didn't help. We had just left something like Gundawingawonga and were heading towards Two Fishes Creek.

We walked for about ten kilometres. None of the seven cars that passed us picked us up. We stopped under a tree when the hot afternoon sun drained us of what little energy we had left. My legs were killing me.

We stood there for another three hours. I tried everything to get picked up. I smiled. I waved. I begged. There was no use making a sign with a destination on it. We had no idea what to write. If we wrote

'Queensland' I supposed we'd at least get a laugh from passing motorists. It didn't help that Mad Dog looked like a cross between a murderous bushranger and freaked-out hippy. My arm was getting tired from holding out my thumb. (Incidentally, if you're hitching in Southern Europe don't stick out your thumb, it means 'Up your arse!'. You might get picked up by the mafioso, though. But then they'd chop off your thumbs and feed them to their cats.)

In Europe I found the Germans were the best at giving lifts. In twelve out of the seventeen countries where I've hitched, I've been picked up by Germans. They'll pick up anyone. Druggies, serial killers, terrorists. 'Ja, hullo, jump in!' The Swiss on the other hand will also pick you up, but then spend the whole journey telling you how dangerous it is to hitch—'I could be a murderer you know!' In Italy I was quite often picked up by young beautiful women who'd waffle to me in Italian for two hours because I said *Buon giorno* when I hopped in the car. However, probably the friendliest and easiest lifts come from the Irish. They will take you miles out of their way to drop you off. The only down side is that you will more than likely have to listen to their whole life story. And even then, you can only understand about every third word.

A man who looked a lot like Mad Dog came strolling up the road towards us. He had a beard and ponytail and was wearing a cheesecloth shirt. He was carrying two tall glasses filled with some sort of drink. 'Good afternoon,' he said brightly, 'I could see you guys standing here all afternoon from up at my house.' He pointed to a farmhouse set about two hundred metres back from the road. 'I thought you'd like a cold drink,' he said, handing me an ice-cold glass of homemade lemonade. It was delicious.

'Where you headed?' he said.

'The Sunshine Coast in Queensland,' I said, in between noisy slurps.

'Oh. You've sort of come a funny way.'

'Yeah, it was sort of an accident.'

We finished our drinks, said thank you about eight times, and he shuffled back up to his farmhouse.

Two and a half hours later he returned. It was starting to get dark. We'd been in this one spot for almost six hours. 'Would you guys like to come up to the house? My wife has made you guys some dinner. You must be starving.' I hesitated for a second then Mad Dog said, 'We'd love to. That would be wonderful.'

Mad Dog immediately felt right at home. It looked as if we'd stepped back to 1975. There were throw rugs and scatter cushions everywhere. The farmer and his wife had the very unhippy names of Scott and Julie. They were both dressed in caftans. Their two kids, on the other hand, were called something like Moonshine and Soybean. Julie served us up a giant dinner of, if I heard correctly, alfalfa sprout lasagne. I noticed Julie had impressively hairy armpits. They were hairier than mine.

'I've set you up a bed each,' Julie said, as she gave me a second serve of lasagne that was bigger than the first.

I am amazed at some people's generosity. Scott and Julie had no idea who we were but invited us into their house, fed us, then asked us to stay the night. This was not just a one-off, either. On my hitching jaunts I've met the most incredibly generous people. A German man (a gay jewellery designer for the pope) drove me about a hundred kilometres. In that time he shouted me a four-course lunch, gave me a hundred dollars and asked everyone in the restaurant if they'd take 'his friend' to Hamburg. I mean, I had to fuck him of course, but . . . only joking! Another time a Danish guy invited me to stay at his house in Aalborg. I left two weeks later. In that time he wouldn't let me buy him one drink. And I tell you, we had many! A Frenchman picked me, and a girl I was hitching with, up in a city bus. 'I will finish my shift soon, zen I will drive you,' he said. We did the circuit of the city of Freiburg twice, then jumped in his car and he took us to the village of Breisach on the Rhine. He took us out to dinner, then picked us up the next morning for a guided tour of wineries and villages across the border in France, including shouting us a gastronomic feast at a marvellous little restaurant. It was his one day off a week, but he was just so excited about showing us around. 'My wife, she is not very 'appy about it, but . . . oh well,' he said.

The next morning, after soybean pancakes and lentil sausages for breakfast, Scott drove us to a major road. 'You'll have a better chance here,' he said. He was right. Twenty minutes later a car pulled up.

'Thanks for the lift,' I said as we jumped in. 'No, thank *you*,' he said, 'I need someone to roll my joints.' He smoked all the way to the Queensland border.

We waited and waited. At this rate we weren't going to make New Year's Eve. There was a good chance we were going to celebrate it on the side of the road in the middle of Shithole, Queensland. One thing was certain, we wouldn't win a 'Hitchhiking Race'. Hitchhiking is a sport in Europe. There are Hitchhiking clubs all over the continent and since 1994 they have held the annual European Championships. In teams of two, the hitchers have to get from one point to another over a few days, passing checkpoints along the way. They all have to wear matching yellow boilersuits. Mind you, I was doing this years before them (holding hitchhiking races that is, not dressing up like B1 and B2). In 1987 I raced a Canadian fellow from Zermatt in Switzerland to Interlaken (the loser had to buy the other one a large beer). He had an hours head start. I had seven lifts and Chad had two. I beat him by two hours. I said that means you have to buy me two beers.

In 1998 the first Around the World Hitching Race took place. The race went for three months. Andrej Kuritsin and Yulya Korbtkova of Latvia won.

A few tips from Andrej and Yulya would certainly have helped us. It took us four hours to get a lift. Maybe we needed the yellow boiler suits. At just after eleven we were dropped off in Ipswich, a satellite town of Brisbane. It was late. We had to find somewhere to sleep. It was a bit chilly and we didn't fancy finding a spot on the side of the road, so Mad Dog suggested we check into a motel.

'How much for a room?' I asked.

'Eighty dollars,' the frumpy lady at reception mumbled.

'Have you got anything cheaper?'

'Nah.'

'For eighty dollars do you get a lobster dinner?'

She stared at me hard for a second. 'You have access to a pool, there is a TV in each room, tea-making facilities and we have a mini-golf course,' she said coldly.

'But we just want to sleep, then we're leaving first thing in the morning. And . . . I promise we won't use the mini-golf course.'

'That's the price,' she grunted.

I crashed out as soon as my head hit my eighty-dollar-a-night pillow. I got my money's worth the next morning, though. I made six cups of tea and coffee that I didn't drink, I wet every towel and I messed up the sheets in the bed we didn't use. And, I did a big poo in the middle of the floor. Actually, I didn't, but I sure felt like it.

We waited 28 seconds for our first lift. Pity he only drove us fifteen kilometres down the road. We were getting desperate now. We weren't going to make it. Another two hours went by without a lift. I was trying not to look desperate. I'd stare at each passing driver in the eye with a pleading look. At last a car pulled up in front of us. We bolted up the road but, just as we reached the car, they accelerated off, blasting their horns. Arseholes. A similar, but funnier, thing happened to me in Switzerland one time. A car pulled up about 50 metres in front of me and I muttered 'Bloody hell' under my breath as I jogged up the road with my heavy pack on. Puffing and panting, I opened the back door, threw my pack in, then jumped in the front seat. The driver gave me a look of total disbelief. He had a large map folded out on the steering wheel. He'd just stopped to find out where he was. He must have thought I was some psycho. He took me anyway, but kept glancing nervously across at me every couple of minutes to check I wasn't pulling out a machete.

I was getting angry now. When a car passed and didn't pick us up I would step out on into the middle of the road, put my finger up and scream out, 'Fucking arseholes!' I did this about 50 times before we finally got a lift. The fellow was going to Maroochydore. That was only ten minutes from Mooloolaba. I sat in the back with a great big drooling dog. He looked a bit scary, but was an absolute pushover. Not like a lift I got just outside of London one time. The guy had an ocelot in the back. An ocelot, in case you don't know, is a slightly smaller version of a leopard. It was the driver's pet (he was a vet who specialised in big cats). Her name was Tabby. She kept trying to nuzzle me through the cage behind the front seat. 'You can pat her if you want,' he said. No thanks. I am quite partial to my fingers.

'I'll take you to Mooloolaba,' our driver said. It was so nice of him to go out of his way. Probably the best 'out of their way' lift I've had was in Germany. An American GI picked me up. He'd just had an argument with his wife and he told her he was going up to the shop. He drove me over 200 kilometres to the German–French border. 'I'd take you further,' he said, 'but I don't have my passport.'

It looked like it was going to take our driver an extra five hours. He insisted on taking us right to the Tallest Man in the World's house but ended up driving around the same block five times before he found it. Finally, at last, we made it to Mooloolaba. It was just after six o'clock on New Year's Eve. I was so tired I was pissed off my head by nine, and trying to snog some girl who looked a bit like the drooling dog by eleven. Shortly before midnight, I passed out.

Moped

Corfu, Greece
May 1987

I was about to embark on a journey around the island of Corfu with two porn stars. Ken was from Melbourne and had blond shaggy hair and a recently grown wispy blond moustache. He already had a deep tan from just two days of lying in the sun. He looked just like a porn star. The second member of our party was Sleazy. He was a waterbed salesman from Rotorua, New Zealand (and no, I didn't make that up). Sleazy was not his full name. It had started as Sleazy-Wine-Bars after an above-average record of picking up girls in wine bars in London. It then became Sleazy-Train-Trips (ditto). Then Sleazy-Graveyards (after he bonked a girl in one). And, as of two days ago, he had become Sleazy-Olive-Groves (figure that one out for yourself). He had an uncanny resemblance to Magnum PI and managed to pick up girls with the worst pick-up lines known to man. He not only looked like a porn star, he also had the bonus of having a great porn star name.

We were fifteen minutes north of Corfu town smack in the middle of an industrial estate. One that could have been anywhere in the world. 'Hey, am I on a Greek island or the western suburbs of Melbourne?' I shouted above the whirring of my vehicle's engine. Ken and Sleazy didn't hear. Well, couldn't hear, actually. I was already lagging far behind. I was on a moped. Ken and Sleazy had opted for more powerful (but for me, terrifyingly frightening) motorbikes. In my defence, I was very excited when I saw that the hire place had Vespas. Ever since I'd seen the film *Roman Holiday*, with the most beautiful woman in the world, Audrey Hepburn, scooting around the Colosseum, I had wanted to ride one. OK, I am also not all that skilled on any two-wheeled motorised contraption. A Vespa seemed the lesser of two evils.

The three of us each had a different agenda for our jaunt around the island. Ken wanted to circumnavigate the whole island in one day and also ride as fast as possible at any opportunity (doing the second would make the first easier, Ken told us). Sleazy wanted to perve at as many women sitting on as many beaches as he could find. He also wanted to 'have a beer or two'. I, on the other hand, wanted to visit 'Bloo-Loo Bay'. I called it this because I didn't know its name. I had a poster at home with a picture of the most idyllic bay I'd ever seen. The water in the bay was a brilliant, almost garish aqua-blue (looking very much like the water in a toilet that uses Bloo-Loo). And, all it had on the poster was that it was on Corfu. I didn't know where it was, but I had to find it. My other mission was a simple one. Since I didn't want to die in a horrible motorcycle accident, I was going to take it easy. Apparently, Sleazy told me with a smile, in midsummer one person a day dies on the roads of Corfu. That can't be true I told him. Well, I hoped it wasn't true. Mind you, I did read this in a guidebook about Corfu: 'The cult of the motorcycle and moped is presided over by a jealous deity apparently requiring regular human sacrifice.'

The others were way up ahead. Sleazy was weaving from side to side all over the road (oh good, it looked like Sleazy was going to be today's sacrifice!). We'd left the industrial area now and were close to where we had started from that morning. We were staying in the small beachside village of Gouvia and had caught the early bus into Corfu town to hire our bikes.

We were following the route notes from my guidebook, *The Traveller's Guide to Corfu*. It had already guided us out of town just fine. It was proving to be a good buy. I'd bought it for only 50p at a car boot sale in London the week before. What a stroke of luck, I thought when I picked it up. There was only one small problem with it, though. It was published in 1969. Back then, scooters were 80 cents a day to hire (it also warns riders to be careful because people habitually walk in the middle of the road). A double room in a hotel (with bath) would set you back 70 cents a day. A luxury hotel room would cost you a whopping $3.

Ken and Sleazy were waiting up ahead for me on the side of the road. As soon as I got close enough, they raced off again. I would have to get used to this. There were mudflats to the right of us, and the mountains on our left were lush green with pine trees. While I was gazing up into the mountains, a bus lurched around the corner in front of me. In the middle of the road. I almost wet my pants. Probably my biggest problem when riding a motorbike is not actually my lack of skill, but my tendency to spend way too much time admiring the scenery instead of looking at the road (having the concentration span of five-year-old doesn't help much either). Strangely enough, being a very keen sightseer is not a good prerequisite for riding a small machine at high speeds on foreign roads.

It was early May and there wasn't much traffic on the road. That was fortunate, because the same guidebook which mentioned human sacrifices also said: 'The greatest cause of accidents in Corfu is overtaking.'

My 1969 guidebook described Ipsos Bay as having 'two small hotels halfway along the beach and also a camping ground. One of the hotels has a jukebox and can be quite lively in the evenings'. Quite lively! On the road that hugs the long narrow pebbly beach of Ipsos Bay, I counted no less than forty bars and nightclubs. In a space of eighteen years Ipsos Bay had gone from 'quiet little seaside hamlet' to a resort full of pubs called the Red Lion with 'Traditional Greek Food' like bangers and mash. But right now the beach was quiet. The planeloads of partying Brits wouldn't be here for at least a month.

As we stopped while I checked my guidebook, I noticed for the first time that the sun felt hot. Riding on the bike it was actually quite cool. 'You got the sunscreen?' Sleazy asked. I was responsible for the sunscreen. I rummaged through my daypack and brought out a blue plastic bottle of . . . shampoo. It was the same colour as the sunscreen I'd left sitting on the bathroom sink back at the villa. 'We'll turn into bloody lobsters!' Sleazy gasped. 'Yes,' I said with a smile, 'but at least we'll have silky arm hair!'

Out of Ipsos the road became steeper as we climbed the slopes of Mount Pandokrátor. Buzzards were wheeling above us in the thermals and the air was pungent with the smell of pine. We laboured up hairpin turns with mighty drops on one side down to the sea. Naturally, I took it easy. Ken and Sleazy had to keep waiting for me. As I tried to explain every time I got near them, I just didn't want to die.

My guidebook described Kouloura as 'the most thoroughly romantic of all the coves along this coast.' Looking down through pale green sprays of eucalyptus (yes, eucalyptus!) and dark jets of cypress, the still water of the bay did look idyllic. But no, it wasn't Bloo-Loo Bay.

I was only just starting to feel comfortable with my Vespa. The last couple of times I'd changed gears, I had finally managed not to rev out the engine like a screaming banshee. I might have mastered the whole clutch and changing gear thing—a simple task in theory—but that didn't stop me panicking each time I tried to put the theory into practice.

The Vespa really is a classic. Even its history is a legendary story. After the Second World War, Italy's broken economy was wrecked and automobiles were not only too expensive, but useless on the war-damaged roads. So, in stepped Enrico Piaggio, the aeronautical engineer. Using old aircraft parts left over from the war (the suspension was originally old suspension gear from a World War Two bomber), Enrico—along with Corradino D'Ascanio, who was responsible for the production of the first modern helicopter—built the first Vespa. Today's model looks very much like the original fifteen Vespas that rolled off the production line in 1946. The 'Paperino' or, as it was better known the 'Donald Duck' was an immediate hit. Within three years 35 000 had been produced. In ten years, one million. In the 1950s Vespas were even being used like a family car. It was not uncommon to see a family of four piled on top. Vespa today has 43 per cent of the scooter market and has sold over 15 million in Europe alone.

Vespa is Italian for 'wasp'. Not because it sounds like one, but because of its rounded and flared tail. The Greeks, on the other hand, call all mopeds *papákia* meaning 'little ducks', because of the noise they make.

My guidebook had the next section of road to the town of Roda marked as 'a minor untarred road' and recommended drivers not to tackle it 'unless your car has good clearance. A careless driver can easily crack the sump of his car'. It is now, of course, like any sealed road in Corfu. A pity, really. Tourists have penetrated to just about every corner of the globe now. Every little beach or village that's made 'accessible' takes away the adventure of discovering the untouched beach or the unspoiled village for those who want to make the effort. According to my guidebook, Roda *was* once worth the effort: 'Roda is a hamlet on a plain by the sea with just one inn, The Avra, in a converted fisherman's house. There are two beachside restaurants as well. Roda is an unspoiled sleepy place where you can bathe and lunch on fresh fish at the two fine little eating places'. Not hard to guess what Roda is like now that it is so easy to get to. A huge, bustling resort.

Nevertheless, we found a nice café on the beach. Sleazy wanted a beer and my feeble 'It's not even eleven o'clock yet' didn't seem to faze him. A beer cost 150 drachmas (in 1969 you could have got a night in a hotel *and* three serves of bangers and mash for that). Sleazy was already checking out the talent and trying to chat up the Greek waitress, 'So . . . do you come here often?'

We skolled our beers. Well, Ken made us skol our beers. He was impatient to continue his quest. Sleazy had given up on the waitress. His quest would have to wait for another time.

Just when I thought I'd mastered my Vespa, I let out first gear too quickly as we were leaving and ploughed into a bush. After pulling a few twigs from my ears, I set off again in dogged pursuit of Ken and Sleazy. We were heading inland now and into the mountains. I soon lost sight of Ken and Sleazy as the mountain road wound its way up through the verdant pine forest. I rounded a bend to find the lads stopped by a roadside religious memorial. 'You can't do it, Ken!' I heard Sleazy say as I pulled up. 'Do what?' I asked. 'He wants to nick the stuff inside the box,' Sleazy groaned. You'll find these religious monuments on the side of the road throughout Greece. There is usually a glass-fronted box displaying small paintings, icons and sometimes even jewellery. 'It looks like gold in there!' Ken protested. 'Do you know what the Greeks would do if they caught you nicking their stuff?' I said. 'They'd crucify you.' Ken reluctantly got back on his bike and with a shower of gravel was off again. For the rest of the day, though, I watched him very closely every time we went past a memorial.

'Let's go bush,' I said as I studied the map. The road (well, track) to the right of us didn't seem to be on the map. Ken looked worried. 'We'll just have a look,' I pleaded. My ulterior motive was my third agenda for the trip. I wanted to find an authentic Greek village and an authentic Greek restaurant (my guidebook recommended the village of Skipero, where the locals regularly eat frogs—today they probably serve pork pies). As soon as we left the main road, the pine trees and wildflowers that ran riot on the slopes of Mount Pandokrátor were replaced by huge shady groves of olive trees. 'This is more like it,' I thought to myself as we passed a pony laden with brushwood being led by a tiny Greek lady dressed entirely in what looked like one giant black shawl.

Up ahead, by the side of the narrow road, stood a row of ochre, white and mulberry-washed houses with biscuit-coloured tiles. There didn't seem to be anyone about. Well, besides a lone goat standing in the doorway of one of the houses. We stopped by the dusty roadside where rickety chairs were set out under the shade of a vine. The vine-trestled patio of what was obviously a restaurant beckoned us. The inside was empty and smelt of wine and cheese. We sat down and an old woman appeared out of nowhere. 'Beer? Do you have beer?' Sleazy blurted out before I had a chance to test out my 'Hello, how are you?' in Greek. A beer was 60 drachmas. It was the same brand of beer we'd bought in Roda only 45 minutes away, but at less than one-third the price. There was no menu. 'You . . . have . . . lunch?' I said in the slow broken English we all tend to use when we speak to foreigners (and, naturally, if they don't understand you, you *shout* exactly what you have just *said*. Because they couldn't simply not understand you. Your new Greek, Somali or Inuit friends would have to be deaf not to understand plain English). Our host looked a little surprised. 'Greek salat, goot?' she said as she smiled nervously with a mouth more full of silver than actual teeth.

'Very . . . goot . . . thank you,' I replied.

We watched as the little old lady waddled to the back of the restaurant and began shouting at a man who was more than likely her husband. Two minutes later I noticed the less than agile husband running up the road. Ten minutes later we heard him shuffling back down again. In his arms he was carrying a bowl full of tomatoes and cucumbers. There were still masses of greenery hanging off the tomatoes. He must have picked them fresh from his garden. Wow, you can't get any fresher than that. Obviously not much call for food in this restaurant.

The Greek salad was the real McCoy (or the real *Khoriatikísaláta*). The fresh tomatoes, cucumbers, black olives, chopped onion and feta cheese were not only authentic but delicious.

'You . . . have . . . baklava?' Ken asked.

'You're not going to eat that crap, are you?' I said. 'It tastes like soggy cardboard dipped in honey.'

'Nah, it's great,' Ken replied.

'What's it like?' I asked as Ken slowly ate his baklava ten minutes later.

'It tastes like soggy cardboard dipped in honey.'

The Greeks make fine savoury dishes, there's no debate about that, but after 4000 odd years of civilisation I reckon they still haven't quite grasped the concept of dessert.

As we departed the restaurant, our lovely hostess handed us a tin full of homemade biscuits. We later discovered why she had no teeth. The biscuits could have been used to build houses.

Oh, by the way, if you're in Corfu and you'd like to visit this wonderful little village, I can't help you. I couldn't find the name on the map, and the sign I saw on the way out said something like ΚΗΓΦΔΣΑΠΥΨ (don't look for this name by the way, I didn't actually take note of it . . . it's just the Greek letters I have on my computer). And anyway, it was probably just a sign saying ALL GOATS MUST BE KEPT ON A LEAD or something.

From the village we headed back to the main road and were soon winding our way down the mountain towards the west coast. Near the base, the road started twisting down through olive groves under great limestone slopes. Suddenly, between the gnarled trunks of the olive trees, we caught a glimpse of water. Incredibly blue, clear water. I'd found Bloo-Loo Bay. Bloo-Loo Bay was Paleokastrítsa.

The beach was quiet. Lines of empty deckchairs were just waiting for the summer throngs to arrive. According to my guidebook, 'Crowds arrive every day in summer and fill the five restaurants'. Five restaurants! I counted that many on the road on the way in. Even back in 1862, after rambling on about 'the perfect quiet except the dim hum of myriad ripples' Edward Lear went on to say: 'Not that it will last. Accursed picnic parties with miserable scores of asses, male and female, are coming tomorrow.' I went for a dip in the perfectly clear waters while the lads had a beer with one of the accursed picnic parties in a beachside café.

Ken and Sleazy sped out of Paleokastrítsa. I didn't even bother to try and keep up. We were heading south now along the coast. Corfu town was only fifteen minutes away to our west. Or, as it's correctly called in Greek, Kerkira (this is also the island's name). I love the way a country or even a city can have dozens of different names depending on which language you speak. Mind you, some English speakers just assume the English name of a country is its official name. To the Greeks their country is not Greece but Ellas (the Germans on the other hand call Greece Griechenland while the Japanese call it Girisha). Some of the names locals call their own country are tongue twisters, though. The Hungarian name for Hungary is Magyarország. The official Taiwanese name for Taiwan is Chung-hua Min-Kuo. Croatia is Hrvatska and Albania is Shqipëria. The Swiss have so many official names for their country—Schweiz, Suisse, Svizzera and Svizera—that the coins and postage stamps have no room for all of them. So the Latin, Helvetia, is used. My favourite, however, is Al-Urdan Al-Mamlakah Al Urdunniyah Al-Hashimiyah. You'd reckon even the locals might prefer the much easier Jordan.

'Hey, do you guys want to check out Mitriótissa beach?' I asked Ken and Sleazy when I finally caught up with them. 'It's only a fifteen minute walk from the road, and it says in the book that Lawrence Durrell once described it as "perhaps the loveliest beach in the world".'

'No, we'll keep going,' Ken and Sleazy answered in unison.

'Oh, it's also Corfu's unofficial nudist beach,' I added. Sleazy's eyes lit up.

'Oh, all right then,' Ken moaned.

We got off our bikes and weaved our way through stunted oaks and wiry shrubs along a stony path to the beach. However, to Sleazy's dismay, there was only one nude and it was a fellow. A German, I suspect (they love getting their gear off).

I couldn't talk the lads into visiting Pelekas. My guidebook glowingly recommended it because 'it has electric light and a few simple rooms to let.' It was probably scarred with yet more Red Lion pubs. I have to admit, I was becoming a little bit obsessed with the changes to the island. I had this vain hope that we might stumble across somewhere that hadn't changed since 1969.

We were flying now, trying to reach the southern-most tip of the island. Moving inland, we sped past the towns of Áyios-this and Áyios-that. My guidebook described the villages in the south as 'unaccustomed to tourists. The villagers do not often display ready charm.' With the 200 000 odd people that visit Corfu every year, I imagine the locals are well accustomed to tourists now. While tourist numbers have grown enormously, the local population hasn't changed that much in the past forty years. In 1961 there were 99 000 Corfiotes (as the dictionary tells me they're known) and in 2001 the local population is only 6000 more at 105 000.

We passed few people and those we saw were locals tending fields of olive trees. We passed fields full of huge green and yellow melons and the air was filled with the scent of mown hay. I wanted to visit Korissíon lagoon. This could be my last chance to find the 1969 Corfu I was desperate to find. I pleaded with the guys to take the turn-off (it's amazing what an offer of a couple of rounds of beer will get you). The road, or track, or goat path was framed in dark cypress as we headed east to the coast again. The track became narrower and bumpier. We passed through green slopes rich with flowering fruit trees. It was like riding down an English country lane (only hotter). The road became even narrower and even bumpier. It didn't look like a proper road any more, but I was on a mission. It wasn't until we ended up in someone's front yard and rode straight through the middle of a bunch of startled chickens that I finally admitted we must have taken the wrong turn. Ahead of us was a long stone wall and beyond that was Korission lagoon. We couldn't get to it. There didn't seem to be a break in the wall anywhere. If I had had the special edition Vespa 150 built for the French army in 1968, we could have got through. It was armed with a 75 mm cannon. I could have just blown a hole in the wall. Ken and Sleazy didn't want to waste time trying to find a way around, so we turned back to the main road.

We rode south through rolling fields. Just as I was thinking how beautiful and untouched it was, we swept around a bend to see kilometres of uninterrupted beach and kilometres of uninterrupted pubs with your choice of bingo, quiz nights, disco or karaoke.

By the time we reached the southern tip of Kavos, it was already five o'clock. We stopped at the lookout for two minutes, then immediately jumped back on our bikes. It was on our twenty-five kilometre journey back to Corfu town that I had my biggest surprise. My guidebook described the village of Benitses as 'a traditional fishing village where you can rent a few rooms in one of the village's houses'. We rode for fifteen minutes past pubs, resorts, hotels and more pubs. It was lager lout heaven. There were already dozens of drunk Brits roaming the esplanade singing, 'Here we go, here we go, here we go!'

The only fishing the locals would do now is fishing empty cans out of the water, and young locals trawling the night clubs trying to pick up (the locals even have a name for this: *Kamáki*, which translates roughly as 'picking up tourists').

It was dusk when we rolled into Gouvia. But that wasn't the end of our adventure. And I'm happy to say it wasn't me who ended it with a bang. Well, more of a slip and a slide really. After going out to the SOS Taverna (SOS stood for 'Serve Only Slowly', I believe) for moussaka and chips (everything is served with chips), Sleazy talked me into riding into the next village to a disco. He had been told by an English guy that this disco was full of girls.

After numerous ouzos and Sleazy's unsuccessful attempts to earn a new variation of his name (he was hoping to become Sleazy-Pebbled-Beaches), we left the nightclub at two in the morning. We walked— well, staggered—outside to find the street awash with driving rain. In front of basically all the nightclubbers, who were streaming out onto the street, Sleazy jumped on his motorbike, started it up, put it into gear and went to ride off. He got about two metres down the wet road then the back wheel locked up. He'd forgotten to take the lock off it. The front wheel began spinning the bike around in circles. Sleazy tried to stay on and control it but just ended up spinning around and around till the bike ended up on top of him with the engine revving loudly. The hundred people or so standing outside applauded him.

I drove home at around three kilometres an hour through the pouring rain. And, as I explained to Sleazy when I turned up at our villa fifteen minutes after him, the reason I went so slow was that 'I didn't want to die'.

Foot

Innsbruck, Austria
June 1987

Everyone in the group had serious hiking gear on. They wore those tweed-like calf-length hiking pants (or are they shorts?), long woollen socks, expensive hi-tech walking boots and micro-techno-fibro-thermo-wanko jackets. And all six of them had one of those fandangous telescopic walking sticks. I stood out just a little bit. I wore bright blue board-shorts with red cartoon dogs all over them and a pair of basketball runners. My walking stick was more of the old-fashioned kind. It was a rather bent and gnarled-looking branch.

Our guide, who must have been eighty, was already leaping up the steep mountain trail like a gazelle. I knew I shouldn't have had all those Jägermeisters the night before. And God, I felt silly wearing the feathered huntsman's hat someone in the bar had told me everyone would be wearing.

Our Austrian mountain guide's name was Hans (I would have been disappointed if it wasn't). A badge on his jacket had the word *Fuhrer* embroidered across it in big red letters. Gee, and I thought he'd committed suicide in a bunker in Berlin, when all along he'd been working as a mountain guide in Austria. No, actually, Führer means 'guide' in German. Mind you, the only guiding Hitler ever did was to guide his country to ruin and damnation.

Hans's English extended to one word. 'Hello'. He would use this for everything: 'come this way', 'look over here', 'stop here', 'be careful' and 'hurry up Brian, you're holding up the group'.

I introduced myself to two fellow members of our hiking party, a couple in their fifties called Hal and Mary.

'Are you from Hawaii?' I asked Hal.

He looked at me in utter amazement, 'Wow! You're clever. How did you know?'

Gee, it was hard. He was wearing a Hawaiian shirt and a baseball cap with Honolulu on it. There was also Clara, a 60-year-old lady from Surrey in England. 'This should be jolly good fun,' she told me, with a basket of plums in her mouth. She looked as if she had borrowed her grandmother's hiking clothes from the 1850s.

Actually, I'm wrong. In the 1850s, women hikers didn't wear pants. They wore skirts (with flannel-lined tweed knickers to keep warm   mmm, sexy). The first woman to scale Mont Blanc (in 1838) did it in a skirt. She might have had an icy wind blowing up her fanny, but she travelled in style. She took an entourage of six guides (I suppose she took that many in case she lost one or two) and six porters. Six porters were *needed*, too, because the provisions they carried included two whole legs of mutton, six ox-tongues, twenty-four fowls, eighteen bottles of fine wine, one large cask of *vin ordinaire* (cheap plonk for the porters and guides), one bottle of brandy, three pounds of sugar and a large supply of French glazed plums (one can never do any serious hiking without a good supply of French glazed plums, I say).

The Ecuadorian couple with us didn't have any French glazed plums, but they did have an enormous bag of 'trail mix'. It looked like something you'd feed to a cockatoo. They knew more English than Hans (but maybe less than a cockatoo). All of two words more. They knew 'thank you' and 'beautiful'. They would answer every one of Hans's 'hellos' with 'thank you'.

And finally, there was Jo—the reason I could join this Hiking Club trip. When I say 'join', I mean 'sneak on'. I'd met Jo, an Australian girl who was working in Innsbruck, the night before. She said I could sneak onto the hike without anyone noticing (I couldn't have stood out more in my lairy shorts).

The first couple of kilometres were a doddle. Well, that was because we were in a cable car. We'd all met at the cable car station in the small town of Igls at 8.30 that morning. I have to say, I wasn't feeling too sprightly. Even though I'd only had four beers the night before, each beer came in a glass the size of a bucket.

'Hello, hello,' our Führer encouraged, as we stepped out of the *Patscherkofel* cable car. The air was crystal clear and just cool enough to be positively exhilarating. With every mouthful of fresh mountain air, my hangover faded. We followed a steep trail straight up the lush green hillside covered in Alpenrose and other wildflowers. Mary seemed to know the names of all of them. The large city of Innsbruck below looked like a tiny hamlet from this height. It was like the view from an aeroplane.

Hans stopped to show us where we were going on his map. It looked like we were going a long, long way—and it also sounded as though every peak and every valley we were going to climb was called 'hello'. The hiking trails were marked in colours for degree of difficulty (blue=easy, red=intermediate, black=difficult). No one else seemed to flinch like I did as Hans kept pointing to blacks. I also noticed on the map that 'hiking' in German was *bergwander*. Sounded like something you could buy at the Innsbruck McDonalds.

We trudged up a steep incline (I know it was steep because we were walking up what had been the downhill ski run during the 1964 and 1976 Winter Olympics). The ski-lifts looked out of place stuck in the middle of green fields. Particularly with fat, lazy-looking cows standing in the middle of the run.

I chatted to Hal and Mary. Well, when I say chatted, I mean gasped in between my puffing and panting. Hal and Mary were members of the Hawaiian Hiking Club (Hal was still amazed, by the way, that I knew they were from Hawaii). They had hiked in 42 countries. This was their sixth hike around the Innsbruck area in eight days. Plastered all over Hal's backpack were badges from, among other places, Milford Sound in New Zealand, Patagonia in Argentina, the Lake District in England and New York City (the only hiking there is hiking away from the muggers, I joked to Hal's blank response).

Still, they weren't a patch on Arthur Blessitt. He has walked 56 005 kilometres through 292 separate nations. He started walking in 1969 and is still walking. I have a feeling that he might be a few pumpkin seeds short of a trail mix. I say this because he's walked the entire 56 005 kilometres carrying a four-metre wooden cross (as in the Jesus variety). It is so big that it has trainer wheels on the bottom so he can drag it along. He is doing this, he says, 'Because Jesus called me to give my life to carry the cross in every nation of the world.' I'm glad I didn't get that phone call

He hasn't had the cross the entire time, though. It was lost for a month by Alitalia Airlines (he should have known better, Alitalia invented the term 'lost luggage'). It was also stolen, ironically, on the most holy day of the year and in one of the most holy places on earth. It was Christmas Day in Assisi, Italy. He did get it back only to almost lose it forever when someone set it on fire in Orlando, Florida.

Amazingly, and quite frighteningly, he's not the only one doing this. He has some competition. Keith Wheeler (whose motto is 'Smile, because God loves you') has only visited a piddly 115 countries with his cross. I wonder what would happen if they bumped into each other. Would there be a fight? Would Keith be mighty pissed off with the upstart Arthur? 'Look, Blessitt, you may have travelled to more places than me, but at least I don't have wussy trainer wheels on my cross.'

I was feeling like I'd walked 56 005 kilometres and we'd only been walking for two hours. It wasn't because I was unfit, I might add, it was just that Jägermeisters and hiking don't really mix. Finally we came to a stop at a . . . bird house. Perched on top of this craggy peak was what looked like a bird house mounted on a wooden pole. Hans opened a little door and pulled out . . . a rubber stamp and stamp pad. Everyone in the group (besides me) plucked out a little green book from their packs. Hans gave me a quizzical 'hello' when he saw I didn't have one. He reached into his pack and brought out a spare one for me. The book had *Fremdenverkehrsverband* written on the front. It probably simply meant 'book'. The Germans like using ridiculously long names to say something simple. Another example I found was the word for 'rise' (as in pay rise). In Germany you would ask for a pay *gehaltsaufbesserung*. The *Fremdenverkehrsverband* was my *bergwanderpass*, or mountain hiking passport. All over the Austrian Alps are hundreds of these 'bird houses' with little stamps and ink pads in them so you can put stamps in your *bergwanderpass*. My first stamp had the name of the peak (Boscheben) and the height (2030 metres). I noticed Hal's book was full of stamps.

The bird box also had a guest book and a pen inside. Hal wrote 'Another spectacular peak, another spectacular hike'. Underneath that I wrote 'If I don't make it back, can someone call my mum'.

Hans was soon off again, leaping from boulder to boulder. We stopped often, but less to rest than to enjoy the view. I was bringing up the rear. Clara, who must have been in her sixties, was striding along next to me. 'Gee, that's an impressive walking stick,' I said.

'Yes. I only just bought it. It really is rather special.'

'Oh, why's that?' I asked, rather stupidly.

'It has a vibration absorption system with anti-shock springs that can be turned on and off,' Clara said proudly.

'You're joking!' (Well, I hoped she was).

'No, and it also has this ergonomic cork handle,' Clara said, handing it to me to for inspection. I handed it back carefully. I was scared I'd drop it. It must have cost at least $200. I thought it looked too nice to take outside.

'I like *your* walking stick,' Clara said, nodding at my beaten-up stick.

Yeah, right.

'Yeah, it's got a vibration absorption system, too!' I said, as I bent it down on the ground to form a bow.

The climb continued for another hour. Far below, the Innsbruck valley gave the impression of being poised above another world. Mountain peaks disappeared into a blue haze on the horizon.

Our second bird box was on the top of a windswept plateau. Patches of snow lay about in dirty clumps on the rocky ground. I wrote in the guest book, 'You can all stick your telescopic walking sticks up your arse'.

Not long after we left the bird box, we were traipsing through a field of snow. Then, within a space of thirty seconds, everything disappeared into a whirling white-out. It came out of nowhere. Only minutes before, we were bathed in sunshine. The air immediately became chillier. A micro-techno-fibro-thermo-wanko jacket would have been handy at this point. Through the gloom I could see Hans skipping through the snow. I could only see a few metres in front of me. Then suddenly the snow deepened as the track climbed steeply through sharp boulders. Naturally, I stepped right into a snow drift. My legs were immediately sopping wet from the knees down, and my feet were soon squishing around in my runners making it hard to grip the wet rocks. 'Hello, hello,' echoed Hans from somewhere in front. Somewhere far in front, that is. I scrambled on blindly for ten minutes.

Then, as suddenly as the white-out had come, it went. There was only one small thing that spoilt my relief at being in the sun again. I couldn't see the group. Oh, great. I didn't even know which way to walk. I hope someone reads my message in the first guest book, I thought. To be honest, I wasn't all that worried about being lost. I was more worried about missing lunch. I was just about to turn and walk the opposite way when I heard a faint 'Hello, hello,' from below. There, about fifty metres below, was the entire group standing together looking up at me.

'They don't like me very much, do they?' I said to Jo, when I finally clambered down to rejoin my hiking pals.

'Oh, yes they do,' replied Jo, with a strained smile.

I was starving. 'Where is *mittagessen*?' ('lunch' in German—it's always important to know meal times in a foreign language) I asked Hans. Hans pointed to a tiny dot in the valley below. That tiny dot was a mountain restaurant.

We dropped below the snowline into a sunlit valley. The trail ran alongside a small, clear stream and we crisscrossed it occasionally on narrow log bridges or stepping stones.

By the time we reached the restaurant I was so hungry I could have eaten my walking stick. Not long after that, I thought I might have to. I checked to see how much money I had in my wallet and all I found was twelve Austrian schillings in coins. That's about $1.20, and wouldn't even buy you a sniff of a goulash soup in Austria. I'd spent all my money on Jägermeisters in a drunken frenzy the night before.

Searching frantically through my wallet, I found an American five-dollar note tucked away behind my driver's licence. An American guy I'd been travelling with had given it to me as a souvenir. Sod the souvenir. When the waiter said he'd take American dollars, I couldn't hand it over fast enough. There was one small problem, though. Five dollars in an Austrian mountain restaurant, miles from civilisation, doesn't buy much. I could only afford the *knackwurstsuppe*, which is a clear broth with a pork sausage floating in the middle of it.

Well, at least I had food. A few years later I went on a long hike above the Swiss town of Grindelwald, to the Faulhorn restaurant that can only be reached by a six-hour return walk. I'd set off early and trekked up a steep, groomed walking track through the snow. With only an hour to go before I reached the restaurant, I stopped to take a photo and discovered I'd forgotten to bring my wallet. I'd been salivating at the thought of a long and ludicrously large lunch accompanied by a few icy cold beers, followed by a casual hike back to Grindelwald. Alas, there was no use continuing. I couldn't last the whole day without food, so I turned back. Yeah, I know we humans can survive days without food (an Australian fellow survived for something like 63 days eating only half a Mars bar and one of his socks), but I couldn't stand the thought of watching deliriously happy people devouring their giant schnitzels. I was hungry and mighty pissed-off so I took what I thought was a short-cut through a forest. It wasn't short at all. I ended up clambering through thigh-deep snow repeating 'Fuck!' over and over for the four hours it took me to get back down to the village.

There was going to be no hunger problem at the Café Fernblick. I took full advantage of the large basket of bread rolls, which eased my hunger but compounded my unpopularity with the rest of the group, Not surprisingly, we were the only people in the restaurant. It was in the middle of nowhere.

After lunch, we made a detour up another steep track and—half an hour later—reached another bird house. Following the stamping ritual, Hans stood on a rock and clapped his hands to get our attention. He then made a short and moving speech ('Hello, hello') before pulling a small clear plastic bag, with what looked like medals in it, from his jacket pocket. He motioned for me to step forward then, to the rapturous applause of my fellow hikers, Hans pinned a bronze medal onto my T-shirt. I'd completed three peaks (which is very good for one day, Jo told me). And I not only received a bronze medal, but also a *Leistungs-abzeichenkasermandl* certificate (it probably meant 'hike'). Clara proudly received her silver medal (for ten peaks), then there was a hushed silence while Hal and Mary stepped forward. Hal looked as proud as Hawaiian punch as Hans pinned a gold medal on his puffed-out chest for conquering twenty bird houses.

I wrote 'Hello, hello' in the guest book.

The remainder of the walk was downhill. The low brush and low conifers gave way to a thick forest of pines. The path became a single-track road and we passed fields of freshly-cut hay with its heady perfume. Farmhouses with traditional elaborately carved balconies and flower-filled boxes bordered the fields.

We reached the small village of Patsch just as I reached my I've-had-enough-of-hiking-for-one-day limit. Innsbruck still looked kilometres away. Just as I was seriously contemplating calling a taxi, Hans motioned for us to hop into a white van which was conveniently waiting for us on the opposite side of the road. We were back in Innsbruck by dusk, and after a long, long shower (I used all the hot water) I hobbled down to the hostel's restaurant for dinner. Sometime after seven o'clock I fell asleep, right into my goulash soup.

Aeroplane

Casablanca, Morocco
October 1988

I love flying. I love everything about flying. I love just being in an airport, showing my passport, checking in, then wandering aimlessly around duty-free stores or tacky souvenir shops. I get a buzz reading the departures board, daydreaming about flying to Johannesburg or Beijing. Once aboard, I'm one of the few people alive who actually look forward to my airborne snack. I love all the little plastic bags and containers, and I'll tear open every single one. I don't drink tea or coffee, but I'll tear open the milk anyway. I'll open the cheese and take a tiny bite. Even on long flights where you're fed every hour, I'll say 'Yeah, sure, why not?' when I am offered breakfast at three o'clock in the afternoon (which makes perfect sense, because you happen to be flying over Turkmenistan, where they happen to be having their breakfast at the time). I put the sticker saying 'Please wake me for meals' in a prominent position on my forehead when I sleep. I even like turbulence. It's like a bonus amusement park ride. Except, of course, when I'm trying to eat one of my 37 meals. That's a bit of a challenge.

I don't even have a hint of the fear of flying (which, when you think about it, really isn't the fear of flying per se, but the fear of crashing). Some people refuse to fly. I bet they would all ride a bicycle (the chances of dying in a bicycle accident are 1 in 88 000, while your chances of dying in an airline accident are 1 in 10 million). Even scarier, in my view, is driving a car. In a typical one-month period on highways around the world, more people will die in automobile accidents than the total amount of commercial jet airline fatalities worldwide since the dawn of jet aviation. Of the 18 million or so flights every year, on average ten will crash. That's just over 14 billion miles flown for each crash. You have more chance of dying after being stung by a bee than by falling out of the sky in a plane.

Goodness knows, if you're still a bit anxious, you can always check out www.amigoingdown.com. This website calculates the likelihood of your plane plummeting to the earth. Enter your flight details, including airline, type of plane, cities of departure and arrival, and time of month and you get the odds of your chances of plummeting to the earth. Funnily enough, Iran Air didn't have very good odds for flying in the middle of winter and in a plane that was 30 years old. Still, even then, you have a much higher chance of dying by falling off a donkey than of dying on a midnight flight from Tehran to Bandar Abbabas.

I'll fly any old airline. I'll quite often just go with the cheapest flight available. I flew to Europe on Yugo Air once. It was *much* cheaper than all the rest. OK, so it was in the middle of a war, and there was a fair chance we'd be shot down flying over Serbian airspace, but boy was it cheap! And, even though it took 37 hours to get from Melbourne to London and the man next to me somehow managed to smoke twelve packets of cigarettes (and, impressively, grow a full beard!) during the flight, I saved 200 bucks!

No wonder I didn't even bat an eyelid when our Boeing 727 Royal Air Maroc flight from London to Agadir in Morocco shuddered slightly on its way down the runway. I was relaxed and comfortable with the knowledge that (most) airlines have amazingly complex and thorough maintenance regulations. Every three to five years a plane is basically stripped and put back together again. Royal Nepal Airlines takes even more precautions. Every October a buffalo is sacrificed. Its head is cut off on the runway and the blood is sprinkled on the landing gear. This is meant to ward off crashes by giving the plane its share of blood so that it won't seek it from humans.

My girlfriend, Jane, and I were off to Morocco for two weeks to get a bit of sun before the English winter stormed in. I'd got our tickets from a 'bucket shop'. When I went to pick them up, I had to navigate my way around an office with no less than 20 desks in a space that would normally fit about four. The whole place looked as if it was set up for a quick escape if the desk police suddenly turned up. Everyone working there looked like those guys who sell dodgy perfume from the boot of a car. But hey, it was cheap. I believe a real traveller is someone who spends as little money as possible in order to keep travelling as long as possible.

The plane lifted off the ground with ease. How several hundred tonnes of steel can rise so easily into the air has got me absolutely stumped. But, then again, I'm still trying to figure out how a ballpoint pen works. Not to mention TVs, microwaves, radios, computers and, well, most things really. Planes amaze me. In my view they are one of the three greatest inventions of the twentieth century (along with the mute button on a TV remote control and midriff-revealing tops for women).

'Brian, what's a six-letter word for sausage?' Jane asked. She hadn't even noticed the take-off. She was already well into a crossword puzzle. I was trying to figure out what the stewardess was saying over the PA. I was actually recording on a tape player at the time and I've played it back over and over again, word by word, and this is what I believe the stewardess said: 'The number of these flights seven five seven. Please shall reach Casablanca chiefs airport, an air service of flight tree hour and fun minutes. First sexual beads fasten your seatbelts under the back of your city and friends no smoking with a take-off. We wish you a flight food. Thank you.'

Out the window, England looked like a patchwork quilt. There were fields of green, yellow, brown and grey. I love the window seat. I love flying over all the diverse and sometimes bizarre landscapes and thinking to myself such excitable thoughts as 'Wow, that's Iran down there.' Suddenly the plane was enveloped by cloud (we were in England after all) and there was nothing to see.

I put my earphones on and started flicking through the stations. The comedy station had the same jokes played on every airline in the world. There will always be some unknown American who'll inevitably say, 'take my mother-in-law . . . someone PUH-leeeeze take my mother-in-law'. I usually listen to each one for five minutes or so, anyway. A warning, though: if you ever fly Royal Air Maroc, don't flick over to Channel 9. It's Moroccan music and it sounds like a drunken rugby team banging pots and pans while taking it in turns to jump on a cat. It really is painful.

Meanwhile, the food was already on its way. I waited eagerly to see what delectable surprises Royal Air Maroc would come up with. The first was that the meat was unrecognisable—was it chicken or pork? (I never did find out!) The second was that the peas were frozen solid. The chicken (or pork) tasted like, well . . . everything tastes the same in the air. The thing is, you lose 40 per cent of your taste sensation at altitude.

Which is just as well in some cases. But, then again, a lobster thermidor from Maxim's would probably taste the same as the chicken-pork-whatever.

A friend of mine always orders the vegetarian meal, but not because he's a vegetarian. He orders it because it usually comes out first and he tells me it's made specially. If he flew on some American Airlines flights, he wouldn't know where to start. As well as the vegetarian option, the alternative meals include children's, diabetic, gluten-free, low-calorie, bland (I thought the food already was, but this is apparently even more so for people with ulcers), lactose-free, low-fat, low-sodium, Moslem, Hindu, kosher and vegan (a cheesecloth shirt and a tambourine are provided with this option).

After opening every packet, including the salt which I didn't use but opened anyway for the hell of it, I'd made a fine mess of my tray. What even I find astonishing, though, is the waste. There is soooo much rubbish, and—whether you open the dozen packets or not—the whole lot gets chucked. Back in the early days of airline travel, meal scraps were simply thrown out an open window in the galley. Lone herdsmen in the deserts of Turkey would have been hit from above with chicken bones, half-eaten rolls and tiny vodka bottles.

'Would you eat me?' I asked Jane.

'What?'

'If the plane crashed, and you had to eat humans to survive, would you eat me?'

I'd just finished reading the book *Alive*, telling the true story of a Uruguayan football team that crashed in the Andes in 1972. The survivors ate their dead team-mates to survive (a recommended read if you're just about to fly, by the way). They ended up eating everything. Hands, fingers, hearts and even brains.

Jane squirmed in her seat, 'No, I wouldn't. Would you eat me?'

I considered for a moment. 'I'd have a go at your boobs,' I smirked.

Before I had a chance to tell her that human flesh is supposed to taste like pork, the movie started. It was some sort of action movie. Five minutes in, someone spoke for the first time and Arabic subtitles came up . . . taking up half the screen.

Next in the flying ritual is using the toilet. Now most people I know are familiar with the concept of using a toilet. The idea is relatively simple. Even my three-year-old nephew, Cooper, can manage it (although his Dad has trouble—he came home drunk one night a few years back and pissed in his sock drawer). Obviously accuracy was not a concern for some of the passengers. If they got vaguely in the direction of the toilet (or hand basin for that matter), they were happy. I'm sorry to say, though, I made it worse. I made the terrible mistake of going to the toilet in my socks, and—in trying not to stand in the wee on the floor—ended up peeing everywhere but in the toilet itself.

In the mirror I looked like a corpse. My face was white, drawn and dried-out. Not only does the recycled air inside the plane make you look like death, but the airline toilet mirrors make you look even worse. Brad Pitt would look ugly in an airline toilet mirror. Back in the old days, you could have at least stepped outside for some fresh air. The passenger plane designed in 1909 by Igor Sikorsky (the man who also built and flew in the world's first helicopter) had a promenade deck. Admittedly this feature was only suitable for a brave minority, because it involved literally walking around on top of the plane.

Back in my seat again, and with Jane now in the children's puzzle page, I picked up the safety card (probably the only person on the plane who had). Not to look for the exits or anything, I hasten to add, but to admire the illustrations. Our plane was a Boeing 727. I always check what type of plane I'm on and think to myself something like, Ah, a Boeing 727 (when I wouldn't know the difference between a 727 and a Cessna).

The Boeing 727 does have a pretty good record, though. The first one was built in 1964 for United Airlines (then passed on to Royal Air

Maroc, I believe). Only 250 were originally planned, but—by the time they stopped production in 1984—just over 1800 were sold. The older ones have flown the equivalent of 3000 times around the world. The 727 fleet alone has carried the equivalent of the entire world's population.

Meanwhile, high over Europe, the sky outside was dark but clear. Below, the lights of towns and villages (Spanish by my guess) looked like an upside-down starry night. I watched for quite a while, mesmerised by the lights. Suddenly the lights stopped dead. We were crossing the Mediterranean and the Strait of Gibraltar. I could see the lights of Africa, fifteen kilometres away, on the other side. From this height it looked like you could jump from Europe to Africa (with a good run-up, of course). The lights on the east coast of Morocco seemed to stretch out for hundreds of kilometres. The visibility was amazing. Not that even the poorest visibility is much of a problem for pilots. With today's technology, pilots can fly virtually blind. In the early days of airline travel pilots not only didn't have radar or radios, but didn't have meteorology services to tell them what the weather would be like. In poor visibility, pilots would fly only a few hundred feet above the ground with their heads out of the window following railway lines or roads into a city. This was more reliable than a compass. But it didn't always work. Once two planes, bound for Paris and London respectively, were following the same road at the same height. Both pilots had their heads out the window looking down at the road. The two planes collided head-on, killing everyone on board.

Being a passenger on the first flights wouldn't have been too pleasant, either. The passengers had to sit in an open cockpit. Each one was supplied with a leather jacket, goggles, flying helmet and a hot water bottle to help them keep warm. At least you didn't have to try and make conversation with the person sitting next to you. Your lips would have been frozen shut.

Our Captain said something over the PA. All I got was 'Hullo …'

then, '. . . thank you.' But I imagined he was telling us we were starting our descent into Casablanca. Jane and I weren't stopping there, though. We were continuing on to the beach resort of Agadir. There was nothing really worth seeing in Casablanca. Casablanca's most famous sight is Rick's Café and that never even existed, except on a film lot in Hollywood. (An interesting note: Humphrey Bogart wasn't the original choice for the role of Rick. Ronald Reagan was. Scary thought.)

Nevertheless, I was looking forward to Casablanca airport, where we would disembark for half an hour. According to my Royal Air Maroc in-flight magazine, I would be 'cordially welcomed into the King Mohammed V Reception Building, the most luxurious air terminal in the world. Aglow with marble, crystal and glass, Casablanca's new airport has every convenience and comfort. Enjoy the new lounges, restaurants, wonderful duty-free shopping and close parking'.

The airport may have been modern and sparkling, but everything was closed and it looked like someone had grabbed the cast of *Ali Baba and the Forty Thieves* and plonked them in the middle of the airport. Men dressed in their bedding were lazing about in the 'new lounges' smoking. Every single one of them seemed to be having a heated argument with someone else.

The 'wonderful' duty-free shops were closed, so we found a relatively quiet spot among a bunch of sleeping Moroccans (they were smart: they were already in their nightshirts).

Two hours later we heard 'Agadir' mentioned a couple of times in an announcement, noticed a few people get up and decided to follow them. We walked down a long corridor. Well, shuffled really. No-one was in a hurry. When, at last, we were led out of 'the world's best airport' and onto the tarmac, all I could see by way of aircraft was a contraption that looked to me like a short step up from Orville and Wilbur Wright's plane. It was a twin-propeller thing. In fact, I'm sure it was the same plane used at the end of the film *Casablanca*.

A smiling hostie greeted us at the top of the stairs. Whoops, sorry, I should correctly call them flight attendants. The original flight attendants from the 1930s were called stewards and were always men. Women joined the ranks when it was decided that stewards also had to be registered nurses (I imagine they would come in handy for cutting up humans into bite-size pieces).

There were only about twenty of us on the flight. The seats were uncomfortable but, luckily, it was only a short flight to Agadir. We have no concept of what a long-haul flight really is. The first ever long-haul flights were looooooooooooong. KLM, which by the way is the world's oldest airline, pioneered long distance aviation. One flight left Amsterdam on 1 October 1924 and arrived in Jakarta on 24 November. Fifty-five days later. OK, so it was held over in Bulgaria for three weeks awaiting spare parts, and for another week in Turkey, but the total actual flying time was 127 hours! Today that same flight would be over in twelve hours (not counting any repairs in Bulgaria). One hundred and twenty-seven hours! That, I figured out, is around 60 movies. And 32 meals (with 256 packets of things to open).

By contrast, the shortest airline service is one from Logan Air which runs between two of the Orkney islands in northern Scotland. Normally the flight takes two minutes. But with a tail wind, it's over in 58 seconds. That's not even enough time for the flight attendant to show you where the whistle is located on the life jacket. Yet I bet they still manage to feed you twice.

The plane clattered down the runway. The engine noise was deafening. The overhead lockers kept swinging open as if the plane was possessed by a demon. Everything shook. Above the noise I could hear my bones rattling. Just as the plane noise reached its teeth-chattering, screaming crescendo, it lifted off the ground. I loved it. Now that was an amusement park ride.

As soon as the No Smoking sign was switched off, every single person, regardless of seating, regardless of age—including, I might add, what looked like a ten-year-old—lit up in unison and began smoking with furious dedication. Within seconds the whole cabin looked as if we were in the middle of a thick fog.

The hostie smiled as she appeared out of the fog and handed out drinks and peanuts that were older than the plane, while the plane shook and shuddered around her. I checked out the safety card. Our plane was an ATR 42 made by Aerospatiale (specialist in the manufacture of the amazing vibrating plane).

Before I had a chance to listen to all the stations on the headset, the plane landed. Well, thumped onto the tarmac, then screamed down the runway. We walked towards the small terminal building and stood in the short queue that had gathered near the entrance. 'Why does that sign say Marrakesh, I wonder?' Jane said as she pointed to a large sign on the terminal building. I looked around. I saw another sign. It too said Marrakesh. We'd got off at the wrong stop. We'd got off one airport too early.

We looked at each other in shock then stepped out of the queue and bolted back towards the plane. Out of the corner of my eye, I saw a group of men running towards us. I turned to see four large men in military uniform brandishing even larger guns that were pointed directly at us. 'Put your hands up!' one of them shouted. 'We're on this plane!' I said feebly. They thought my blonde-haired, blue-eyed and flowery-summer-frock-wearing girlfriend and I were terrorists. A scary-looking chap pointed his gun only centimetres away from my face. Then, just as they were about to strip-search us, our smiling stewardess called out from the top of the stairs.

'We could have been shot,' I said calmly as we sat back in our seats, 'Cool, hey?'

An hour later, I checked with the stewardess before we stepped off the plane. Then I checked the sign on the side of the terminal building.

Yes, this was Agadir airport. No wonder the Moroccans consider Casablanca airport to be the best in the world. Agadir International Airport consisted of a large shed. Your common or garden variety, corrugated iron shed.

The baggage carousel sounded terminally ill. It coughed and spluttered like a dying man. Our bags (when they finally appeared) looked as though the bag handlers had been playing a quick game of five-a-side soccer with them.

The customs fellow looked like a terrorist. A cigarette dangling from the corner of his mouth dropped ash inside Jane's bag as he rifled through her knickers. He picked out a carton of cigarettes, opened it, took out a pack and shoved them into his trouser pocket. He looked at us, smiled, then reached into the carton and grabbed another pack. 'Hey, what do you think you're doing?' I muttered. Jane told me to let him have them. She just wanted to get out of the airport.

It's funny how when I fly it doesn't even cross my mind that the plane might crash. Not even for a millisecond. However, a few years after our trip to Morocco, I saw a story in the paper. A Royal Air Maroc ATR 42 went down on the identical flight that we took to Agadir. The aircraft entered a steep dive and crashed ten minutes after take-off. The pilot was blamed for disconnecting the autopilot and deliberately causing the crash. He committed suicide and took 43 people with him. It did make me think, though. I'll keep on flying, but—if you look at the odds—I'd better keep away from donkeys and bees.

Hire Car

Agadir, Morocco
October 1988

Agadir–Taroudannt

I found it quite difficult driving on the right-hand side of the road to begin with. It didn't help that the condition of the road—well, the haphazard trickle of asphalt—made our teeth chatter, and that I had to dodge camels, donkey, mules, goats and hundreds of people dressed as Obi-Wan-Kenobi. However, what I found most annoying (not to mention dangerous) was that every time I went to change gear, I'd find myself opening the window. I was so used to the gears being on my right.

Luckily, driving out of the seaside town of Agadir was relatively easy. The roads were wide and straight. Agadir is a new city. In February 1960, an earthquake collapsed the whole previous version of Agadir like a pack of cards. It was reduced to rubble in a matter of seconds. Twelve thousand lives were lost. Afterwards, for fear of epidemics, the whole town was bulldozed flat and rebuilt as a modern lifeless city. If I'd had to drive through a maze of old narrow streets, all the while trying to change gears with a door handle, I would undoubtedly have hit something or someone on the way out.

Jane and I had decided we wanted to see the real Morocco, so we hired a car and, without any preparation at all, drove straight out towards the desert. And it wasn't long before we got there. No sooner than we'd left the suburbs of Agadir, actually. After only fifteen minutes we totally lost sight of Agadir behind us. We were completely surrounded by desert. To the north, I could just make out the Atlas Mountains in the morning haze. Being in the middle of endless desert really does give you a feeling of being small and insignificant. I wasn't thinking about that, though. I was too busy thinking about what would happen if we ran out of petrol or if there was some sort of mechanical problem (I consider changing a tyre nothing less than mechanical genius). Jane, on the other hand, was worried that we'd be mugged and raped by marauding bandits. A broken fuse scared me a hell of a lot more.

We'd hired our car—well a Fiat Uno which is like a ride-on lawn mower with a roof—from a company called Africar. I hired it from there simply because I liked the name (working in advertising, I'm a sucker for a good pun). There was a Hertz across the road, but I was sold on Africar. Hertz are everywhere. They have over 500 000 cars to hire in 140 countries around the globe. The company was originally called Rent a Ford when, in 1918, an eighteen-year-old fellow from Chicago began renting out twelve Model-T Fords. In 1923 he sold the company to John Hertz. Today it's just another one of those bloody giant American conglomerates that are slowly taking over the world. It's enough to make you hire a car from a dubious outfit with a half-clever name.

As soon as I had the stressful gear-changing caper out of the way, I began to play with all the bells and whistles in the car. What's this button do? What's this bonnet-release button do? Oh, it opens the bonnet. Back in the car after shutting the bonnet I began my usual flick around the radio stations. The only two I found were both playing Moroccan music. I soon turned it off. It's quite disturbing listening to someone singing as if they're in terrible, agonising pain.

We passed a donkey on the side of the road. Well, I think it was a donkey. It had so much greenery piled on top of it that only its legs were poking out the bottom. It was plodding wearily along, being led by a man who was probably taking it to Agadir, at least an hour's walk away. A bit further up, a couple of camels were being used to plough what looked like barren desert. Then a bit further on there was another four-legged shrub. This donkey was stacked even higher. There seemed to be a lot of action going on considering we were in the middle of a desert.

To the east ominous dark clouds were gradually drifting towards us. Up ahead a purple haze lay along the horizon (incidentally, Jimi Hendrix spent a lot of time in Morocco but, in his case, I suppose the 'purple haze' was in his brain). We were heading for the town of Taroudannt. It was, according to my guidebook, a 'real' Moroccan city with 'magnificent and well-preserved red mud walls'. It hadn't changed in hundreds of years. I'm a firm believer in reading up on a place before you visit it. However, now and again it's an adventure and sometimes a wonderful surprise to just turn up somewhere without knowing a single thing about the place. All I knew about Taroudannt was that it had magnificent red mud walls. I was hoping, though, that it wasn't like a village further to the south which had also remained unchanged for a hundred years. Up until the 1920s every European that came near that village was ambushed, kidnapped and strung up by the ears and left to die.

The road turned to red dust. The huge dust clouds behind us stayed hovering in the air for ages. Amazingly, the dirt road was smoother than the asphalt one. 'I've thought of some other names for companies,' I said. 'You know, like Africar. You could have a company that sells snorkelling equipment in Helsinki and call it Fin-Land. Or, how about shop called Tie-Land in Bangkok. Or . . .' Before I could come up with another witty pun, we came to an intersection. I pulled over to the side of the road while Jane looked at the map. As we all know, women cannot read maps, so after Jane dithered around for a few minutes I took it off her. 'It doesn't make any sense,' Jane protested. She was right. I don't think that even the person who designed this map would be able to read it. According to my interpretation, we would have to go via Algeria and through the Sahara desert. We couldn't possibly be lost this early in the trip.

Mind you, if we were in a Hertz car that was installed with NeverLost we wouldn't have had a problem. An onboard computer provides turn-by-turn driving instructions to where you want to go. If you take a wrong turn, the computer-generated voice will tell you, 'Hey, stupid! It's the next left.' Or something like that. But, that would take away the fun of screaming at each other over whether to go left or right.

The signs didn't help either. What signs there were looked to me like a homeboy had graffitied his tag on them. Distances were hard to figure out as well. In Arabic 0 means 5 and 7 means 3, etc.

'Is that twenty-seven kilometres to the next scribble or seventy?' I asked Jane.

'Twenty-seven, I think.'

'Right. Twenty-seven kilometres to where though?'

I didn't want to take the wrong turn. I didn't want to end up in the town where they string people up by their ears. Jane finally figured it out. 'It's straight ahead.'

'Yeah, I knew that,' I said.

We hadn't seen anyone for a while when Obi-Wan-Kenobi (a man wearing a traditional Moroccan djellaba which, with its large hood and long brown robe, makes him and half of Morocco look like a Jedi knight) jogged by us. We couldn't see any nearby houses or farms, so where had he come from? Have you, like me, ever wondered why the Moroccans are so damn good at long distance running? It's probably because they walk, or run, everywhere. And if that means trudging 80 kilometres through the desert to get the morning paper, then so be it. In fact, in the last hour we'd seen dozens of people wandering in the desert, but only two cars.

Some dark clouds were closing in. The sky to our right was pitch black. On the left, it was a perfect blue. Suddenly the clouds were over us and let loose a monsoonal downpour. The Fiat's wipers were flapping crazily for their little lives. Well, they were eventually—after I activated the indicators, headlights, high-beam, window washer and the cigarette lighter, and opened the bonnet again. Then, as suddenly as it started, the rain stopped. The sun came out immediately, reflecting brightly on the wet road.

In the distance, Taroudannt looked like a gigantic red sandcastle. The city was totally encircled by high red mud walls. It really did feel like we were stepping back a thousand years. Until, that is, a Moroccan boy rode up noisily beside us on a motorbike. 'You want nice hotel for you?' he said, while riding only centimetres away from my window.

'No, we're OK. We have a hotel.' We actually hadn't booked one, but I had the name of one from my guidebook. It was called Hotel Saadiens (which hopefully wasn't a reference to its cramped rooms).

'I show you. I take you,' he insisted.

We had no choice really. There only seemed to be one gate into the city and he was riding in front of us. As soon as we entered the city, the road was teeming with brightly coloured life. There were people pushing carts piled high with oranges, melons and bags of spices. One guy even had a cart piled high with microwave ovens. Our guide offered to unload our car, take our bags in and even prepare a hot bath. It finally took a wad of cash and a desperate cry of 'For God's sake leave us alone' to get rid of him.

Taroudannt–Marrakesh

We were on the road by eight, under a blanket of low hanging cloud. Both of us were tired and grumpy. The early morning prayer (or, as it should be renamed, desperate call for singing lessons) which is blasted around the city at five in the morning seemed to be coming from inside our wardrobe.

It rained right through the two days we had in Taroudannt. And I mean rained. We spent most of our time in restaurants (I had camel—tastes like old shoes and each bite takes about ten minutes to chew) and wandering around the souks ('NO, I don't want a FUCKING carpet!').

The major problem with a guide showing us the way into the town was that we didn't know how to get out again. Not that it took me long to find the gate—it just happened to be the wrong one. After all the rain, the road had disappeared under a mess of mud and camel shit. I circumnavigated the walls three times trying to find the road beneath the quagmire.

I wanted to take the Tizi-n-Test mountain pass to Marrakesh but the chap in the hotel had told us, 'Road is much danger. Car go . . .' He then whistled and with his hand mimicked a car going over a cliff—well, it was either that or someone was going to drop bombs on us . . . 'so is no good.'

'We'll go,' I enthused. 'It will be all right.'

Jane gave me a pleading look, 'Brian, we're not.'

In hindsight it was probably a wise move not to. We later learnt the road had collapsed down the mountain in a mudslide.

The torrential rain had turned the desert a deep chocolate brown. It was peppered with stark white rocks. It felt like I was driving on a huge lamington. We passed small mud-brick farmhouses surrounded by fences of cactus plants. They looked uninhabited but for the occasional bright piece of clothing hanging out to dry.

Half an hour after leaving Taroudannt, we passed through a small village. It consisted of a couple of mud-brick houses and a service station. About 500 metres before the service station, there were maybe a dozen people milling about a car on the side of the road. It had crashed into a pole. I noticed, as we drove past, a man lying on the grass. He looked dead. No-one was even looking at the body. They were all watching two policemen trying to get the other person out of the wrecked car. Like every person who passes a car accident, I slowed down. And, like every person who passes a car accident, I felt sick in the stomach. And, like every person who passes a car accident, I tried to get a good look.

There are around five million car accidents a year in the world, with close to 500 000 deaths. And not all road accident deaths just involve one or two people. The world's worst car accident happened in Afghanistan in 1982. A petrol tanker crashed in a tunnel and just over 3000 people were killed.

The service station fellow seemed totally oblivious to the crash only metres down the road. He gave us a huge beaming smile as he filled our tank. Nowadays even having someone else fill the tank seems a bit old-fashioned to we westerners used to self-service, but for the first twenty years or so of automobiles, petrol stations didn't exist. Everyone had to buy their petrol from chemist shops. At least Molotov cocktails would have been easy to make. Most chemists sold petrol in large bottles.

I went to the toilet. Well, calling it a toilet is much too kind. While I was away, our smiling service station attendant asked Jane to be his wife. 'It OK,' he said. 'My wife she won't mind. She will very much like you.' Having a few wives is not that strange in Morocco. The former Prime Minister of Morocco, Madani El Glaoui, had 50 wives and 64 children. When he died, his brother Thami took all of his wives and added them to his own harem of 96. That's over 150 wives. By the way, Jane declined his tempting offer. Later on in Marrakesh I would be offered 1000 camels in exchange for her.

Not long after our pit stop the scenery changed to a moonscape of yellow rocks. Huge boulders lay scattered about as if thrown around by capricious giants. In the middle of this nothingness we came to a river. There were about twenty people—we're still in the middle of nowhere, let me remind you—standing around watching it. This river was obviously new. It must have been created by all the recent rain. I have to admit that it looked impressive. There was one major problem, though. It flowed right across the road. And, boy, did it flow. It was a virtual torrent. We stopped. I stared at the fast-moving water. We couldn't cross that. We would have to go back. A boy of about sixteen or so stepped up to my window. He started waffling to me in French. 'I don't understand French,' I said in perfect French. 'It OK for you to go,' he said in not-so-perfect English.

'No, it very dangerous,' I said in that broken English we all use when we speak to foreigners.

'No, it OK. Many car go. I help. It OK.'

There was a very good chance the 150 kilogram Fiat Uno would be swept away down the river, but I couldn't stand the thought of driving back. I reversed for a few metres, took a deep breath and moved slowly forward. 'If I take it in second gear, we should be fine,' I said confidently (as if I'd had plenty of experience fording turbulent rivers in tiny cars). I glanced around at Jane as we hit the water. She had her eyes firmly closed. Immediately the water was halfway up the outside of the door. This probably wasn't a good idea. I could feel the car being pushed to one side. I surged forward. Don't stop and don't speed up, I thought to myself. Take it easy. Out of the corner of my eye I noticed the rest of the Moroccans staring at us in total disbelief. The Moroccan boy was behind us pretending to push. I stayed calm. After what seemed like fifteen minutes, but was probably only two, our little Uno rose out of the water and back on to the road. 'You can open your eyes now,' I said. My heart slowed down a beat or two. The Moroccan boy shoved his hand through the open window towards my pocket, 'You give me 50 dirham (about A\$8)'.

'What for?' I said, still shaken from the crossing.

'I help you. I push you,' he hollered. I sped up, but he began running to keep up.

'No, you didn't. You did nothing,' I said. I wasn't giving him money for walking beside our car.

'Give me 50 dirham!' he demanded repeatedly, as he tried to force his hand into my pocket.

'NO!' I repeated just as often. He was now sprinting to keep up with us. He still had his arm in the window. I was worried that if I really sped up, I'd tear his arm off. He began grabbing at my shirt. Sod it, I thought, I'll take his bloody arm off. I sped up even more. Just as I was trying to figure out what I was going to do with a dismembered arm, he pulled his still-attached arm out of the car and collapsed on the road. I looked back through the rear-view mirror to see him making a feeble attempt to throw a rock at our car. The Moroccans may be great runners, but luckily they can't throw rocks.

After all that excitement, it was back to the endless emptiness of the desert. The High Atlas mountains loomed in the distance. We passed a village that was set well back from the road. The mud-walled houses looked like gigantic beehives, and collectively they were just like Luke Skywalker's village in *Star Wars*. (Ah, so that's where all the Obi-Wan-Kenobis came from!)

We knew we were getting closer to a city. Rubber tyres and oil drums were piled on the side of the road. A line of very tall palm trees with dry, moth-eaten leaves led us to the crimson ramparts of the city of Marrakesh. The walls of the city rose high above us, then suddenly we entered the gate and were surrounded by dozens of Moroccans on pushbikes. Plus the usual array of donkeys, goats and carts piled high with brightly coloured fruit. I dropped down to a walking pace. The speedo wasn't even registering. Mind you, back in the early days of automobiles this was as fast as you could go. In 1878 the law prescribed that on English roads cars should go no faster than a blistering two miles per hour. They also had to be led by a man carrying a red flag to warn pedestrians and horsemen. Some old people today still abide by that speed limit. They must have also had a law back then that you had to drive with an indicator on the whole time, because a lot of old people still do that, too.

Amazingly, I not only found the hotel I was looking for, I scored a car park right out the front. In between a donkey-drawn cart and huge pile of old cabbages.

Marrakesh–Essaouiria

We had four days in Marrakesh (for dinner one night I had sugared pigeon pie—it was like eating chicken-flavoured sticky-date pudding) and we spent many hours wandering around the souks ('NO, how many times do I have to tell you, I don't want a FUCKING carpet!').

About an hour after leaving Marrakesh, we were almost run off the road by an overtaking Peugeot station wagon. The engine screamed as it went past. It was a taxi. I counted no less than ten people crammed into it. It swerved all over the road in front of us. Ten minutes later I was waved down by a policeman who was standing by his car in the middle of nowhere. He waffled to me in a mix of Arabic, French and English. I caught something about a fine, or was that 'I am fine', or 'isn't the weather fine?' Then he handed me a piece of paper with scribbles all over it and pointed to a number (damn, is that 250 or 597?). He was fining me for . . . I had no idea what. I wasn't speeding, so it must have been that I wasn't swerving all over the road. He took the cash, smiled and walked back to his car. I'd hazard a guess that the money went straight into his pocket. Oh well, it could have been worse. A friend of mine was sold some hash by a Moroccan fellow in Tangiers who then confronted him twenty minutes later dressed in his police uniform. He gave him a huge fine and took his hash back.

After passing through a dramatic landscape of stark rocks that towered against the dark blue skies we drove by a large cluster of trees filled with goats. I slammed on the brakes. There were about ten trees, all with around six goats happily munching leaves high up in the branches. There wasn't a single goat on the ground. Were they tree goats or was it a goat tree? Two shepherd boys came running out from under the shade of the tree to greet us.

'*Stilo, stilo!*' the boys chorused.

They were asking for pens. This wasn't the first time we'd been asked for pens, either. Nearly every child we saw in Morocco asked us for a pen (for some reason the teenagers wanted not pens, but Bob Marley cassette tapes). If you are planning on visiting Morocco, I recommend you raid your stationery cupboard at work. You'll make a lot of Moroccan children very happy. They will hassle you for twenty minutes to give them a pen. One of the shepherd boys pointed to the goats in the tree and said, 'Goats!' He then put out his hand for money. He wanted me to pay him for stopping and looking at his goats. They'll be asking me for money for the sun rising next. I was getting used to it. In the souks you get asked for money every five minutes. For the other four minutes someone else would be asking you to be their friend, your guide or your boyfriend—both of us got asked this.

Not long after the tree goats we came to the end of the earth. The road we were travelling on took a sharp left at the edge of a cliff. We must have been climbing steadily for the last few hours. Far below us as far as the eye could see, the Atlantic Ocean was covered in a blanket of thick sea mist. It must have only been metres above the water. It truly was an astounding sight. It looked like cotton wool. It looked like the end of the earth. We got out of the car. I could smell the sea even though we must have been at least 1500 metres above it.

When we finally wound our way to the base of the cliff and into the valley below, we were no longer in the desert. In fact, it couldn't have been more different. We were driving through the middle of a lush green banana plantation. Small villages were scattered over the landscape—ochre splashes on a green backdrop.

It wasn't hard to spot the town of Essaouiria. The whole town seemed to be glistening white. With the whitewashed houses and their blue windowsills and doors, it looked more Greek than Moroccan. Essaouiria was a maze of narrow lanes and tiny tranquil squares (there is one *huge* square in town though which, fittingly, is called Place d'Orson Welles).

We checked into the Grand Hotel. And it was very grand indeed. Although, it probably should have been renamed the Former Grand Hotel. The dusty foyer was a vast four-storey high courtyard. The giant domed roof above wouldn't have looked out of place in a Renaissance cathedral. A formerly grand staircase took us up to our formerly grand room. It was huge. The large bed had clean white fine cotton sheets on it. Well, clean in 1973 when the bed was last made. We could hear the pounding surf of the ocean crashing on the wall below our room. The hotel was built on a sea wall overlooking the Atlantic. From the front of the hotel, you wouldn't even realise you were near the water.

We thought we were the only people staying there until we saw a German couple in the foyer later on that night. Being the only two couples in the whole place we felt a kinship with each other and stopped for a chat. When I asked, 'How are your sheets?' they both looked at each other strangely. Then the fellow said, 'They are . . . they are OK.' They said goodnight and hastily scurried off. Later in our room it clicked as to why they all of a sudden behaved so awkwardly. They had thought I'd asked, 'How are your shits?'

Essaouiria–London

We had two days in Essaouiria (I ordered prawns for dinner one night and a colossal ceramic bowl came out filled with—I'm not exaggerating here—at least 50 giant prawns. Not one to waste food, I ate the lot and lay in bed for hours groaning about how full I was). We also spent many hours wandering around the souks (what part of 'I don't want A FUCKING CARPET' don't you understand?).

On the way out of town I had to do an eighteen-point turn around a corner. I know it was eighteen, because I counted every single bloody one of them. We had come to a corner where the front walls of the houses sat right on the road. The road was no wider than a bathtub. Jane had to get out and bark instructions. Either I didn't hear or Jane didn't tell me to stop (we never did finally establish which one it was— even though we did debate it for the next two hours) and I scraped the car against the side of a building. There was an almighty long scratch and dent down the passenger's side of the car. Ten minutes later we finally turned the corner, with Jane cursing my lack of skill at driving and me cursing Jane for her lack of skill at giving directions. In 1901 Carl Benz—the man who designed and built the world's first car—said that driving was such a difficult skill to master only a million people around the world would ever be able to do it.

On the outskirts of Essaouiria we passed a Jaguar that looked brand new. Its driver either didn't do much driving in Essaouiria or he was very good at eighteen-point turns. It was immaculate. For the average Moroccan, though, the car would cost the equivalent of twenty years wages. Mind you, it would take 60 years of wages for the average Australian to buy the world's most expensive production car. The McLaren F1 6.1 costs around $1.9 million.

The five-hour journey back to Agadir was uneventful. There were no monsoonal rains, no flooded rivers to ford, no dead bodies on the side of the road, no goat trees and no wandering Obi-Wan-Kenobis.

On the way back to the office of Africar, I had a stroke of genius. I parked on the opposite side of the road. The chap in the Africar office looked out the window, saw that the car looked fine, signed the form and let us go. The long scratch and dent was on the opposite side. Three hours later we were on a plane back to London. I know, it's not a nice thing to do, but what do they expect if they insist on having streets as wide as bathtubs?

Taxi

Belfast, Northern Ireland
September 1988

'Down theirt lane there is a popular plairce for knee cappin', my tour guide said, with a big grin. 'That's where they put a gon to tha back o' ya knee and blow tha focker off.'

David (or, as he pronounced it, Dare-ved) was not only my tour guide, he was also my taxidriver. I'd flown to Belfast that morning for a meeting (I was working at an advertising agency in London at the time), and then I was to fly straight back when it finished. The meeting only lasted an hour. I still had two-and-a-half hours before I needed to be at the airport. As I jumped in the cab, I had a brilliant idea. 'Look, I've got two hours before I have to be at the airport,' I said to the cabbie, 'would you take me on a guided tour of Belfast?'

'Yeah, whoy not?' he said, with a this-sucker-will-make-a-great-fare smile.

There were two other good reasons that made a guided cab tour seem like a great idea. The big one was that I had a company Cabcharge card. Work could pay for it; they were used to big taxi bills. Only a few months earlier we'd had a big boozy lunch in Greenwich and I'd shared a cab back to central London with my boss, the creative director, and two other workmates. 'I need another drink,' our creative director announced, 'let's stop at a pub.' He told the taxidriver to wait for us while we staggered inside. Naturally, the meter stayed running. When the boss spotted a couple of pool tables his eyes lit up and he sent me outside to tell the taxidriver that we'd be a bit longer. Two hours longer, to be exact. When our patient (and-soon-to-be-wealthy) taxidriver finally dropped us off back at the office, the meter was sitting on £72.45 (about $220).

So really, my soon-to-be-rather-expensive journey back to the airport shouldn't even raise an eyebrow. And anyway, I could always say the taxidriver went the long way. Mind you, when it comes to a hard-to-explain fare, I would have nothing on a Dutch fellow I read about. He was in Frankfurt for the Frankfurt Book Fair and had caught a cab back to his hotel after a string of parties. He was smart, though. He'd taken the business card of the hotel with him, knowing he was going to have a drink or fourteen, and he simply handed it to the taxidriver. He promptly fell into a drunken stupor. The next morning he was woken by the taxidriver, outside his house in Amsterdam. He had handed over his own business card with his home address on it. His little taxi ride was just over 450 kilometres.

The other reason that encouraged me to take a cab tour in this particular cab was that I could understand the driver. In the cab from the airport, I couldn't understand the driver at all. He may as well have been speaking Hungarian. He had the thickest Northern Irish accent imaginable.

'Where's your Bergornta?' he asked, as I stepped into the taxi.

'Sorry?' I said.

'Where's your Bergornta?' he repeated.

What the hell's a Bergornta, I thought? Was it some sort of special entry pass I needed? Was it Northern Irish slang for baggage? Was it a type of gun?

'I'm sorry, what's a Bergornta?' I asked warily.

He looked at me strangely for a minute. 'Where . . . are . . . you . . . be . . . goin' . . . to?' he said slowly, and a little angrily.

'Ohhhh,' I said, 'I'll "bergornta" 28 Jamisons Road.'

I had no trouble with David's accent. He had that beautiful lilting Northern Irish accent. Even if they say something like, 'I'll kull yer, yer fockin' bearstard!' it sounds delightful.

My tour started with the large and grand Europa hotel. David told me it had been bombed more than fifty times. 'The rooms must be cheap, then,' I said.

'Nah, foreigners have no idea that it's used fur bomb practice.'

The tour continued as we passed a boarded-up shopfront. Black soot covered the surrounding shops. 'They'll fockin' blow up anythin,' David grunted. He was right. It was a fish and chip shop.

David kept turning around (taking his eyes off the road) to talk. 'A fella got decapitated here,' he said, pointing to an innocent looking family home. I had to lean forward out of my seat to hear him. It was a black London cab and the back seat was quite a distance away from the driver. This was the instantly recognisable Austin FX-4. I love London cabs. When you think of the symbols of London, you think of red double-decker buses, red telephone boxes, bobbies and black cabs. They're great-looking cars in that clunky, old-fashioned sort of way. These venerable machines had been unchanged since they were specially designed and built in 1959 (sadly, in 1997 they finally stopped manufacturing them). There are over 24 000 black cabs in London. Mind you, that doesn't make getting a licence to operate a black cab in

London easy. All cabbies have to acquire 'The Knowledge'. This involves two years of riding around London on a scooter, trying to memorise 24 000 streets (so they can quickly find the longest route) and learning the whereabouts of every hospital, theatre, hotel and train station in central London (which they all seem to promptly forget). Back in 1636, when cabs first appeared on the streets of London, licences were even harder to come by. King Charles only gave out 50. These, of course, were for horse-drawn carriages (or cabs, hence the name). By 1654, under the rule of Oliver Cromwell, the number of licences was increased to 200 and regulations were introduced. Since modified versions of those rules still operate today, they must have included such clauses as: Ye cabdriver shall not wash or use deodorant; thou shalt take the longest route; thou shalt not speak the language of thy passengers; and, if thou does happen to speak the language, thou shalt share thy outrage over politics, sport, economic reforms and the state of the traffic.

I have to admit, I was a little pensive getting into a black cab at Belfast airport. The last time I'd seen a black cab in the streets of Belfast was on the television news in Paris two months earlier. The footage was of a black cab surrounded by a large angry mob in a back street of Belfast. The taxidriver had somehow ended up in the wrong place and he was frantically nudging forwards and backwards trying to force the cab through the dense crowd. As he reversed madly up the kerb, the cab stalled. Within seconds, and right in front of the TV camera, the mad hordes dragged the driver out of the smashed window and kicked him to death. So you can perhaps imagine the sense of foreboding that crept over me as we drove down a gloomy street full of bomb-damaged and blackened houses. The ground was still wet from the morning rain, but even the shiny new cars and rose gardens couldn't make the streetscape look anything more than dreary and depressing.

Graffiti was scrawled here and there. Among all the usual illegible scribbles were slogans for the UDA, the RUC and the INLA. I had no idea who these groups were. I only knew of the IRA.

'A copple o' fellas were machine gonned down in this pob,' David said, matter of factly as he pointed to a quaint little pub, with cute little flower pots, called The Happy Fiddler. It seemed as unlikely a place as any to find cold-blooded killers. I couldn't figure out if David was a Protestant or a Catholic (or a cold-blooded killer for that matter). I listened carefully for any clues, but he didn't give anything away. I couldn't tell by his taxi ID tag either. David had a yellow tag dangling from his rear-view mirror. This was a pass to both sides of the sectarian divide. A green badge meant you could only go to ply for trade on the Catholic side. No badge meant the Protestant side (which is a bit silly, because a Catholic could just take off his badge and go the Protestant side).

We drove through a pair of giant metal gates that used to separate the two clans, and entered Falls Road. The red, white and blue of the Union Jack was replaced by the orange, white and green of the Irish flag. We passed the headquarters of Sinn Fein. I was looking for signs of 'The Troubles', but just saw normal shops and normal houses and normal people shopping and walking their dogs. 'The Troubles' started in 1968. For the past twenty years, barely a month had gone by without a blown-up car or body having been shown on the news.

'Are there any, like, famous old buildings or monuments to see?' I said. It was turning into nothing but a House of Horrors tour.

'Ah, yes. The City Hall is a grand old build'n,' David said with enthusiasm. 'Except, it was bombed three month's back,' he added. Suddenly, David whipped his head around with a huge smile on his face, 'I've thought of a great plairce t' take ya!' He wildly swung the steering wheel around and turned off down a side street. Hopefully, this 'great place' wasn't where some poor bastard had got his limbs hacked off with a butterknife.

On the way to the 'great place' we passed the prison. There was a queue of wives out the front waiting to visit their bombing, shooting, slashing, knee-capping husbands.

We were now in the suburbs. The continuous line of terrace houses looked like any other street in London, Leeds, Liverpool, Lincoln or Lower Slaughter. Even in a tiny village in the countryside, the Brits string all the houses together. It's scary to think that the whole country has an intimate knowledge of their neighbours' toilet habits.

Gee, we must be going somewhere good, I thought. We'd been driving for almost twenty minutes through nondescript suburbs when we pulled up across the road from a pub. A giant banner read '50p PINTS!'.

'Yer won't get a fockin' pint in London fur *that* price!' David said proudly. He'd taken me all the way to the outer suburbs of Belfast to show me a pub that had cheap beer (very cheap too, I might add—a pint in London was about £1.50). 'We might as well go in,' I said. Sod it, I thought. No use coming all this way for nothing. When else would I get a chance to have a beer in an authentic Belfast pub and, more importantly, when would I get a chance to buy a beer for 50p?

It was only 11.30, but there were already a dozen or so locals taking full advantage of the cheap beer. There was no one under the age of fifty. Most of them had tweed caps on. I had a pint of lager and David had a half. He downed his before I'd even finished my first sip. A man at the bar next to me mumbled something to me. I couldn't understand a single word he said. It might as well have been Norwegian. I agreed with him wholeheartedly, then quickly turned back to my beer.

David introduced me to his friend, the publican (I wonder, was he a republican publican?). He was an ex-opera singer and had lived in Italy for almost twenty years (he must have eaten lots of pasta by the look of him). He had retired and returned to his old suburb and bought a pub. David asked him to 'sing a piece for my Australian friend'. The most amazing sound came out of his mouth. He had a beautiful tenor voice and each note was carried to perfection. The whole pub listened in awe. I totally forgot about my taxi ticking away out the front.

The meter had just clicked over to £49 (about $150) when we got back into the cab.

Still, I was not even close to my boss's effort. And not even close to the longest black cab ride on record. A cabbie once drove from Piccadilly Circus to Cape Town, South Africa. And back. A total distance of 33 908 kilometres. When he finished, the meter read £40 210 (a tad over $120 000!). Luckily, he didn't try to pick up a fare in South Africa. Only recently, seven people were killed and thirteen were wounded in an ongoing feud that ended in a shoot-out between rival taxi operators over who should ply the trade on a particular street.

Everything looked bright and cheerful as we left the pub. The sun had come out and kids with smiling faces were playing football on the street. It's amazing how a bit of sun and a pint of lager can make the whole world look cheerier.

On the way to the airport we passed the Mill Town cemetery. 'This is the mairn site for IRA burials,' David said, 'There's probably a few heardless bodies in there es well.' Quite a fitting end to my tour really. I'd had all the places where people had been killed, and I'd finished off where they all end up.

Verdant hills lay on either side of the motorway. The city behind us, lit by bright sunshine, nestled at the head of a sheltered valley. The setting looked so peaceful.

In the distance, the waters of the harbour glittered in the sun. 'Down there is the Harland and Wolff shipyards,' David said, 'It's where they built the Titanic.' I was waiting for something like '. . . and six people got their legs chainsawed off last week' but that was it. That was the first site on my whole tour (besides the cheap beer), that didn't involve loss of life. Oh, wait a second . . .

Hovercraft

English Channel, France
November 1989

I wasn't going to be sick. The water was calm, so why the hell was the hovercraft vibrating and shuddering so much? It was supposed to be hovering. While it wasn't actually throwing us around the cabin or lurching from side to side, it was definitely (as an old rocker might have put it) shaking all over. The shuddering was quite normal apparently— so why wasn't it called a shuddercraft? I grabbed the 'complimentary' sick bag. I'd been staring at it for about ten minutes, thinking that if I took it I'd be admitting to myself that I was going to be sick. Now that I held it in my hand, I found there was no way I was going to open it. That would mean I was definitely going to be sick.

Earlier on, I had been looking forward to my trip on a hovercraft. For a start I just love the name. Hovercraft. It sounds like something George Jetson would drive to work in. Sorry to interrupt, but the

American spellcheck on my computer keeps underlining hovercraft to tell me it's spelled wrong. That's because the Americans have their own name for hovercraft: the very imaginative Ground Effect Machine. I'm sorry, but it doesn't quite have the same ring to it. The Americans just don't get it sometimes, do they?

Despite the shuddering, the hovercraft really is a wonderful piece of machinery. And to think, when Sir Christopher Cockerell designed the first hovercraft in 1956 it was based on a model he built out of a hair dryer, a pair of kitchen scales and two empty Kit-e-Kat tins (actually, I think it was an accident. I reckon he was really trying to make a sex aid for his wife. One of the first hovercraft models was called an Air Lubricat, after all).

Cockerell made a model of a hovercraft, minus the tin cans, and took it to the government. Back in the 1950s if anyone had an invention that might have military value, then by law they had to contact the government. Accordingly, Cockerell's model hovercraft flew over many Whitehall carpets (and a few family living rooms too, I bet) in front of ministers and government experts. It was promptly taken out of the Cockerell's hands and put on the 'secret list'. There it sat idle for a year while the Swiss went ahead and built one.

I once met an American fellow who had built a hovercraft in his garage. This guy Daryl spent two years locked away most nights constructing the four-man hovercraft from scratch. When the big day came for the launch, he took it down the beach to show it off. A Los Angeles television news crew got wind of it (so to speak) and came down to film the inaugural run. Daryl drove it about 30 metres then crashed head-on into a pier. Well, at least he made the news.

Boarding the hovercraft had been like boarding a plane (and in fact, a journey on a hovercraft is called a 'flight'). After we'd checked in and been given our boarding passes we'd walked out onto a tarmac. And there, in all her glory, was *Princess Anne*. No, she wasn't there to greet us. That was the name of our hovercraft. *Princess Anne* was huge. Only her sister, *Princess Margaret* came close in size to *Princess Anne's* wide beam. Built on the Isle of Wight, *Princess Anne* is the largest hovercraft in the world.

Once aboard her royal highness, we had allocated seats just like we would in a plane. And the seats themselves were identical to plane seats, with a pouch behind the seat in front holding a 'safety card' and that sick bag I was trying so desperately not to use.

The hovercraft wasn't as flashy as the cross-channel ferries, with their restaurants, massive duty-free stores and cinemas. The *Princess Anne* only had a small bar, snack bar and a tiny duty-free store. You couldn't go out onto the deck above, either. Well, I suppose you *could*— but you'd more than likely get sucked in by the giant fans and turned into shark food.

The *Princess Anne,* however, did cross the channel in half the time of a normal ferry. In fact, the *Princess Anne* holds the record for the fastest crossing in a time of 22 minutes. Not bad for an old lady (she was built in 1969).

The sound of the four giant propellers (known as propulsion units) starting up had been deafening. The whole hovercraft had started to vibrate. Suddenly, we had begun to rise as the titanic air bags filled. Then, with a horrendous noise and even more vibrating, the mammoth machine had floated across the tarmac and slid into—sorry onto—the English Channel.

It was not long after that, that I started to feel sick. It wasn't just me, either. There was mass giddiness. Most people were holding their sick bags as well. I closed my eyes and tried to concentrate on the image of a spirit level inside my head. The sick bag was still in my hand. It was OK, though—I was feeling all right. That was until . . .

'Ey Brian, yer 'arvin a beer then?' Steve, a mad Geordie (a native of Newcastle-upon-Tyne) said, as he shoved a can of Heineken in my face.

'Nah, I'm all right,' I groaned.

'Wus wrong wid yer mun. Is yer a poof?'

'Are you the only person on this pathetic excuse for a boat who isn't feeling sick?' I whimpered.

Steve and I were workmates. Thirty of us from the advertising agency I was working at in London were being shouted an overnight trip to France. It was a thank-you for all our hard work (well, for everyone else's hard work, at least).

'Smell this, then,' Steve said, as he waved the beer in front of my nose.

'Fuck off, or I'll be sick on you!'

He slunk off to annoy someone else.

'Hey, do yer want a nice greasy 'amburger then?' he added.

This type of cruel tormenting had happened to me before, on a ferry to the Greek island of Santorini. My two 'friends', Ken and Sleazy, and I had just left the party island of Ios. Well, when I say 'left', I mean escaped from. No one ever leaves Ios. You only escape. I'd even met a couple of guys who'd been there for three months. They'd only planned to stay a week. The problem was that the ferry only left in the morning. That was the hard part. No one got out of bed till lunchtime.

Ken and Sleazy were waving food in front of me and telling me it was a maggot burger. They were also kindly offering me a fish milkshake and a phlegm sandwich. Admittedly, my seasickness was hangover-induced, but I thought that not only my stomach, but my head as well were going to explode. My stomach finally did. I spent the next hour in the bowels of the ferry clutching a dirty toilet bowl. I missed the ferry's arrival at Santorini, one of most stunning approaches by sea in the world. I got them back, though. I put their passports into the washing machine in our villa.

The approach to the grey and dismal industrial port of Calais wasn't quite in the same league as Santorini. However, this time I wasn't going to be sick. Maybe if I stood up it would help. No, it made me feel worse. No one else was up and about except for Steve. He was trying to talk someone into having a beer with him. That bloke's face was the same colour as the can of Heineken Steve was holding.

I turned my attention queasily back to the sick bag and noticed a list headed 'How to avoid seasickness'.

> Eat wisely *(a bit hard when the snack bar only sells greasy hamburgers and chips)*
> Don't watch others being sick *(again, a bit difficult when everyone else is being sick around you)*
> Stuff cotton wool up your nose *(now they're taking the piss!)*
> Don't look at the sea *(what, and look at everyone being sick?)*
> Don't travel by hovercraft *(I made that up, but it's probably the best suggestion of all)*

The hovercraft was shuddering even more now. Shuddering a little dangerously, I thought. The hovercraft was close to shuddering itself into bits. Still, I wasn't going to be sick. I kept staring straight ahead. Then again, if I'd known then what I now know I would have been feeling fine. A few years later I discovered a good way to tackle sea-sickness. Lie flat on the ground and look straight up. This had worked on a dodgy ferry across the Red Sea. Everyone on board the boat was lying down on the deck looking up into the sky (including the captain, I think, judging by the way the boat was thrashing around out of control).

Steve came back with a hamburger. It smelt like I imagine the bowels of hell smell. He was already into his third can of beer. We'd only been seaborne for twenty minutes. Fiona, an Irish lass from work who was sitting in front of me, had thought drinking a sports drink would help her feel better. Uh-uh. She projectile-vomited a bright red mess into the back of the chair in front and all over her lap.

Mind you, when it comes to a good chuck, she had nothing on my friend Stuart MacPhee. He was travelling around Europe with his parents, in a kombivan he'd bought in London, when he went out for a night on the piss in the south of France. He hadn't had a big night out for a month, and he was soon pissed off his head. Staggering back to the van in the middle of the night, he clambered all over his parents on the way up to his bunk bed above their double bed. When he finally woke up the next morning, his mum was making breakfast. She didn't look very happy. 'I think you better apologise to your father when he comes back from the shower,' she said. Uh-oh, he thought. What have I done? Did I stand on his head on the way to bed? Did I say something to him? No. His dad had got up in the middle of the night to see if Stuart was all right. Stuart had been making a groaning noise in his sleep. As he stood up, Stuart leant over and threw up all over his dad's head. He then rolled over and went back to sleep.

The story is so well known now that when people meet Stuart they say, 'Oh, are you the Stuart MacPhee that threw up all over his dad?'

There was no way now I was going to be sick. Even with the cacophony of vomiting groans and heaves around me, I was going to make it. There was only five minutes to go before we reached Calais.

I held out. When the hovercraft finally came to a shuddering and noisy halt on French soil, I'd never seen so many relieved people in my life. Including me.

I was so happy I hadn't been sick. Ironically, it was Steve who eventually was sick. But that was eight hours later, after eating a dozen snails and drinking ten pints of lager. That'll teach him.

Helicopter

Grand Canyon, USA

October 1990

At last I'd found an advantage to being a skinny weakling. I got to sit in the front seat of the helicopter with the pilot. The lightest person got the prime seat which was surrounded by a floor-to-ceiling bubble window. I couldn't believe my luck, particularly as the other three passengers were girls. These three girls from California, with the very Californian names of Candy, Sunny and something like Twinkle-Twinkle-Little-Star, sat complaining in the back seat. The reason not one of them got the front seat was that their collective arses could possibly have filled the Grand Canyon—that we were, hopefully, about to fly over.

The girls thought everything was either 'totally rad' or 'totally awesome'. I'd never in my life seen such 'totally awesome butts'. The three of them would fill all the podium spots in the World's Biggest Butt Competition. They actually looked rather surreal. Their butts were so way out of whack with the rest of their bodies. It was as if they'd shoved king-size quilts down the back of their pants. And—while I'm certainly no fashion guru—I would have thought that if you have a butt the size of a Volkswagen you might think twice about wearing leggings. It was frightening enough to scare off small children.

I was still trying to come to terms with my first sight of the three girls at breakfast. They were ploughing through their meals (and, seemingly, other people's) like there was no tomorrow (or even much left of today, for that matter). I couldn't believe the size of the breakfasts. My plate (or should I say platter) was stacked with about a dozen large rashers of bacon, six eggs worth of scrambled eggs, six extra-large hash browns, six whole fried tomatoes and a pile of pancakes that looked like the Leaning Tower of Pisa. There was enough maple syrup to fill a bathtub. There was also a rack with eight slices of toast in it. I ate till I was full, but it looked as if I hadn't even touched my plate of food. The waitress stared at me as if I had an eating disorder. 'Are you sure you're finished?' the waitress asked me. No human being could finish that meal—besides the three girls who had those bottoms to maintain.

This was my first time in a helicopter. I'd always said that when I became very wealthy, I'd buy myself a helicopter. Buying a helicopter is easy if you've got the cash. So easy, in fact, that you can buy one over the internet. I found a website with over 500 helicopters for sale. All you have to do is give them your credit card number and they'll deliver (they land it in your front garden, I guess). The rather terse descriptions looked like they were selling $2000 used cars instead of $500000 helicopters. For example: *BELL 206 JET RANGER III, 1980, New paint, new interior and reconditioned engine. Windshield wipers and heater. Very good condition. Works everyday* (you would bloody well hope so!). *Price – $715 000 (US).*

The most expensive helicopter for sale was $1.2 million—what a pity that's just over my credit card limit. The cheapest was a mere

$16 000—called an 'Indian helicopter', the reason it was so cheap was that you got sent the bits and pieces in the post and had to build it yourself. When finished, it is just below the weight of a 'true helicopter', so you don't even need a licence to fly one—although they 'recommend' you have a lesson or two. It's an extra $120 for the plans. It's probably a good idea to get them—now where does this blade thing go?

Our pilot looked like Chuck Yeager. He was wearing the standard issue mirror glasses and he had the standard issue moustache. According to the 'The Grand Canyon. The Ultimate Experience' brochure, he 'learned his trade while serving in the armed forces'. I just hoped he wasn't going to have a flashback and think he was back in the jungles of Vietnam, scream out hysterically about 'goddamn Charlie', then smash us into the nearest Vietnamese restaurant. Maybe I'd seen too many Sylvester Stallone movies. I think one of the spaced-out Vietnam vets had written the brochure, too. It described the trip as 'man's relation to nature becomes a vivid reality'.

The whole helicopter piloting caper looked easy to me. All Chuck did was give the joystick the slightest nudge, and the helicopter lurched forward and lifted off the ground. I'd seen more difficult amusement arcade games. He nudged the joystick once more and we climbed slowly above the pine trees. It felt as if we were floating in the air (which I suppose we were). Thankfully, I couldn't hear the noisy blades of the chopper at all. We'd all been issued with industrial-strength ear mufflers and we were listening to music through our 'stereophonic headphones'. It was classical music. It sounded suspiciously like the soundtrack from *Apocalypse Now*.

There were pine trees as far as I could see. The helicopter rushed forward only metres above the trees. The shadow of the chopper over the trees changed from small to massive as Chuck did his best to scare the shit out of us. We passed so close to the top of one tree that instinct made me lift my feet.

A red line sat on the horizon in front of us. The helicopter seemed to be skimming along only metres off the ground as we sped towards the lip of the canyon. Quite suddenly, we dropped. My stomach popped up and tickled my tonsils. Should we be dropping this fast? As we plummeted towards what I imagined was going to be a pretty gruesome death, I glanced up in time to notice the most beautiful sight I'd ever seen. The Grand Canyon at sunset.

The helicopter seemed to be free-falling down the wall of the canyon. Just as I was about to scream abuse at the girls for ending my life, Chuck gave his joystick a good tug and the helicopter levelled out. We were inside the canyon. We were ringed by sheer walls tinged with a hundred shades of orange.

The Grand Canyon looked, words fail me here . . . grand. It's sheer beauty and size can't be described. Can you just imagine being the first white person to stumble across it a couple of hundred years ago? I wouldn't be surprised if the first words were an expletive followed by a religious reference.

Chuck pointed out lots of buttes (tall, thin mountains of rock poking up from the canyon floor). 'This one up ahead is one of the largest buttes,' Chuck told us. 'But not as large as the three butts in the back,' I wanted to add. The buttes all had rather grandiose names, there was a Cheops Pyramid, a Buddha Temple and even one called Confucius Temple.

Chuck was weaving in and around the buttes. I could do that, I thought. I mean, I once got the second highest score on a helicopter flight simulation game called 'Kill Everyone and Everything' or words to that effect.

Way down at the bottom of the canyon, the Colorado River looked quite piddly. It's beyond my comprehension to think that this tiny-looking river made a hole this big. But then again, when I was kid my dad would tell us, 'Don't leave the tap dripping. That's how the

Grand Canyon was formed, you know. A boy left a tap dripping.' We believed him, too. He also told us that if we bit our fingernails we'd end up like him. He's got three fingers missing.

The girls were 'oohhing' and 'ahhing' in the back. 'This is the most romantic thing I've ever seen,' one cooed. There is, however, an even more romantic helicopter trip over the Grand Canyon. You can get married in one. The helicopter takes off from Las Vegas (where else?) and you get married as you fly over the Grand Canyon. For $1846, you get a minister and a video. There isn't much room, so the videographer also acts as the best man.

As part of our 'The Grand Canyon. The Ultimate Experience' trip, we would get to land on the canyon floor and wander around aimlessly for half an hour. We landed not far from the river (another dead-easy manoeuvre, I thought).

Chuck told us to keep our heads down as we stepped out of the helicopter or 'we might lose you'. A couple of years later I found out exactly what 'lose' meant. I was heliskiing in New Zealand and the pilot told us about one fellow who, when he stepped out of the chopper, tried to grab his cap, which had blown off. The blades grabbed his arm and sucked him in. 'He was sliced into thin pieces, just like ham in a deli-slicer,' the pilot said.

I wandered down to the river. It didn't look quite as piddly close up. The rapids looked ferocious. On the way back, I couldn't help thinking of Bobby and Cindy. When the Brady Bunch went to the Grand Canyon, Bobby and Cindy snuck off in the middle of the night with a torch filled with baked beans to give to an Indian kid. I hoped I didn't bump into any Indians. I'd forgotten to bring a torch, let alone some baked beans.

The girls were sitting on a rock when I got back to the chopper. I squeezed on next to them. We started talking about music, and they asked me had we heard of Michael Jackson in Australia. 'Michael . . .

Jackson?' I said vaguely, 'No, never heard of him.'

'Madonna?' one of them asked.

'You mean from the bible?'

'They're both really, like, totally huge in the States.'

'Nah, never heard of either of them,' I shrugged.

In my three months in America I got asked many a dumb question by Americans. A fourteen-year-old boy asked me if we had 'stores' in Australia. 'No,' I said, 'we hunt and grow our own food and make our own clothes.' 'Wow! Really?' was his reply. Another time, after spending five hours at a party in Long Beach, California, two girls said to me, 'Gee, you did real well tonight.'

'What do you mean?' I asked.'

'By speaking English all night.'

Another time, I was in a hire car in southern Florida when I pulled up to a service station and the attendant said, 'You've sure got a funny accent. Where's you from? Up north?'

'No, I'm from Australia, actually,' I said.

'Gee, how long did it take yous t' drive here?'

'A couple of months.'

Back in the helicopter, Chuck did the easy joystick thing again and we lifted up, as easy as you like, from the canyon floor. I'd had a quick chat to Chuck before we got back in the chopper (I'd had enough of talking to the girls—there's only a certain amount of winding up of Americans one can do before you start to feel sorry for them). Chuck wanted to be a helicopter pilot after watching Vietnam War movies. It turned out that the brochure writer was the victim of a minor misunderstanding. Far from being a hardened war veteran, Chuck was just (like me) the veteran of too many war *movies*. He had trained to be a helicopter pilot after seeing the opening scenes of *Apocalypse Now*. A few years later I met a bloke in Norway who was inspired to become a helicopter pilot after watching every episode of *Skippy, the Bush Kangaroo*.

The buttes threw long shadows across the canyon floor and up the sheer, now bright red, walls. It was beyond breathtaking. When we landed back at the base, I wanted to go back up and do it all again. The girls, on the other hand, almost pushed me over in their rush to get out of the departure lounge. I suppose that was fair enough. They had six fried chickens, three extra-large fries, four pounds of lard and nine chocolate sundaes to eat.

Jeep

Oahu, Hawaii
November 1990

As the man in the car hire place told us not to take the jeep off-road, we gave each other a 'like hell, we won't' look. I was already imagining driving up volcanoes and stuff. I mean this was a JEEP. During the war, well, during war *movies* at least, they drove over sand dunes, through mine-infested fields and dodged enemy fire while clambering over ruined buildings. A few bumpy dirt roads and the odd sand dune couldn't be too difficult. Could it?

I'd met my two travel companions (Johnny and Eddie from Liverpool, England) the night before, over way too many $1 Mai-tais (an extremely tasty but brain-numbingly deadly cocktail). We had decided we were going to hire a jeep and drive into a volcano. Eddie tried to talk two Californian girls into joining us. They were close to coming until Johnny told them they would only be allowed in the jeep if they wore bikinis. I think he thought we were in an Elvis Presley movie.

Eddie drove first. I sat in the back nursing the surfboard Johnny had hired. 'If I can't 'ave bikini-clad girls,' he'd said, 'then at least I can 'ave a surfboard' (their Scouse accents made me feel like I was travelling with Ringo and George). We'd hired a Jeep Wrangler. I asked Eddie before we decided to take it, if it was a good jeep. 'As long as it can drive over a foockin' mountain it doesn't matter what sort it is.'

It could have been any one of twenty jeeps that are manufactured in the US, obviously, but also in the UK, Germany, France, Italy, Russia, Brazil and, of course, Japan. The original jeep was commissioned by the US army in 1940. They asked 135 different automobile companies to design and provide a running prototype of a fast, lightweight, all-terrain vehicle. They were given all of 49 days. Only one company was able to produce a prototype in that time. The Bantam Car Company's prototype was tested over 5000 kilometres of unpaved roads. It worked a treat (one noted army officer who tested it said, 'It can do everything except bake a cake'). But alas, Bantam was gypped. The army asked Ford and Willys-Overland to create a jeep using Bantam's plans. Willys got the gig and, in a space of four years, supplied the army with 1.3 million standard green army jeeps.

Our Jeep Wrangler was similar in one way to an army jeep. It had no roof. Luckily, it was overcast. I didn't fancy a full day of the sun frying my head. We were soon out of the high-rise hotels of Waikiki and driving past Diamond Head—the headland where all the cashed-up locals live. So cashed-up in fact that one old couple had built a $20 000 airconditioned kennel for their poodle. We can only hope that they set the airconditioner too low and the pooch froze to death.

I was looking forward to getting away from Waikiki and the honeymooning Japanese in matching outfits, and the loud Americans in even louder shirts. After Diamond Head we drove through the lushest green landscape I'd ever seen. Everything was emerald green. The surrounding mountains looked like they were covered in thick, green shag pile carpet. We drove through plantations of bananas and papayas and the omnipresent coconut palms. Stuck in the middle of all this loveliness was a 'mock' Hawaiian village with a gaudy sign announcing 'Hula shows'. How naff. Mind you, if it really was the 'traditional' hula show, I might have gone. The original hula celebrates the genitals of the chief. The women dance the hula while flashing their genitals. Now, I'd go and see that. Strangely, it's not performed too often today. Well, unless you go to The Hawaiian Pussycat niteclub.

We stopped for a drink at a stand by the roadside. A very large, and I mean *very* large, Hawaiian lady suggested we try the papaya juice. I was too scared to say no. She crushed the papayas as if they were made of tissue paper.

'Try saying that five times real fast,' said Johnny, when we were back in the jeep.

'What?' I asked.

'The name of the highway we're on.'

The highway was called the Kalanainaole highway. I couldn't even say it once. The highway hugged the coast. It had no choice really. The Pacific Ocean sat only metres away on one side, while on the other mountains shot almost straight up like massive green velvet curtains.

Johnny wanted to surf Waimea bay. He'd only surfed once before. There was a pretty good chance he would die. He had no idea that the waves can get as big as a five-storey building, and that underneath the shallow water there was razor-sharp coral that could tear his body into strips. It was at the very least going to be interesting to watch. Even though I surfed a bit as a kid, there was no way I was going out there. There were three good reasons I didn't like surfing any more. The first was that I had once been standing in waist-deep water holding my surfboard when suddenly my feet were pulled out from underneath me.

I had been standing on the wing of a giant manta ray. I ran out of water quicker than you can say Kalanainaole highway. The second reason was that, on another occasion, I wiped out so badly that I swallowed three times my body weight in salt water. Last, but not least, I was shite at it.

Walking on to the beach at Waimea Bay was like walking on to the set of Baywatch. I'd never seen so much tanned skin and bleached-blonde hair. There were more people on the sand watching the surfers than people surfing. It was only the start of winter, so the waves weren't really big yet. They were *only* the height of a two-storey building. We sat on the sand. It was lucky that I had good sunglasses on. Johnny had taken off his shirt. His skin was so white it was almost translucent.

'Have you got any sun-block on?' I asked, concerned that he would turn bright red in a matter of minutes.

'No,' he said, 'I'll be all right.'

I suppose it didn't matter. His skin was probably going to get torn up by the coral, anyway.

'So, are ya goin' in then?' Eddie asked Johnny.

'Yeah, juz giz a minute.'

Twenty-five minutes later, we all trudged back to the jeep. Johnny hadn't even put his foot in the water. 'I didn't want to show the locals up,' he told us.

Incidentally, Hawaiians were surfing hundreds of years before us whiteys took it up. When Captain Cook spotted the world's first surfers he was 'impressed with their skill and agility'.

Not long after we passed the town of Mokuleia, the road came to a sudden dead end. Beyond it was a rough dirt track. The Waianae ranges loomed in the distance. 'Now let's see if this jeep can climb a foockin' mountain then,' Eddie announced as he sped off the road and on to the track, 'That's what it's built for.'

I suppose he's right. The definition of 'jeep' in the dictionary is 'a small off-road military vehicle'. The name 'jeep', according to the most widely accepted theory, came from the slurring of the acronym GP for General Purpose vehicle (there must have been a lot of drunk GIs). Actually, the jeep's official name was 'quarter-ton command reconnaissance vehicle'. Not a very good name in the middle of battle, though. 'Quick sergeant, get the quarter-ton command reconnaissance vehicle.' By the time he had finished saying that, the war would have been over.

Our quarter-ton command reconnaissance vehicle bumped and lurched along as bushes brushed the underside of the chassis. I was bouncing around in the front while Johnny was doing his very best to keep the surfboard from taking flight.

After a bruising half-hour we came to a clearing. Sitting in the middle of it was a light plane. How the hell did it get there? A film crew were shooting up into the cockpit while a couple of other crew were shaking the wings, simulating flight. Sitting in the cockpit was the actor, Richard Chamberlain. 'Oh, my God,' I laughed. I couldn't believe it. Richard Chamberlain had been sitting at the table next to me in a London restaurant only a month earlier. It's rare enough that I spot a celebrity (well, of sorts anyway), let alone see one for the second time in a matter of weeks, on the other side of the world. I was tempted to go over and say hello to my new friend, but they were now blowing smoke all over him and he was yelling 'mayday' into his mike. I'd hazard a guess that it wasn't a big-budget blockbuster. They only did two takes before the smoke machine broke down.

By this stage the terrain was getting a little rougher. The track cut its way through thick jungle. Now and again we'd fly over a boulder. Eddie must have thought we were in the Paris to Dakar rally. The air had turned sticky. Away from the coastal breeze, the air was muggy and still. Seeing that we were 'off-road', it was difficult to figure out where we were on the map. Using the map I had, and my somewhat dubious navigational skills, I figured out we were very near a large area that was used for bombing practice by the military.

'The US army throw bombs around here,' I told Eddie.

'So what? Fuck 'em!' he shouted over the screaming engine.

I knew we were in a quarter-ton command reconnaissance vehicle, but I didn't think we'd quite pass as members of the US army. And, anyway, I didn't fancy trying to fend off hand grenades with the surfboard. Our camouflage wasn't too good, either. Eddie and Johnny were wearing the loudest Hawaiian shirts I'd ever seen. They even made the ones worn by the American tourists in Waikiki look understated.

Finally it was my turn to drive. It was my turn to scramble over volcanoes and storm over sand dunes. I was going to show them how to go 'bush bashing'. I roared up over a small rise and there below me . . . was a road. Oh, great. I'd managed to accomplish all of 400 metres of bush bashing.

The road was a single lane. There were pineapple plants (or trees, or bushes or whatever the hell they grow on) as far as the eye could see. I drove about 500 metres and when I went to change into top gear, I couldn't find it. In fact, I couldn't find any gear at all. It was like stirring a pot of porridge. The jeep rolled slowly to a stop.

Before I even finished saying 'It's not my fault', it started to rain. The rain soon turned into something that resembled a monsoon. We were drenched in less than a minute. Eddie tried the gearstick. It could now do a complete circle. Johnny grabbed the surfboard out of the jeep, 'Come on, there's no use 'anging around 'ere.'

I tried to figure out where we were on the map. It showed a vast area of pineapple plantations. We were in the middle of that. Somewhere.

We walked down the middle of the road for half an hour. There was no traffic at all. The rain was still coming down, but it was actually quite refreshing. It was like being in a warm shower.

We finally came to a T-intersection. This was a step up. The road here had two lanes. We stuck out our collective thumbs and the first car that came along pulled over. It was a pick-up truck driven by a giant, smiling Hawaiian man. Johnny threw the board in the back and we all squeezed in the front. The Hawaiian man took up half the seat. 'What are you guys doing out here?' he said, chuckling, 'there's not much surf.' He then started laughing his head off.

'So, where are you headed?' he said, still laughing.

'Waikiki,' we chorused.

'Ha, ha, ha, haaaaaaa,' he chortled, 'you're going the wrong way.'

We got out. We could still hear him laughing as he drove off.

Eventually we got another ride. Going the right way this time. A nice couple from Nebraska with matching shirts drove us all the way to Waikiki.

Back at the hostel, I had a quick shower then met the lads for a farewell drink. They were flying home to England the next morning.

'What did you do about the jeep?' I asked Eddie, after our third $1 Mai-tai. The jeep was in Eddie's name.

'I put the keys in an envelope, drew a rough map of where the jeep was, and slipped it under the door of the car-hire place.'

'But you don't know where the jeep was' I said.

'Yeah, I know.'

Yacht

Somewhere near Albania
July 1992

I'd only ever been sailing once before. Apparently I was one of the crew. I had been invited along to a 'social' race on Port Phillip Bay. I was fully expecting to do nothing more than sit on a deckchair drinking G&Ts surrounded by girls in string bikinis (well, maybe a touch of wishful thinking on the last one). However, it was all rather ghastly. It was windy and cold and my hair got terribly messed up. Worst of all, I had to do crew-type things. What made this task even more difficult was that I couldn't understand what the skipper was yelling at me to do. 'Hey Brian, grab the guy and put your luff tackle in the hawse hole and spanker.' Which guy? Whose luff tackle? He might as well have been speaking Dutch. Which he just might have been, since *yacht* is a Dutch word. Yachts were originally called jaght schips. The Royal Melbourne Jaght Schip Club doesn't quite have the same ring to it though.

At one point our skipper asked someone to hoist or do something to a golly wobbler. I'm sure he was taking the piss. A golly wobbler! These yachting people can't be serious. Anyway, we lost the race. Probably because I wasn't spanking hard enough.

Back at the yacht club it was like walking into a *Gilligan's Island* theme party. There were grown men dressed like the skipper. Canvas shoes, white pants, colourful polo shirts and, I'm not joking, skipper hats. One older chap was even wearing a cravat. No-one else even batted an eyelid at the fact that he was an absolute dead ringer for Thurston Howell the Third.

The gibbering about jibbing continued on here as well. I still couldn't understand them. I overheard a conversation behind me that went something like, 'Yeah, my seacock was beginning to sag so I tried a tiller extension. In the end I had to marry hank to one of the guys.' (Gee, I hope Hank didn't mind.) People who are into yachts are *really* into yachts. Now, I consider myself a skiing nut and I hang around with other ski nuts, but I've never had anyone say to me, 'How's your control precision on short radius turns with the densolite core?' I know skis are nowhere near as complicated as a yacht, but when you ski, at least snow is snow. Yachting people have their own names for the weather, the water and even the toilet.

But what really hoisted my gaff-mizzen and set my mainsail aflutter was an incredibly large book I found in the library entitled *Yachting terms. The language of sailing*. This book was full of thousands of words only a handful of people could understand. Half of them sounded like medical ailments: aneroid barometer, baggy wrinkle, gallow bits, gammon shackles, jam cleat and clove hitch. The definitions made even less sense. For example: '*A-cock-bill*. When the foul hawse hangs cat-head, or from the futtock hoop it is a-cock-bill'. Yes indeed.

Sadly, it's all a bit too late to be reading these yachting books now.

I should have read them before I decided to play skipper and very nearly kill myself and my fearless crew off the rocky coast of Albania.

I'll set the scene for you. This was my first trip as a tour leader to Greece. I'd done the central Europe loop quite a few times, but this was my first trip which included an interlude during which, as the brochure put it, '... after a couple of quick lessons, you'll cruise away for three glorious days of sailing'. We had six 25-foot yachts in the flotilla. There were six people to a yacht. Our 'flotilla skipper' had his very own 'lead' yacht. However, I had to somehow find skippers to take charge of each of the six boats. This was not an easy task. I found only four with sailing experience. The other two skippers' maritime experience was not extensive: one fellow had actually stayed up to watch Australia II win the America's Cup, the other guy caught the Manly ferry to work every day.

Being tour leader meant I had the advantage of choosing who I wanted on my yacht—I didn't want to be lumbered with the boring passengers, or the Manly ferry commuting skipper, for that matter. Our skipper was Donna (who actually knew where to put gallow bits and gammon shackles). The crew were Donna's boyfriend, Dave, Matt and Tim (two blokes I'd become good friends with) and (Tim and Matt talked me into this, I swear) the best-looking girl on the bus. Matt said she'd look the best in a bikini.

On our first day of sailing we didn't do any. We motored across a sea of glass the whole day. We started out from the north-east coast of Corfu and headed for the Greek mainland. Our yacht didn't have a name (they all had MG Spring 25 painted across the front, or foul hawse, or bow or whatever) so we christened ours *Taramasalata*. The other yachts became *Tzatziki*, *Moussaka* etc.

At 10.30 a.m. Matt and Tim opened a beer. 'The sun's over the yardarm,' Matt declared. I couldn't argue with that. What the hell's a yardarm? The fridge was full of beer. Stupidly, I'd put Tim in charge of buying supplies. Our lunch menu for three days consisted of dry biscuits and tinned sardines ... and that was about it.

We spent the afternoon diving off the boat into the clear blue waters of the Mediterranean. It was just heavenly. On the surface, the water was warm and clear. When you dived off the mast, into the deep water below, it was icy cold. It must have been at least ten metres deep. We anchored the boats in a big circle and spent the entire afternoon happily splashing around in the middle.

Incidentally, here's an interesting story. When tourists, lured by the sea, first arrived in the Greek islands, the locals looked at them in amazement as they swam in the water. The Greeks did not know how to swim. Greek children could paddle in the shallows, but they weren't allowed to swim. An old Greek proverb says: *There are three things to fear in the world: fire, women and the sea* (I'd probably put women first).

Our first port of call was the tiny seaside village of Syarta. When we were still over 500 metres away from shore, I caught a whiff of cooked fish and barbecued lamb on the offshore breeze. After our lunch of biscuits and sardines, I was looking forward to anything that didn't come out of a tin. It was late afternoon, and the setting sun flooded the small cluster of villas hugging the shore and washed the surrounding mountains in gold. A couple of other yachts gleamed in the snug harbour.

'Is there anywhere for my passengers to shower?' I asked the proprietor of the one and only restaurant. 'You can use the shower here,' he said. He was a little surprised when 37 of us then trooped into his bathroom. We made up for it, though. We dined like Greek gods in his restaurant and downed many a cold beer and cloudy ouzo. I've never seen a man with a bigger smile when I handed him a huge wad of drachmas to settle the bill. We finally left at around one in the morning after Spiros, the restaurant owner, had taught us all how to do 'Greek dancing'. One of these 'dances' involved doing the twostep with a table in your mouth. I'm not exaggerating here; you clench your teeth around the edge of a small table, lift it up, then do something that resembles the hokey-pokey. I'm sure it's not a real dance and Spiros would have had a good laugh about it later with his mates.

The boat was hot and stuffy. I didn't know what was worse: the overpowering smell of sardines or the even more overpowering smell of Tim's feet. Tim, Matt and I slept on the folded down kitchen table. Donna and Dave were up the front in the triangular shaped bed (you have no choice but to have your feet touch each other's), while the bikini girl had a bed to herself at the back.

I awoke in the night to the boat rocking. I wondered how the water could be so rough in a protected harbour. But no, it was just Donna and Dave being rather amorous after a few too many ouzos. I slept fitfully all night. If I, at any stage in the night, tried to move—let alone roll over—I'd fall out of my narrow bed. A real bed would have been lovely. I'd always imagined myself aboard one of those luxury yachts. I saw a yacht on a television program once that was 500 feet long (twenty times longer than the one we were in). It was the Saudi Arabian royal yacht and had everything from fourteen TVs to solid gold toilet brushes. I'd hazard a guess those aboard weren't served sardines, either.

Day Two was more motoring on glassy water, more beer and sardines and more dips into the refreshingly cool sea. By afternoon, enough of a breeze had sprung up for us to hoist our sails. Our flotilla skipper organised a race. First one to port. Donna soon learned to shout orders in normal real person's language. Big sail, little sail, rope holder, large blue rope, etc. I even got to have a go at the steering stick thingy. It's called a tiller, I believe. See, I did learn something.

We soon hit the front. We must have been travelling at 50 knots an hour. Or is it just 50 knots? A knot is based on the length of a minute arc (one sixtieth of a degree) of the great circle of the earth. It is not exact, because the earth is not a perfect sphere. It would undoubtedly be simpler to use kilometres per hour. But hey, that would be too easy.

Just so you're not confused, there are also stationary knots. Knots that you use to tie the yacht to a jetty. One yachting book says to be a good seaman it is important to know a few knots. Most of the diagrams look like the workings of your small intestine. The 'running clove hitch bight knot' looks like something Rubik of Rubik's cube fame might have made up.

We must have been doing something right because we were miles ahead. How many miles exactly, I'm not sure. A mile on land is different to a mile at sea (can't those damn yachties have anything normal?). One reason we were so far ahead—well, probably the main reason—was that we were racing not to Plataria, but to a military port in Albania. Our flotilla skipper calmly suggested we avoid gunfire and head to Plataria. This involved a lot of Donna shouting at us to 'tack' and 'jibe'. Well, more like shouting to move the big sail to the other side of the boat and tighten the blue rope on the rope holder thingy. We finally motored into the port dead last and half an hour later than the last boat.

Day three and the water was glassier than glass. This meant, of course, that there was a constant, and annoyingly loud, noise from the engine as we motored our way back to Corfu. However, I devised a way to motor along and get away from the noise. Tying the small dinghy we had to the back of the yacht (naturally using the running clove hitch bight knot), I simply got towed along behind. Twenty metres away from the boat, I dozed off in the sun, with the only sound being that of water lapping against the side of the dinghy.

We stopped for lunch in a sheltered cove on a small uninhabited island. Incidentally, there are over 2000 islands that belong to Greece. Only 154 of those are inhabited. Halfway through our sardine lunch, our flotilla captain's voice came over the radio, 'The wind's picked up. You can go for a sail if anyone's interested.' There was only a slight breeze in the protected cove. I looked up from my sardines and biscuits, 'I'm keen.' Only Matt and Tim seemed interested. Everyone else was more than happy to sit back, relax and swim in the clear waters. Donna, Dave and the bikini girl jumped aboard *Tzatziki*.

As we motored out of the cove, the strengthening wind cooled the hot blue day. A few strips of high cloud raced by in the breeze. I nominated myself the skipper and immediately started barking orders to my crew. 'Hang 'em up from the yardarm!' I shouted. 'Jib the hoist, Ahoy there, all hands on deck, anchors aweigh!' I was having a ball. By the time we got the big sail hoisted, the wind had picked up to gale force. I sent my fearless crew off to the bow (see, I even talk like a skipper) to put up the little sail. *Taramasalata* was really moving. She began to lean heavily to one side. Wow, I thought, this is like yacht racing I've seen on the telly. The boys lost control of the little sail and it began flapping around as if possessed. *Taramasalata* was plunging her bow into the water and totally smothering the lads in spray. They were holding on for their life. Sod fixing the sail, they just wanted to stay on. I tried to slow us down. I steered away from the wind. That should do it, I thought. Wrong. It made it worse. The sail was now virtually horizontal to the water. We were flying. We must have been doing at least 150 knots. The boys were clutching onto the rails as if their lives depended on it (probably because they did).

I could hear the flotilla skipper shouting from the radio below deck, 'Hoist the spinnaker abaft!' (or something like that). There was panic in his voice. He said something else about golly wobblers, then eventually gave up and used our language, 'Take down the fucking sail!' It looked like poltergeists were having a food fight in the kitchen (OK, galley ... but it is a kitchen, for God's sake). Sardines, biscuits, empty tins and dirty plates were flying about with no-one there to throw them.

We were also heading back to the Albanian military port. I was struggling to hold onto the tiller now. OK, we are going to die. The boys were now screaming with fear. So, what did I do? I laughed. I laughed and laughed. I started crying, I was laughing so much. I was laughing because I had no idea what to do. The boys looked at me in amazement.

All of a sudden the big sail swung clean to the other side of the yacht, and instantly we slowed down. Tim came clambering down to the back, 'Bloody hell. You tried to kill us, and you're pissing yourself laughing!' Yes, I may have been laughing—but that was because I was hysterical. I thought my luff tackle and gallow bits were well and truly golly wobbled.

On my next Greek sailing trip we were having lunch in the same secluded cove when our flotilla skipper's voice came over the radio, 'You can go for a sail if anyone's interested.' There was silence for a second then, 'All except you, Brian.'

Ferry

Stockholm to Helsinki
September 1992

The Silja Lines Ferry service is the official carrier of Santa Claus. Official carrier? Who sanctions that? Unless I've been terribly misled all these years, Santa Claus doesn't exist. Still, it's amazing other companies haven't jumped on the bandwagon (or sleigh!) as well. There's a couple of obvious ones. McDonalds could be the 'official restaurant of Santa Claus'. Just look at the size of him. He clearly doesn't mind a Big Mac or two. With those red rosy cheeks and all that ho-ho-ho-ing, he'd also be perfect for Absolut Vodka. 'The official tipple of Santa Claus'.

Anyway, if he does travel by Silja Lines, I bet he doesn't stay in the tourist class cabins. For a start, there's only three beds and he's got twelve reindeer. The cabins should be renamed 'claustrophobia class'. They are tiny. Three people couldn't even fit into one at the same time. Sorry, I tell a lie. They could, it's just that one person would have to stand in the shower.

I was sharing one of those glorified broom closets with my driver and cook. I was the tour leader for 22 Hong Kong Chinese passengers on a four-week tour of Scandinavia and Russia. Already one week into the trip, we were taking the overnight ferry from Stockholm to Turku, Finland (near Helsinki). Mind you, only a few hours earlier I wasn't sure we were going at all. I couldn't find the ticket office. I wandered aimlessly around the streets of Stockholm for over two hours. Not only did every street name sound like an ice-cream company, they all sounded the same. There were, in one block, streets named (and I swear these are all true) Hangovägen, Hallönbergen, Hügdalen and Hägerstensäsen. I eventually found the office on the corner of Hägen Daaz and Norgen Vaaz.

This was my first time on this ferry and I was looking forward to it. The brochure I picked up at the ticket office promised 'International atmosphere with delicacies galore in the buffet restaurant', plus 'There is lots of fun and lots of cruise program'. Oh, I was also looking forward to it because the ship would be full of partying Swedish girls (I had visions of sharing a spa with the under-21 Swedish netball team).

The brochure also claimed 'that all cabins are equipped with automatic wake-up'. I was intrigued to know how they knew what time you wanted to wake up.

After spending ten minutes trying to figure out how all three of us could fit into the cabin at once, we made our way to the buffet restaurant. Everyone we passed looked happy. They all looked Scandinavian. They were either blonde and beautiful or brunette and beautiful. I fell hopelessly in love seven times before I even left our floor.

I both love and loathe buffets. I love them because you have so much food to choose from, and I loathe them because you have so much food to choose from. I feel I should try everything, and end up heaping my plate with fourteen different dishes. And I can tell you with some authority that Thai red curry chicken, spaghetti marinara and sausage rolls don't taste that flash all mixed in together.

I thought it odd that the brochure called it a buffet when its common name is Swedish anyway. It's amazing someone hasn't told them that we call it a smorgasbord, too.

My passengers were already in their seats. They were all eyeing off the piles of food just waiting for me to give them the go-ahead. What happened after that was sheer madness. I have to admit that I've been known to stack up the odd prawn or two at a buffet, but my passengers would have even out-stacked Santa Claus. One fellow had created a feat of engineering that rivalled the Great Wall of China. He'd somehow managed to pile at least 50 prawns on to one plate. On second thoughts, maybe it looked more like the Eiffel Tower.

The massive display of smoked salmon was gone in seconds. Other diners looked on in horror. I wouldn't be surprised if it became forever known, and often talked about, as the Great Salmon Riot.

Then again, I suppose it could have been worse. On a ferry to Swatow, China in 1921, residents of two Chinese cities started a riot (probably over the buffet—it must be something to do with who gets the most prawns). It started as arguments and fist fights, but when the ferry was forced to land in Amoy (home to half the people on the ferry), the Swatowians went berserk and started smashing furniture. The captain ordered all of his crew to help quell the now-totally-out-of-control passengers. What nobody had realised was that the ferry was drifting towards a razor-edged reef. Within seconds, the reef opened a huge gash in the ship's hull. The passengers, now stricken with fear, set upon each other in earnest. Knives, hatchets and axes fell (just the sort of thing one carries on a ferry) and hundreds were murdered. My passengers didn't quite go that far though. There was a bit of pushing and shoving to get to the last smoked herring, but that was about it.

I think the passengers got 'All you can eat' confused with 'Can you eat all?'. Dessert was another free-for-all. Even the normally sensible piled their plates high with cheesecake, apple Danish and chocolate mousse. And the not-so-sensible ones? Well, I thought I mixed odd food combinations together at a buffet. One guy had smoked eel on his Black Forest chocolate cake.

I'd promised my group that I'd take them to the ship's karaoke bar after dinner. They'd been looking forward to this for the past few days. So much so in fact that they'd been practicing—to the dismay of our neighbours in the campsite in Stockholm. To be honest, I was excited too. I don't mind a bit of karaoke. Sadly, I've sung karaoke in about fifteen different countries. My highlights and lowlights include being congratulated for my singing by a man who I was sure was Boris Yeltsin in a ritzy karaoke bar in Moscow; and falling off the stage onto a tableload of Japanese in Waikiki, pissed off my head, trying to do the twist while singing 'Twist 'n' Shout'.

My driver and cook left the food frenzy just as one of my passengers returned to the table with his fifth serve of cheesecake. They were heading back to the cabin (to grab the best beds, I bet, and leave me with the one on top of the cupboard).

I left too, and told my passengers to meet me at the karaoke bar. The bar was quiet. There were only a few beautiful Scandinavian types propped up at the bar. No one was singing yet. I moved several tables together so my group all could sit together. An hour and a half later I was still sitting at the now-very-large table by myself. Not one single passenger had turned up. They couldn't possibly still be at the buffet— they'd already eaten every prawn on the ship. They must have got lost. I'd better find them, I thought. Besides that, I was getting tired of saying, 'Sorry, these 22 seats are taken.'

I found them in the enormous duty-free store. They were spending the equivalent of a small country's GDP on perfume and stuffed toys. 'Yes,' they told me, 'we are coming to karaoke soon.'

Three came. The rest collapsed in their rooms under the weight of prawns, cheesecake and perfume fumes.

I sang first. My old karaoke favourite, 'My Way' (every karaoke bar seems to use the same video discs with accompanying bizarre videos. The one for 'My Way' involved a lot of paedophilic-looking clowns frolicking around on a pier). My three remaining passengers got up together to sing. They did an extraordinarily accurate impression of a dying cat. After that, they tended to hog the microphone with various more impressions of dying animals. They also managed to scare away half the people in the bar. One, however, did do a delightful Elmer Fuddesque version of 'Moon River': 'Moon wivver, bwighter dan da sea.'

Finally, at around two o'clock, my passengers waddled off to bed. I was drunk. I had no idea how much I'd spent. To buy a beer in a bar in Sweden, you just hand over the biggest wad of notes you can hold and hope they don't ask for some more. I didn't feel up to clambering over my driver and cook to get to my bed yet, so I went to see if I could find another bar (or that spa with the under-21 netball team). The bar probably wasn't a good idea. Another couple of drinks could send me into bankruptcy.

It was in my wanderings that I stumbled upon the 'Fun Fun Disco'. It was like walking into a shampoo and toothpaste commercial. Everyone had shiny hair and shiny teeth. They were all pissed off their heads.

I was there only one minute and a Swedish girl asked me to dance. Well, she said, 'flop-de-flop de floop-de-plop' first, before I told her I couldn't speak Swedish. Halfway through our first dance she leant over and said, 'You can if you like, kiss me. But not fuck me.' Gee, and I was just happy to have a dance. Her name was Ulna. Or Olna, or Alna or something like that. She, like a lot of the drunk people in the Fun Fun Disco, was on the ferry solely to get pissed. They would stay a half a day in Helsinki, then get pissed again on the way back.

Three hours later (with four weeks worth of wages given to the barman) we staggered out of the disco. My new best friend (an incredibly drunk Finnish guy I'd met) invited Elna and me (plus two Finnish girls) to his room. 'We can go to his room, but no fuck OK?' Ilna told me.

The Finnish guy (he told me his name about ten times, but I couldn't pronounce it. It sounded like he had a mouthful of prawns) had a deluxe room (a bit of a waste really. He would have all of two hours in his 'deluxe' room before 7.30, when the boat was due to dock).

The sun was just beginning to rise. I knew that because the room boasted a massive window. It was a pity that I was so drunk and I couldn't really appreciate it. The desolate islands that are dotted around the Finnish coast loomed out of the sea like blue ghosts in the dim morning light. Well, I have vague recollections of something like that, anyway. I'm not too sure what we all did for the next hour or so. I seem to remember the Finnish fellow shouting *skål* (cheers in Swedish) a lot. Every time he yelled this, we had to skol some *akvavit* (a horrible Swedish schnapps).

I crawled back into my own cabin sometime after six. And no, Olna didn't let me fuck her. Or kiss her for that matter—but that had probably something to do with the fact that I was a blithering wreck and that I could hardly stand up.

I had a horrifying dream about an old Swedish lady wearing rubber gloves who was shaking me and screaming at me in Swedish. Then I woke up. It wasn't a dream. A cleaning lady was shaking me awake. I guessed she was telling me to move my arse and get out of the cabin. My driver and cook had already packed up and left. Why hadn't my driver and cook woken me? And what the hell happened to the 'automatic wake-up'? It was 8.30 and the ferry had had been safely moored for over an hour.

I didn't have a hangover. That was because I was still pissed. I fell out of bed and grabbed my bag. Luckily, I still had all my clothes on (because I'd been too out of it to take them off). I bolted down the empty corridor. The *akvavit* was still swimming around in my stomach. I stopped in front of a cleaner, who looked like the Swedish version of Meatloaf, vacuuming in front of the now empty duty-free shop. He didn't understand 'Where's the gangplank?' I tried using hand signals. I couldn't believe it. The ferry was about to head back to Sweden, and here I was playing charades with Meatloaf.

I found the gangplank with only seconds to spare. The crew were just about to pull it up. My bus wasn't hard to find. It was the only vehicle left in the massive car park. They had been waiting over an hour for me. 'Why didn't you wake me?' I asked the driver. 'I did,' he said, 'and you said "If I can't fuck you, can I at least play with your boobs?"'

Bus

Bournemouth, England
October 1993

Frank Bruno (well, a guy who looked like Frank Bruno, the boxer) stepped onto the bus and immediately lit up a joint. Ten guys struggled aboard behind him carrying enough beer to last a year or two. We were going away for one night. I knew then I'd made a big mistake. I should never have taken the trip on. As a tour leader, I'd had plenty of experience keeping paralytic Aussies under control but, only ten minutes into the Bucks Party Weekend, I knew this was going to be very different. I had no control at all. As we stopped at traffic lights in High Street, Tooting, in busy mid-morning traffic, one of the guys stepped out in the street and casually pissed into the gutter. This certainly wasn't going to be a nice little Cliff Richard-type summer holiday.

I was taking this rowdy bunch to Bournemouth, on the south coast of England. Their ultimate destination was a nightclub called The

Zoo (or The Cage, or something else to do with a place that held wild animals). Apparently, the best man told me, it would be full of girls (and blokes acting like wild animals). He had read, in a recent nationwide survey by a major condom manufacturer, that Bournemouth beach had been voted the best place in England for an alfresco bonk. He was a bit optimistic there. This was October in England. It was bloody freezing.

We were all going to sleep on the bus—a double-decker that had been converted into a cosy travelling holiday home for 24. Luckily, there were only thirteen of us (we needed the other eleven beds to store the beer). Besides Frank Bruno, who was an East Ender (who ended every single sentence with, 'yunnowoteyemean?'), the rest were Kiwis (who ended every sentence with 'eh?').

I'd been warned about taking a bucks party weekend trip. The company I worked for had only ever attempted one before. It wasn't very successful. Well, for the tour leader at least. The passengers had literally thrown him off the bus halfway through the weekend.

We'd only been on the road for half a minute and my lot were handing me a can of beer. My driver, Nial, would get offered a beer every ten minutes all the way to Bournemouth. The best man's name was Tum (Tim in English). He was carrying a jug full of money. 'Thus uz our kutty money for beer,' he told me. There was enough money in the jug to buy beer for the entire population of Bournemouth.

Our old beast of a bus spluttered down the motorway as the lads danced on the tables. The bus may have spluttered, but it was a reliable old thing. Built sometime in the 1950s by the Bristol Tramways & Carriage Company, it wasn't unlike the first double-decker buses that appeared on London streets back in the 1880s. Back then, each bus was pulled by twelve horses. By 1900, over 50 000 horses were being used to transport two million people a day. The first motorised double-deckers appeared on the streets in 1905. By 1914 there were already 3000 chugging through the streets of London. Most of the horses were then sent off to the war (amazingly, over 500 000 horses were killed in battle during the First World War). Not surprisingly, there were no more horse-drawn buses on the streets of London after that.

Even the old motorised double-deckers saw some action in the war. They were used to transport troops across the muddy fields of Northern Belgium. Most of them still had their destination boards on the front, and ads for soap and stockings on the side.

Buses like the one we were travelling in had seen a bit of mud, too. These reliable old beasts had taken overland trips everywhere, from ploughing through the deserts of Sudan to climbing over the Khyber pass in Afghanistan.

Well, I thought they were reliable. I was sitting upstairs when I heard a loud bang and a horrible fizzing noise from below. Oh shit! I rushed downstairs just as another loud bang echoed up the stairs. I got below just as Frank Bruno was setting off . . . another firecracker. That is, letting off a firecracker *inside* the bus. He was attempting to shoot skyrockets at other cars on the motorway. I went back upstairs. I wasn't telling Frank to stop it. He was the size of a small house. And every bit as smart.

We'd only been on the road for an hour and the groom had passed out upstairs. 'I'm just having a rest,' he told me, before he collapsed onto one of the bunks. Mind you, if he was on a trip with Rotel tours (or coffin tours as they're affectionately known), a German company that also has travelling beds, he wouldn't have been able to just pop upstairs for a nap. The beds on those tours are in a trailer that is hauled behind the bus. The beds are stacked on top of each other and are pulled out of the trailer like drawers in a morgue. Then again, it's probably a good idea. They do take a lot of old people. If one of them snuffs it on a trip, they can simply leave them in the mobile morgue in the back.

We stopped at a pub for lunch. Two of the lads had to carry the groom in. Thirteen servings of cod and chips didn't even put a dent in the kitty. We stayed to watch some rugby game. England versus Burkina Faso or something like that.

Frank Bruno stepped back on board carrying a large hat-rack. He'd stolen it from the pub. 'I fought it might come in 'andy,' he said, as he set it up in the corner of the bus. It did. Everyone hung their jackets on it.

Half an hour later we stopped at another pub for a drink. They once again carried the groom in and plonked him on a bar stool. He immediately fell off and slumped at the feet of a group of menacing looking bikies playing pool. Lucky we had Frank Bruno with us or they would have beaten him to a pulp with a pool cue. The bikies were listening to heavy metal on the jukebox. The songs were mostly about how Satan would kill us all. Just before we left, Frank and I put on Kylie Minogue singing 'I Should Be So Lucky'. By the time it came on we would have been safely up the motorway. It would have almost been worth a beating just to watch their faces as Kill All You Mother-Fuckers' was replaced with 'Lucky in Love'.

We parked in a massive car park by the Bournemouth seashore. Tum and I ran across the road to a telephone box to order pizza for dinner: 'Yes, that's right . . . deliver the pizza to the double-decker bus . . . in the middle of the car park!'

The smell of aftershave in the bus was overpowering. Well, at least it got rid of the pizza smell. The boys were getting ready to pick-up. We arrived at the nightclub to find a queue of people waiting to get in. They were mostly girls. 'Foockin' all right!' Frank said, rubbing his hands together.

'Sorry. No jeans allowed,' grunted the bouncer. Eight of us were wearing jeans. We had no choice. We went to the other nightclub down the road. There was hardly a girl in the place. It was full of blokes wearing jeans. The groom promptly fell asleep in the corner, while the rest of the lads did their very best to spend the entire beer kitty.

I crawled back to the bus sometime after two. Most of the lads had already crashed. I was just about to doze off to sleep when Frank Bruno shouted out from the other end of the bus, 'Who's got me foockin' blanket?' No one answered. I knew it wasn't the groom. He hadn't even made it to one of the bunks. He'd collapsed on the floor. He would have been warm, though. He was totally wrapped in toilet paper. 'Who's got me foockin' blanket?' Frank screamed, 'Who's got me foockin' blanket?' This went on for twenty minutes. I couldn't stand it any more. I stumbled out of bed and found him a blanket. I was just about to doze off again, then . . . 'Who's got me foockin' pillow?'

The lads had beer for breakfast. I passed it up. The three-hour journey back to London involved more drinking, smoking, dancing, fireworks and the inevitable browneyes at passing traffic. Just before noon, I dropped the lads off at The Church in Kings Cross. No, don't worry, they weren't going to mass. They were going to The Church, which was a regular Sunday event that involved comedians, strippers and a lot of people throwing up.

They all staggered off the bus and waddled inside. Oh, except the groom. They carried him in. It was his bucks party and he'd been conscious for about ten minutes of the whole thing.

Cruise Ship

Luxor, Egypt
November 1993

How good was this going to be? Our three-star cruise up the Nile wasn't running so we were going to be upgraded to a five-star *deluxe* cruise ship. Wow. I'd stayed at a few flash five-star hotels before (well, two anyway) and was very impressed—as only someone who's spent most of his travelling life staying in cheap dives can be—with the fluffy robes, the chocolates on the pillow, the TVs in the bathroom and phones in the toilet, and those tiny packs of shampoo (I have a rather impressive collection of these at home). So what would five-star *deluxe* have to offer? Champagne baths? A wall of TVs in the toilet? Naked women on the pillow? Not quite. Thanks to the ship's salad bar, my then girlfriend (and now-wife) Natalie ended up in the London Infectious Diseases Hospital in such strict quarantine that I had to wear a plastic coat to visit her. But that's getting ahead of the story.

As we stepped out of the scorching Luxor midday heat and onto the *Royal Boat*, we were offered white face-towels by a smartly dressed Nubian boy. The towels were cool and wet and lying on a bed of ice and rose petals.

The foyer of the *Royal Boat* was small and simply, but stylishly, furnished. The ship (or boat—I never know which is which) hadn't looked much from the shore, though. More like a small block of flats than a boat. Mind you, who wouldn't enjoy a flat with constantly changing water views?

There were well-dressed staff buzzing about everywhere. We were greeted by our very own cruise director, Mohammed. I'd never seen such a big smile in my life. It must come with the job. Besides the facts that he was male and Egyptian, the big beaming smile made him look like Julie McCoy from *The Love Boat*.

Mohammed McCoy lead Natalie and me to our suite. The piped muzak that was playing in the foyer was playing in the corridors as well. They were playing an instrumental version of 'Tie a Yellow Ribbon Round the Old Oak Tree'. It was worse than any elevator I'd ever been in.

Our suite was quite posh. Even the sheets on the large bed smelled fresh (a nice change from some of the hotels we'd stayed at in Egypt, where the sheets smelled like my dad's socks). By the way, the word 'posh' comes from the early Atlantic crossings of the early 1900s, the most expensive cabins on the ship were the POSH cabins. Because ships had no airconditioning, these cabins would be on the side of the ship away from the warm sun. On the return journey, you would move to a cabin on the other side. They were the Port Out, Starboard Home (POSH for short) cabins.

If you want to travel really posh today, you could always book the deluxe penthouse suite on the *Crystal Symphony* cruise ship. Your palatial suite features personally monogrammed stationery, bathrobes and slippers. And, if you want the aforementioned slippers while you're playing the white grand piano, or when you've just stepped out of the suite's private gymnasium, you simply buzz for your very own personal butler. All this, however, comes at a price. It's a whopping $1700 a night. The 102-day round-the-world cruise would set you back $1.7 million (you could buy a small cruise ship for that!). You do get unlimited drinks, though, and the bar fridge is full of Moët & Chandon (I'd be pouring bottles of it down the sink just to get my money's worth).

I checked out our bar fridge. I always check out the bar fridge in hotels. Mind you, I never buy anything. I just like being amazed at the prices.

'Look at this, Natalie. The bottled water is $10!'

'Oh, really.'

'Bloody hell, this tiny bottle of Johnny Walker is 32 bucks!' I moaned.

'Yes, Brian.' Natalie smiled.

'Jesus, the fuckin' peanuts are twelve dollars! Can you believe that? Twelve dollars!'

'Yes, Brian.'

Natalie is so patient. I go through this little routine in every single hotel we visit.

Actually, it reminds me of a funny story. Two friends of mine had a layover in Singapore on their first overseas trip. The airline put everyone up in a hotel for the night. They hadn't stayed in a flash hotel before and were quite surprised to find a fridge full of drink. They had a couple of beers, then piled the rest—including the champagne, vodka, gin, whisky, wine, port, brandy and even the peanuts—into their bag. When they checked out, they were given the bar bill. It was $475. They were too embarrassed to hand it all back, so they handed over the cash. The funny thing is, neither of them are particularly keen on a drink.

We freshened up (as one does on a five-star deluxe cruise ship) and went to meet our tour guide, Brad, in the dining room for lunch.

This cruise was part of a two-week tour of Egypt. The tour was run by the same company we both worked for in Europe. It actually worked out very well indeed. Not only did we get the tour half-price (staff discount); we didn't have a large noisy group to contend with either. Besides Natalie and I, there was only one other passenger in our group: Lisa, a lovely girl from Sydney. It was like having our own personal tour guide (they don't get that on the *Crystal Symphony*, so ner!).

The muzak now playing in the corridor was an instrumental of 'Feelings'. I made a mental note to cut the speaker wires later that night.

The dining room was not even one-third full. There were only us and a group of middle-aged people sitting together. That was it. The large group were all French. I would say 'bonjour' at least 100 times over the next four days. Most of them thought they were on the French Riviera. Well, they were dressed that way, at least. One lady had even brought her bloody poodle along (I made a mental note to throw it in the Nile when she wasn't looking). Salvador Dali went a few steps further than bringing a pet poodle on one cruise he went on. He booked two suites on the QE2—one for him and one for his two pet cheetahs.

Brad looked very flustered as we sat down. There was good reason, too. He'd lost our passports. He'd gone to check in and couldn't find them. Oh well, it looked like we'd have to spend the rest of our lives on a five-star deluxe cruise ship . . .

Lunch was a veritable feast. Countless waiters scurried around us piling our plates with food. For entrée there was tahina, hoummos, baba ghanough and torshi meshakel (pickled vegetables). Our very Egyptian entrées were followed by a very un-Egyptian main course of roast chicken and roast potatoes.

After lunch we waddled ashore and wandered aimlessly around the markets. The market vendors were terrifyingly persistent. One guy spent over an hour trying to sell me exotic herbs and spices. You may well wonder why I stayed for over an hour when I wasn't in the market for a bag of basil. That was because I was having a ball watching him work through every selling technique known to man just in order to sell me five kilos of cumin. 'You will never, ever in your lifetime be able to buy cumin as good as this, my friend.'

Back aboard the boat, I went for a wander to check out our new home, while Natalie went to our cabin to get changed. The entire top deck of the boat was covered with green carpet intended to look like lawn. It looked like green carpet. About twenty banana lounges surrounded a small swimming pool. There was also a bar and a spa overlooking the water. I strolled downstairs and peeked into rooms (startling the kitchen staff at one point). I stumbled upon an outside area and walked into about a dozen crew chuffing away on smelly cigarettes, including a couple of Nubian boys who couldn't have been older than twelve. The ship was quite small. Not that I'd know, I hadn't even been on a cruise ship before, but it seemed small compared to the *Sea Princess* from *The Love Boat*. Speaking of large cruise ships, the *Queen Mary II* will be launched in late 2003. It will be the largest passenger vessel ever built at a cost of, wait for it . . . $1.4 billion. It will rise as high above the water as a 23-storey building. It will have libraries, casinos, horseracing (expect a heavy track), six cinemas, an ice-skating rink, a couple of full-size basketball courts and a golf course (with an incredibly large water hazard!). The only problem is, most passengers will probably spend most of the cruise trying to find their cabins.

Finding my cabin would be the last thing I'd be worried about if I was on *Titanic II*, which is due for completion in 2004. While the original interior design for the *Titanic* will be faithfully reproduced, there will be one major change: the passenger-lifeboat ratio will be four times that of the original. I'd still be hanging around the lifeboats most of the time, though.

I joined Natalie, Brad and Lisa for a beer on the deck. The boat was moving now. It was good to leave the endless stone quays attached to riverside hotels and the flanks of cruise ships behind. We sipped our beers as the setting sun turned the Nile into a river of pure gold.

This was the life. I could get used to this, I thought. To be honest, though, I never thought I'd go on a cruise. 'I could think of nothing worse,' I'd say. I'd seen cruise ship passengers disembarking at ports all over the world and they were always the same people. Everyone would look like they got dressed in the dark. They'd be wearing green checked pants, purple spotted shirts and orange socks. No one would be under 112 years old. Cruise ships don't have the nickname 'hearses of the high seas' for nothing (in fact the *QE 2* carries 27 coffins aboard . . . just in case).

They would come ashore for two hours, buy over-priced trinkets and the crap you see in souvenir shops and always wonder who the hell would buy, then rush back to the boat for G&Ts in the Wild West theme bar followed by a cabaret night starring someone like Des O'Connor singing 'Tie a Yellow Ribbon Round the Old Oak Tree'. No, thank you.

But this cruise seemed all right. Well, besides the muzak and the beer, anyway. The muzak was now 'Love is a Many Splendoured Thing'. I think the tape was 'The Worst Songs Of All Time'. I was also drinking the worst beer of all time (well, on a par with some of the well-known Australian beers, at least). It was horrible. It tasted like rusty pipes. It was an Egyptian beer called Stella. Definitely no relation to Stella Artois. It was made using Nile water. There were bits of shit (I don't mean that literally—except that now I come to think of it . . .) floating in the bottom. As we watched the sun set over the Nile, the carcass of a dead buffalo floated by. It was very bloated, with what looked like hamburger mince coming out of gaping hole in its side. Not surprisingly, I didn't finish my Nile-water beer.

I was looking forward to dinner. I wasn't disappointed. We were treated to another feast. Friends of mine who had been on cruise ships before had returned saying the best part of their cruise was the food (one couple didn't leave the dining room the entire trip). The people who travelled on what is considered to have been the first ever cruise ship wouldn't have said so, though. In 1536, a ship was chartered to sail from London to Newfoundland with the dual role of trawling for cod and providing an enjoyable cruise. Sixty people signed on. It was a disaster. They caught no fish, and the journey took so long that they ran out of food and resorted to cannibalism.

We sailed through the night. I awoke in the wee hours for a wee and peeked out through the closed curtains. We were motoring though a gorge. The wide and leisurely Nile had contracted suddenly to a massive gorge. Peering into the night, I could just make out the cliffs towering above the ship. We actually didn't travel all that far during the night. We spent five hours in a lock. Mind you, before locks and canals were built, this part of the river would have been unnavigable. In fact, before the Suez Canal was built in 1869, P&O passengers being transported to India had to disembark and travel across the desert on camels and pick up a different ship on the other side. With luggage and mail as well, there were sometimes as many as 3000 camels in the train.

I hopped out of bed in the morning and turned on the giant TV. Well, opened the curtains anyway. The large cabin window was like a giant TV screen. As the boat slowly floated down the Nile, we lay in bed and watched Egypt go by (most of populated Egypt can be seen by boat, since the strips of fertile land, where most of the 47 million Egyptians live, are confined to a few kilometres either side of the Nile).

A mighty sweep of palms and sand dunes beyond the cultivated land disappeared into a distant haze. In the water, brown-skinned children were splashing in the shallows among fishing boats of all shapes and sizes. Dragging ourselves away from the riveting TV show, we got dressed and ready to visit 'the largest and most completely preserved Pharaonic temple in Egypt'—the temple of Horus at Edfu.

Our local Egyptian guide told us that Geb was the god of the earth and husband of Nut. He was, the guide insisted, not to be confused with Khons, who was the god of the moon and son of Mut. Yeah, right. Egypt has just way-too-much history for my way-too-short attention span.

We did, however, see something quite special. In one of the tombs we peered through a dark gap and saw a broken mummy at the bottom of a shaft. Our guide took this opportunity to tell us how mummies were made, 'First, an iron instrument was inserted into the nostrils and their brains was, how you say? . . . sucked out. Next, with a sharp stone knife, they would make an incision in the body and empty all the stomachs and fill it with sawdust and spices, then sew it back up. The body was then washed and wrapped in bandages of fine linen.' Our guide told us all this with big smile on his face. He also went on to say, 'Wives of important men or women who are beautiful are not given to the embalmers straight after death but wait one week. They did this to stop the embalmers from having intercourse with the dead bodies.'

After our lunchtime feast we lumbered upstairs to lie in the warm sun. Being November, the temperature was only in the high twenties. In the middle of summer it would be in the high forties. We drifted past groves of palms, acres of sugar cane, and fields worked by oxen. Men were sowing the earth while women were baptising the family laundry in the Nile. The speakers mounted around the deck were blasting out 'Feelings' again. I had a *feeling* they only had one tape on the entire boat. It was the third time I'd heard it. The staff must be immune to the muzak. Or dedicated masochists.

The French arrived en masse. In fact I hadn't seen them separated at all on the entire cruise. They all lay next to each other on the sun-beds. One lady looked like she'd seen a bit of sun in her time. The mummy in Edfu had better skin than she did. One of the men went in the pool. The rest soon followed. The pool was the size of a king-size bed, but sixteen of them squeezed in and splashed about. When they got out, they used the ship's towels like tissues. One larger chap used five to dry himself. Another one dipped her toe in the pool then picked up a fresh towel, dried her toe, threw it in the basket and picked up a new towel.

The French left the deck en masse just as the sun started to set. Brad and Lisa left Natalie and me to have a romantic dip in the spa. As the sun went down, the river turned pink then, only a few minutes later, a beautiful soft grey. With twilight, a calm descended on the river. The only sound was the gurgling of the spa. There was no muzak—when 'Feelings' had come on for the fourth time, meaning the tape was starting again, I'd pulled out the wires from the speakers.

We motored past endless walls of ochre sand with mountains of mauve and rose in the distance. It was only the smell of the impending dinner feast that dragged us away from our little slice of heaven.

We woke up to the TV again. The story just carried on from where we had left it the previous day. Huts of mud and straw sat among palm trees, while along the banks of the river, white herons frolicked in the reeds. After breakfast we visited another temple. Komombo was so old, so grand, so awesome—and so hard to tell apart from the other dozen temples we'd seen.

At lunch we made a terrible, terrible mistake. We ate the salad. We let our guard down. This was a five-star deluxe cruise, so we just assumed the salad would be OK. Even though our guidebook told us 'to avoid salad at all times'. Even though the guidebook goes on to say, 'Egyptians sometimes fertilise their fields with human excrement. This waste has a way of sticking to the produce, and the food isn't always well-washed before it reaches the plate.' But still we ate it.

Pharaoh's revenge took only an hour to hit us. It hit Natalie a lot harder than me. She had a fever and lay in bed fully dressed, shivering violently under a pile of blankets. We both lay on the bed moaning. 'You don't understand, I'm really sick,' I whined (men can't take pain). I was soon in the toilet, and half an hour later I had mastered the art of pooing and throwing up at the same time.

Two hours later, I thought I felt well enough to attend the final night 'Egyptian Banquet'. 'You go,' Natalie gasped pathetically, 'I'll be OK.' It was fancy dress. An Egyptian theme night (how clever!). I put on my gallabiya (I'd bought this in Luxor) and shuffled to the dining room. Brad was sitting on the huge table by himself. Lisa had also taken sick. The French were all dressed up. One lady had come as Cleopatra. She must have brought the outfit with her from France. Not only are theme nights big on cruises, so are entire theme cruises. They offer everything from 1920s themes to naked cruises. You can even go on a 'Love Boat' cruise based on the TV show—on the original ship! Accompanying you on the cruise are cast members from the show. Doctor Adam Bricker, Vicki Stubing and Issac Washington (the barman!) were aboard the second cruise that went in February 2002 (the first one in August 2001 had sold out in days). I'd go if Julie McCoy and Gopher went along. I always wanted to shag Julie and I always wanted to king-hit Gopher.

There is also another cruise I wouldn't mind going on—to watch. It's called the Lesbian Girl's Party Cruise, and by the look of the photos on their website, the bar looks like a good place to be. There's naked bodies in positions that would make the author of the Karma Sutra blush. The closest we had to that on our cruise was a middle-aged French woman dressed as a belly dancer.

The first of the 28 courses was brought out. It was *Molokhiyya*, a green slimy soup made of God knows what. One smell of it sent me scurrying back to my cabin.

I wandered back to the dining room when dinner had finished. Brad had gone to bed and the French contingent were all pissed. Every single one of them was up on the dance floor. They moved en masse like Siamese octeenuplets. The belly dancer was close to popping out her huge breasts. Every male crew member was staring in hope of a bit of nipple action. I slunk off to bed.

On the next (our last) day, I was feeling better. Natalie was still feeling a little how's-your-father. We sat on the top deck in the shade. Mohammed McCoy buzzed around Natalie asking if she was OK. 'You want chamomile tea?' he asked, 'it's very good for . . . if you have shits.' He brought Natalie a chamomile tea every fifteen minutes after that. He also showed us a photo of his girlfriend in Australia. She was a pretty blonde. 'She loves me,' he told us (two months later Natalie received a letter from Mohammed asking for a photo—no doubt so she could be flaunted as his new girlfriend).

We pulled into Aswan among a sea of fluttering white felucca sails. The chamomile tea must have worked because Natalie felt a lot better as we stepped off the boat. Felt better, that is, until ten days later, when we got back to London. That was when she started (how do I put this nicely?) um . . . er . . . pooing blood and mucus.

It was then that she was admitted into the London Infectious Diseases Hospital. The doctor had no idea what she had. 'It could be anything,' he told me, as I stood by Natalie's bedside wearing my plastic quarantine coat. Anything? He reckoned it could have been dysentery, giardia, hepatitis A, cholera, polio, typhoid or even the black plague.

A week later they let her out. The doctor said, 'Look, I don't know what you had, but whatever it was, it's gone.' Yeah, that's what the doctor in the film *Alien* said, too.

Felucca

Aswan, Egypt
November 1993

'Our three-day felucca trip down the Nile was fantastic,' my friend had told me. 'Oh, except when my girlfriend woke in the middle of the night to find the Captain leaning over her, having a wank.' He also went on to add that when they stopped for dinner, a couple of hours earlier than normal (because of favourable winds), he rushed off to the 'toilet' (Egyptian food does that to you). When he climbed up over the sand dune and saw the 'toilet', he couldn't believe his eyes. Most people only ever used this toilet in the dark. What he saw was a virtual minefield of shit, with strands of well-used toilet paper gently blowing in the breeze. People would normally be stepping through this poo-field in the pitch black of a desert night.

No, I was happy to skip the wanking and The Great Poo-fields and just do a one-day felucca trip. Indeed, I couldn't go to the Nile without going sailing in a felucca. That's like going to Paris and not going to the top of the Eiffel Tower, or going to Amsterdam and not smoking a large joint and having sex with a prostitute.

Aswan was the perfect place to take a felucca trip. Nowhere in Egypt is the Nile more picturesque. The river, full of islands and white-sailed feluccas, threads through the town between banks of smooth granite and yellow sand.

Brad had booked all four of us (Natalie, Brad and Lisa—from the cruise ship) on a felucca owned and captained by a man named Allah Din. He didn't look at all like a wanker (in either respect!). Allah Din was tall and dark-skinned, and dressed in a simple white gallabiya, that looked freshly ironed. He greeted us formally and elegantly, in a manner that suggested we were not only his guests, but revered friends.

Allah Din was Nubian. The Nubians, from southern Egypt, are darker skinned and quite different from the Arabs in both physical features and dress. And what makes them very different to the Arabs is that not once did I meet a Nubian who tried to sell me a carpet. They wouldn't make good carpet salesmen, anyway. 'Nubians are a fine, gentle, noble people with graceful manners and generous hearts,' my guidebook said. Not very good qualifications for offloading dodgy carpets on gullible foreigners.

The small passenger deck on the felucca looked like something straight out of an Ikea catalogue. Bright-coloured cushions and hand-woven rugs were carefully arranged around the raised planks that served as benches. The felucca was small, maybe five metres in length. It's bow was just long enough to house the roughly hewn wooden mast on which the triangular lateen sail was hoisted. The design of the felucca hasn't changed in a couple of thousand years, and once upon a time they were the most important form of transport and communication in the country. In fact, it was the Egyptians who first took up sailing as early as 6000 BC (minus the G&Ts and boat shoes).

Allah Din introduced us to the 'steerman', a young Arab boy called Al-Azziz-Azziz. 'What a great name!' I said to the boy. 'Thank you,' he said humbly, 'Brian is a lovely name, too.' Yeah, right.

We sailed slowly past the Corniche el Nil, which was buzzing with noisy cars, donkeys, bicycles, horse-drawn carts and horse-drawn cart drivers trying to sell rides to the tourists. The four of us lounged on the cushions, soaking up the sun and the view. We passed Kitchener's Island, which looked like paradise itself. The island was given to Lord Horatio Kitchener in the 1890s, when he was consul general of Egypt. Indulging his passion for beautiful flowers, he turned the entire island into a botanical garden, importing plants from as far away as India.

We could no longer see Aswan. The surrounding desert and hills were the colour of ripe apricots. After an hour we beached on a dirt bank. Above us was a small village. Already our arrival had drawn a crowd of children who huddled around us shouting, 'What's your name' non-stop. They insisted I take their photograph and several of them wanted to show me how they swam, so they stripped off and dived into the Nile. I was more impressed that they were game enough to swim in the somewhat dubious Nile water than by their swimming technique.

This was Allah Din's village. We were very privileged, our tour guide Brad told us. He had never taken people to his house. The village, although built of simple mud brick, was extraordinarily beautiful. With barrel-vaulted roofs and domes, the houses were set out around a broad shaded courtyard. The village lanes twisted between walls painted a vivid shade of blue.

We entered Allah Din's house and were greeted by his mother. Her warmth and affection was almost overwhelming. She welcomed us as if we were lost children. I almost thought she was going to hug me and give me a big grandma kiss. We were shown into a large room containing a couple of brightly coloured sofas (Ikea Summer Catalogue, page 28), an extra-large coffee table and, in the corner, the latest flat-screen television. The walls looked as if they were painted yesterday. But what made this whole scene look odd was the floor. It was covered in the finest deep yellow sand, soft on the feet and immaculately clean. There wasn't much use for a Hoover here. It actually looked quite good—and I suppose if there's nothing on the telly, you could always build a sand castle.

We were served ice-cold flower juice. The juice was made from the flower of the hibiscus. It was delicious and surprisingly refreshing in the heat. 'Allah Din, would you please tell my friends your story of when you worked for a Kuwaiti Princess,' Brad asked. Allah Din smiled and said, 'Yes, if you like.' He settled comfortably into his chair and spoke softly.

'One evening, eight years ago, I was tying up my felucca on the banks of the Nile when a beautiful lady called out to me, "Excuse me, can you take me to the other side?" I told her, "No. I am sorry, madam, but the felucca is not for hire. It's my own felucca." (Allah Din had saved for years to buy his own felucca). "Oh, please," she asked me again, "I have to get to the other side." I took her across and she then asked me if I would wait for her. I waited for an hour, then took her back. She tried to give me money but I said, "No, it is my pleasure". She then told me she was a princess from Kuwait and asked if I would take her across the Nile again the next day. I said yes. The next day she asked if I would like to come and work for her as her personal assistant. I said yes. I travelled the world for two years seeing the most beautiful places on earth, but I said to her I would like to stay in one place so she made me manager of her estate in Switzerland. I only ever saw her now and again. Sometimes she didn't even know where she was. One time she awoke on the sofa and asked me where she was. I told her we were in England. She had a very big shock. She thought she was in Switzerland. She had had many drinks the night before and had asked me to organise her private plane, which was always on standby, and accompany her to her house in England. She did not remember asking me . . . or going over on the plane.'

'Was she a nice person to work for?' I asked.

'Oh, yes. A very kind and generous lady. She was very kind to me. One time she left a note and an envelope for me when she was leaving the house in Switzerland. The note said, "Go into town and buy yourself something nice". Inside the envelope was 10 000 Swiss Francs (about $10 000).'

Allah Din didn't brag or gloat when he told us this. It was just matter of fact.

'I managed the Swiss estate for one year, then spent another year at her large estate in England. But the houses were mostly empty and there was nothing really to do. I also got very homesick, so I asked the princess may I go home. She offered me a job running a very big oil company in Egypt. But I said, no, I want to go home to my village.'

So, after four years of working for one of the wealthiest women in the world, earning more money that he could ever imagine, staying in the best hotels and eating in the best restaurants, Allah Din returned to Aswan and his simple mud-brick house with sand as the floor. He didn't do too badly for himself, though. He now owns fourteen feluccas.

After a light lunch of warm bread and delicious homemade dips, Allah Din's mum gave us all a hug goodbye and told us we could drop in any time. We said yes, we would—as if we pass by this Nubian village in the southern Egyptian desert quite often.

Allah Din dropped us off at the Hotel Pullman Cataract, the stunning and elegant turn-of-the-last-century hotel overlooking the Nile. Most Egyptians could live for a week on the price of just one of the cocktails at the bar. This was where Agatha Christie wrote the book *Death on the Nile*. We asked Allah Din to join us for a cocktail on the verandah, but he declined. He had spent four years living a life like that and he was much happier just to potter around in his felucca.

Later that night we saw him in a small, cheap riverside restaurant having a drink with friends and he invited us over. As I watched him chatting and laughing with his friends, it occurred to me that he was the most contented, happy man I'd ever met.

Camel

Sinai Desert, Egypt
December 1993

My camel sounded like Linda Blair—well, Linda Blair when she was possessed by the demon. It was a horrifying low guttural cry that would have done Satan proud. I was just waiting for the camel's head to spin around and spit green vomit at me, when suddenly a large pink swollen tongue, alive and slobbering, popped out between its yellowed teeth. It must have been a foot long. However, this wasn't the only thing that was worrying me. Our camel safari guide didn't seem to have a camel. There was Natalie and me and only two camels. Was he going to walk? Or was he simply going to send us off to wander the desert aimlessly by ourselves?

Our camel guide stood with his arm draped around Natalie's camel with a huge smile on his face showing off teeth even Sir Les Patterson would have been ashamed off. One thing was certain, dental hygiene was obviously not a priority here. I smiled back. He gave me even a bigger smile. I think he was proud of the fact that he had better teeth than his camels. 'Hello, I'm Brian,' I said. Our camel guide smiled. 'Hello, I'm Brian,' I said again, this time trying to match his smile. He kept smiling, but this time he nodded his head. OK, so we were about to spend ten hours in the middle of the Sinai Desert with a camel safari guide who didn't speak English and, more importantly, didn't have a camel.

Our hotel manager had recommended 'Cough Up Nasty Phlegm' Tours—well, that's what it sounded like, anyway—to us the day before. In our first three days in Dahab, we'd been hassled hourly, minutely and sometimes even secondly to go for a short ride by the camel owners who congregated along the waterfront. But no, I didn't want an hour's stroll. I wanted to be Lawrence of Arabia. I wanted to be a famous explorer. I wanted a camel safari.

Abdul (for that is what I christened our camel guide, because it sounded like a good camel guide's name) pointed to what was to become my new best friend and worst enemy. My camel. I immediately christened him Colin. Colin the camel. Colin sat in the brown dust gurgling, belching and grinding his teeth. Abdul smiled. He could have been anywhere between 25 and 75 years old. He had his own personal contour map of the Sinai on his dark and wrinkly face. Slip, Slop, Slap was obviously not a priority here. Abdul, like most Egyptians, wore a simple white gallabiya and no underpants. Every couple of minutes he'd a have a go at his old fellow. And let me tell you, he wasn't subtle. To be scrupulously fair, I suppose I do it almost as often. It's just that I have the luxury of pockets for that sneaky jiggle.

Abdul was a Bedu, one of 50 000 or so. The Bedouins are an ancient people who have been living in the desert for centuries. Wealth for a Bedouin is measured in children and camels. Indeed, camels are more than an animal to a Bedouin. They are a method of transportation, a friend, a companion and a source of milk and meat (like all good friends!). Their hair is used to make tents and clothes, and their dung can be burnt to keep warm (the dung is so dry it can be used as fuel as soon as it leaves the animal). One book describes it this way: 'In the eyes of the Bedouin there could be nothing more perfectly designed to have as a comrade during a solitary existence in the desert. Bedouins will talk for hours about their breed of camel, about their fine coloured hair, elegant looks and sturdy capabilities.' No wonder Abdul had his arm around the camel, a big smile on his face and couldn't keep his hands off his old fellow.

Colin was now snoring like a dirty old man. Abdul stood patting the saddle (well, *khorj* if you want to get technical) indicating that I should climb aboard. Colin didn't look particularly smart. Rather dopey, in fact. As I stepped towards him he let loose a horrendous noise. You can write down the sound a cat makes which is, of course, meow. Just as a dog woofs or a duck quacks, etc. However, if you had to write down the sound a camel makes, it would be something like this: Ergghharergggh.

Colin did have beautiful long eyelashes, though. Eyelashes that girls would kill for (I bet they wouldn't mind a boyfriend with a one foot tongue, either!). The fact is, the camel is an incredibly well-designed beastie. The long eyelashes keep sand out of their eyes. They also have three eyelids to protect themselves from blowing sand. Looked at side-on, camels appear exceptionally large, but head-on they look slim and streamlined. This helps them keep cool, because they will turn towards the sun to minimise solar heat. A camel can survive a water loss of about 40 per cent of their body weight and survive a couple of months without water. Let me put that into perspective. If humans lose 10 per cent of their body weight in water, they can no longer move, drink or speak. Water can only be administered intravenously or via the rectum. Camels have no such problem. They can drink 100 litres of water in a matter of minutes.

No matter how much water they take in, though, camels don't store it in their humps (or two humps if it's a Bactrian. A one-humped camel is a dromedary). The humps are, in fact, stores of fat, and if the camel doesn't eat for absolute ages, it's hump (or two) will disappear. All things considered, then, the camel is rather clever for something that looks so dopey. But then again, I'd probably look dopey too if I walked around in 40 degree heat everyday.

Getting on a camel is easy. It's the next 30 seconds or so that require the utmost skill and balance. Just to stay on. Colin was crouched right down in the sand, so all I had to do was step over him and sit down. That was the easy part. Abdul gave Colin a quick poke with his stick and Colin awkwardly raised his rear legs. I lurched forward, ending up hugging his neck. My face was only centimetres away from Colin's slobbering mouth. Then I caught a whiff of his breath. Christ, what did Colin eat? Vomit? Pal dog food? Just as I tried to pull away I was jolted sharply backwards as Colin straightened his front legs. This threw me back in the saddle again. Colin groaned—sounding very much like my father when I told him the police had caught me shoplifting—then stuck his slobbering tongue out again.

Mind you, at this point, if I had known what I know now I would have been in a mild state of panic. You see, the slobbering tongue is the first stage of a male camel's attempt to attract a female. Luckily for me, he didn't move on to the second stage. Particularly since I was sitting on him. What usually happens next is that the male camel urinates all over his tail then splashes it all over his back. Thank God (or Allah) he didn't find me, Natalie, Abdul or the other camel worthy of his full mating ritual. Which, I might add, also includes the camel salivating copiously so its mouth is covered in foam and all the while making a 'blo-blo-blo' sound (I've seen drunk guys try this in nightclubs, and it doesn't work).

Natalie was up and moving before I had a chance to figure out how to get Colin going. Suddenly, from behind me, if I wasn't mistaken, I heard what sounded like Abdul sucking on an extra-thick shake. It was that loud slurping sound we all love to make when we reach the bottom of the cup. Abdul was making this pleasant noise with his mouth. He would continue to make this noise for the entire day. Non-stop.

Abdul scurried up along to the side of me, 'Slurp, slurp, slurrrrrrrrrrrrp.' Colin started walking, or more accurately, started shuffling forward. It was a little after eight, and the morning was clear and fresh. It was bound to heat up like a furnace later. Something to look forward to. At least I had my Lawrence of Arabia hat-cum-towel thingy on my head.

'Hey Natalie,' I called out, 'I think mine's busted.' This was definitely not like riding a horse. It was more like riding a slow-motion version of a rodeo bull. There was no rhythm at all. I was being thrown sideways, then forwards, then backwards. All in the space of about ten seconds. My spine was taking a battering. 'I think I've got a dud one,' I moaned, 'I think one leg's shorter than the other.' I now know why camels are called ships of the desert. It was like being on a small boat in a tropical storm.

After only a few minutes of excruciating pain we were at the outskirts of the village of Dahab. We passed by one of the many 'camps' (a cluster of ridiculously cheap huts full of hippies). This one was named Happy Land Camp. There was also Lovely Days Camp, Lazy Days Camp, Crazy House Camp and New Life Camp. Gee, I wonder if hippies are their target market. Initially I didn't want to come to Dahab. 'It will be full of bloody hippies, smoking dope, eating alfalfa sprout burgers and staring into space,' I moaned to Natalie. So imagine my delight when I found a quiet seaside village with swaying palms and brilliant coral reefs only metres offshore in the Red Sea. There was also cheap accommodation (a dollar a night—the insects in the bed came free) and cheap food (the insects came free here also).

On the horizon were row upon row of barren, jagged red-brown mountains and between us and the mountains was a relentlessly dry desert, broken up by the odd lone acacia tree or a patch of shrub. Out of what looked like a dust storm appeared an old jeep with about eight Abdul look-alikes sitting in the back. It stopped in front of us. Greetings were exchanged, then Abdul said something and the Abdul look-alikes looked at Natalie, then at me, then burst into laughter. My guess was Abdul had told them he'd get 500 camels for the girl, but he'd be lucky to get a goat for the scrawny fellow who can't even ride a camel. Don't scoff, it could be true. The thing is, I was once offered 1000 camels for an ex-girlfriend by a carpet salesman in Morocco. 'What do I want camels for?' I said, 'But give me two brand new BMWs and she's yours!' In hindsight, though, the camels were a pretty good deal. A cheap, used camel costs around $400, while a low-mileage VGC camel will set you back about $4000. Even 1000 dodgy camels would be worth $400 000! Mind you, if you're talking racing camels, that's a different matter altogether. The best racing camels (always female by the way) fetch up to five million dollars. Sheikh Zayed, the president of the United Arab Emirates, owns 11 000 racing camels and spends over a million dollars *a day* for their upkeep. I looked up the official camel racing website (FICRA—an acronym for 'Fuck I Can Race Anything', I believe) and they had some great training advice like: 'It is not advisable for a trainer to race his camel if it is fat' (gee, I wouldn't have guessed that one). Also: 'Examine your camel's sweat after training'. That sounds like a fun job (camels, by the way, sweat under their armpits like humans). And finally: 'You can tell if your camel is frightened, because it will produce loose stools where it should normally produce hard, dry pellets similar to those of a giraffe' (how many Saudi camel owners—or camel owners anywhere really— would be intimately familiar with the discharges of a giraffe?).

At any rate, if I'd been offered 1000 of just your basic run-of-the-mill racing camels for my ex, that (at about $100 000 a shot) adds up to a tidy 100 million dollars. Damn, I knew I should have sold her.

Shortly after leaving the Abdul look-alikes, I had to dismount. My back just couldn't take it any more. I was sure I'd end up with major spinal damage if I didn't get off the wild-yee-ha-rodeo camel ride. As I stepped to the sand, the heat struck. It was only a little after nine, but the hot desert sand was soon burning through the soles of my sandals. This was going to be a bloody long trek. After 500 metres of Colin trying to kick sand in my face, I thought I'd give riding another go. I didn't know which was worse. Ending up with heat exhaustion and a mouthful of sand, or spending six months in traction. Back aboard, I still couldn't get comfortable. Who designed these bloody things? I now knew why Abdul was walking. I tried sitting up, down and even side-saddle. Then, thankfully, mercifully, after trying just about every position in the Kamasutra, I finally figured out how to get comfortable. OK, I tell a lie. Natalie said, 'Why don't you try it like this?' I mumbled something about being a bloody contortionist, put my legs up on Colin's neck, and what do you know? It worked. At last I could take an interest in my surroundings instead of being solely preoccupied with my spine's wellbeing. We were now skirting the Gulf of Aquaba on the Red Sea, which wasn't red but an intense blue, and washed along the flat desert shore in a long line of white foam. Tropical fish were swimming among the bright coral in the limpid aqua waters just metres offshore. In the distance the water twinkled as if strewn with diamonds. Inland and across the desert, violent mountainscapes jutted out of the lunaresque landscape. It was all rather surreal. The Red Sea on one side, and the Sea of Tranquillity on the other. It was weird and wondrous.

At one point we zig-zagged our way through dunes covered in the tangled, rusted remnants of barbed wire. These were leftovers from Israel's occupation of the Sinai (well, *one* of Israel's many attempts at occupation—which only ended in 1982). This area of the Sinai desert had been the scene of some of the worst fighting during the war between Egypt and Israel.

While we're on the subject of fighting, camel fighting is a popular sport in some parts of the world. In Selcuk, Turkey the 'Melbourne Cup' of camel fighting attracts up to 20 000 spectators. Before each bout a handler confronts the male with a 'wife' in heat, then whisks her away to leave a rather frustrated and angry male. He then goes ballistic when he's put in front of another male. (Sounds like your average nightclub to me: Girl flirts with bloke all evening. She walks away. Bloke gets angry and leaves. He goes outside and starts a fight).

All of a sudden we veered right. Well, Natalie and Abdul did. Colin kept shuffling along the shore. How do you steer these bloody things? 'Hey, Colin, where are you going? Turn right!' I pleaded. Colin wasn't listening (or, like Abdul, didn't understand English). Eventually Abdul noticed I wasn't veering right along with him and Natalie and bolted back with a beaming smile on his face. Without warning, and in what undoubtedly would have been a pretty good circus trick, Abdul leapt up over the rear of Colin and ended up sitting snug right behind me. Phew! Abdul may have had better teeth, but Colin had better breath. Abdul indicated that I should give Colin a poke in the neck with my right foot. I did and Colin magically turned to the right.

After about ten minutes the country changed from flat pebbly sand to rolling, open dunes peppered with what looked like polystyrene rock formations. It looked like a bad set from *Lost in Space*. 'Danger, danger,' I blurted out, as I waved my arms about wildly, 'Aliens approaching!' Abdul ran over, thinking there was something wrong. 'It's OK,' I said. It might have been a little difficult to explain to Abdul. I don't think he would have been too familiar with the antics of Doctor Smith and the Robot.

For the next two hours it was trot and walk, walk and trot, slurp-slurp-slurp, smell of hot camel, smell of hot self, blinding glare, slurp-slurp-slurp and walk and trot. The going was slow—camels walk on average 4km/h and are lucky to get to 10 km/h at a trot. As we approached midday, the sun was burning so fiercely it turned the sky pale, pale blue. The sand and nearby mountains were bleached almost white. It was as if someone had turned down the colour on a television.

Ahead there was a gap in the rock formations forming a gully in the rising cliffs. As we entered the gully, the temperature soared. It was worse than the open desert, because there was a breathless stuffiness between the rocky walls. As we continued, the rocks on either side rose to the height of cliffs. It was silent, except for the plodding of hooves and Abdul sporadically having trouble getting the last of his chocolate milkshake. It was so dry Colin was kicking up what looked like moondust. (How's this for an interesting fact? Some parts of the Sinai have never had rain. Some locals have never even seen rain. How weird is that?)

I was parched. (Here's a handy hint if you happen to go on a camel safari in the middle of the Sinai desert: take more than one bottle of water between two people.) I was desperately looking forward to the oasis where, according to the hotel manager, we would be stopping for lunch. Ahead the gully widened. Colin quickened his pace. He knew he was soon to stop for a rest. We rounded a bend and there it was. The oasis. However, it was clear at a glance that we were entering a mirage. It looked too perfect to be a real oasis. It had swaying bright green palms, a stream trickling down a shiny silver boulder in the centre and veiled dark skinned harem girls were waiting to lead us thirsty explorers to a pool of sweet water. OK, I made up the harem girls, but the oasis looked as if it had been lain out meticulously by a landscape gardener. Indeed, with the date palms an almost fluorescent green against the pale sky and pale desert, the whole thing looked like an oasis from a Bugs Bunny cartoon.

Colin dropped himself down onto the sand next to a simple shelter held up with what looked like sticks. It was set into the side of the cliff. The roof was a haphazard collection of dried-out palm leaves.

As I stepped off Colin, he promptly started grinding his teeth and making a contented gurgling sound. Abdul tied up the camels, then lifted his sleeve to reveal a rather flash watch. He pointed to it and smiled at me. Was he trying to sell me his watch? 'No thanks,' I croaked. '*La, shokran*,' I said in two of the four words I knew in Arabic. Abdul kept pointing to his watch. 'Ah, you want us to leave at two o'clock!' I exclaimed. Abdul trotted into the shelter, lay down in the sand and readied himself for his midday nap.

Natalie and I wandered deep into the oasis. There was not a sound. I expected to hear something. A bird tweeting or at least Arabian drums or the clatter of swords. There would have been at least 50 palms all huddled into an area no bigger than a soccer field. We followed a trickling stream until we stumbled upon a pond set among a series of large boulders (the landscape gardeners had excelled here). The water was only above our ankles, but it was splendidly cool and tasted better than any water I had ever drunk. We both stripped off to our underwear and splashed each other like naughty little children, then lay in the pool dozing in the warm sun.

Abdul cried out to us from below. 'What's he saying?' I asked. 'It's lunchtime,' Natalie responded confidently. 'How ... do you know?' I said, quite surprised at Natalie's sudden grasp of the Arabic language. 'Because it *is* lunchtime,' Natalie responded with a cheeky grin.

Abdul had lit a small fire in the centre of the shelter. A beaten old tin can sat on the fire looking very much like an Aussie billy. From under his robe Abdul pulled out a dirty cloth bag and lay it in the sand next to his feet. Scooping out a large handful of tea leaves he threw them into the billy. Three tin mugs were also produced from the inside of his gallabiya. They were all different shapes and sizes, looking for all the world like something left over from Rommel's desert campaign. Goodness knows where it all was coming from, but Abdul then produced a plastic bag full of flat bread and threw it straight onto the fire (that's the bread, not the plastic bag). It is interesting to note that the fire was probably fuelled by Colin's dung. I, of course, didn't know this then. I don't think I would have been too keen on eating the bread if I'd realised it was cooking away nicely right in the middle of burning camel shit.

Mind you, it could have been worse. A lot worse. Some Bedouin tribes drink camel blood ... as a meal! Here's the recipe, so you can prepare it at home: Find a camel. Milk it of both milk and blood. The blood is to be extracted from a facial vein (you'll be happy to know you can take up to five litres at one time). Oh, it also helps to extract milk if it's a female camel. Mix the blood with the milk. Let it sit for a few days until the blood coagulates and the milk curdles, so it's nice and thick. Then serve. Hmmmm. Yum.

The bread was burnt in spots and looked rather unappetising. Surprisingly, however, it was decidedly tasty and was filled with nuts and dried fruit. Abdul smiled, 'OK, OK?' '*Ma'fish ma'sculla*,' I replied in the last remaining Arabic words I knew, 'No worries'. Abdul's eyes lit up. He would say *Ma'fish ma'sculla* to me every five minutes after that for the rest of the trip. The bread *was* tasty, albeit full of sand. The obvious horrible crunching noises we made with our teeth didn't seem to bother Abdul.

Abdul poured us a dark-coloured tea then reached under his gallabiya again. I wonder if he's got any sugar and milk under there? Or some shortbread biscuits to dip in the tea perhaps? Out came a packet of cigarettes. They were Cleopatra brand (in Egypt, you can also buy Cleopatra brand toothpaste, fruit juice, toilet paper and I even saw a Cleopatra brand screwdriver set!). Abdul offered me one (a cigarette, that is, not a screwdriver). Hesitantly I accepted it. Perhaps it was another use for camel dung. I coughed and spluttered as I took a drag. It tasted a little bit like the dried pine needles rolled in newspaper we used to smoke as a kid. If it *was* camel dung, it actually wasn't too bad.

Natalie and I left Abdul to the dishes and headed back up into the oasis. We found ourselves a cool smooth boulder in the shade of a huge palm and lay sprawled on top, content with a belly full of bread and sand.

Being the intrepid explorer I like to pretend I am, I led Natalie back to the shelter the long way. Clambering over a large rock, I spotted a Coke can sitting up against a palm tree. My heart sank. Can't you go anywhere on this Godforsaken planet without stumbling over a damn Coke can? I glanced around fully expecting to spot the ubiquitous Big Mac container as well. Bloody hell, there was probably a camel drive-thru on the other side of the date palms. 'Would you like some pita bread cooked over camel dung with that, sir?'

The journey back to Dahab was slow. The rows of granite walls in the gully changed colour with every passing minute. It was the same noises, same smells and same glare. The shadows began to get longer and longer till they seemed to stretch out forever. The mountains were now a rich yellow colour, looking like massive mounds of molten gold.

With probably only half an hour of light left, we shuffled into Dahab. As Colin lowered himself onto the sand, out came his slobbering tongue. As I stepped off my new friend, he batted his three eyelids and long lashes at me and began making the blo-blo-blo sound. He kept staring at me. 'I think he likes you,' Natalie quipped. 'Doesn't he know?' I said, 'a man is not a camel.'

Skis

Wengen, Switzerland
January 1994

In the annual Wengen World Cup downhill ski race of 1991, a nineteen-year-old Austrian racer crashed, and split himself in half. With only 200 metres of the 4.26 kilometre race to go, he flew so high off the final steep section that he sailed over the padded bags into the netting above it. One ski got caught in the netting. The rest of his body kept travelling. Travelling, that is, at 100 km/h. The force of the sudden stop split him in half. Right up to the bottom of his rib cage. The medical staff pumped litres of blood into him, but he died on the way to hospital.

Three years, and four days, after that fateful crash I thought the same thing was going to happen to one of my clients. I was working as a ski guide (yeah, yeah, I know, it's not really *working*) in the Jungfrau region of Switzerland, skiing in the resorts of Wengen, Mürren and Grindelwald. I was leading my flock of eight clients down the famous

Lauberhorn downhill course. The race had been held four days earlier, and the whole run had only re-opened that day.

Unlike the racers, my lot didn't get off to a good start.

The starting gate sits at the top of the busy Wixi ski run under the shadow of the mighty Eiger, Monch and Jungfrau mountains. I got everyone to clamber, one by one, up to the top of the wooden ramp that provides the flying start. 'Wait till it's clear of skiers below,' I said, 'then go for it.' I didn't set a good example. In my defence, I was a wee bit excited. I'd watched the race and seeing those racers jump out of the gate gave me delusions of being an Alpine racer. The thing is, though, that the racers reach a speed of 100 km/h in around four seconds. Just let me put that in perspective. Your average family car would be lucky to get to 50 km/h in that time.

I shot out of the gate onto the piste. I went dead straight for about 50 metres then threw in a few frantic turns to slow down (and to avoid cleaning up the merry holiday-makers pottering down the hill). In the actual race, the competitors go straight down for about 300 metres before taking a sharp right. This is exactly what Noddy, a 22-year-old East Londoner, attempted to do. However, he lacked one small thing. Skill. I watched in horror as Noddy careered down the slope completely and utterly out of control. On the way down, he collected an impossible-to-miss Japanese fellow (for some bizarre reason, the Japanese wouldn't be seen dead in any winter wonderland without multi-coloured fluoro ski suits with gold and silver sparkly bits) and scattered a ski school class of six-year-olds, all of whom could ski better than he could.

I know I hadn't set a good example, but Noddy took everything to the extreme. Noddy was on holiday with his friend Doddy (I jest not). They were both unemployed and had financed their trip by selling headache tablets as Ecstasy in nightclubs in London (there would have been a lot of kids waking up with nice clear heads in the morning, Noddy told me). He was a nutter. He'd already frightened off one older chap from my group the day before by telling him that he 'skied like a cunt'—whatever that meant.

I considered myself a pretty good ski guide. Others might not have been so sure, though. On a couple of occasions, I have to admit, I really stuffed up. On one such occasion, I was guiding a group down a winding track that, in the summer, became a asphalt road. We were all flying. The problem was, half-way down the track it turned into its summer role. There was only a slither of snow running down the very side of the road. It was all right for me, I managed to stay on the snow. The rest of the group, on the other hand, skied straight down the road. It made a sound similar to a tabletop grinder. Thank God they were only wrecking hire skis.

On another occasion, I took the wrong turn and led my entire group down into a huge valley that I didn't even know existed. There were no other skiers, or even a ski run for that matter, in sight. It would have been too difficult to turn back, so I led them down through deep snow, hoping to find a way back to the village below. Four out of my five clients floundered in the deep snow and fell every ten metres (well, at least one paying customer and I were having a hoot, but I didn't want to tell them that). Finally, in the distance, I could see the village. However, there was one little obstacle in the way. A cliff. Personally, I love skiing off cliffs, but the two guys in my group who were in their forties, looked like they were about to wet their collective pants. They didn't ski it. They climbed down (well, technically they *fell* . . .). By the time we all reached the restaurant below they looked like five mobile saunas. Even though it was minus eight degrees, steam from all their sweat was pouring off them. Strangely enough they didn't come out with me the next day.

I did my very best to make sure my group on the Lauberhorn run knew what was coming up ahead. In fact, I did very well in stopping Noddy from racing ahead. I didn't really want to see him launch himself

50 metres into the air—which is exactly what the racers do. With a 41 degree gradient and a 30 metre drop, the racers hit the top of the *Hundschopf* ('dog's leg' in English) at around 120 km/h, then fly through the air for 50 metres. If they misjudge the leap, they sail into a rocky outcrop (which is spectacular, albeit messy).

I led the group along the top of the *Hundschopf* then dropped down where it wasn't so steep. This is the favoured spot from which to watch the race and spectators sit in the cold snow for hours to get the best viewing position (numb bums are de rigueur). The Lauberhorn World Cup ski race is by far the biggest sporting event in Switzerland. Almost 100 000 fanatical spectators, clanging cow bells and yodelling, line the run. Another 30 million people around the world watch it live on TV. The Lauberhorn is just one event of eleven World Cup races in a season. Skiing was the second sport, after soccer, to hold a World Cup (now there are hundreds of World Cups for everything from sailing to tiddlywinks).

The course itself is amazing. In the week leading up to the race, an army of skiers (literally—I'm talking a couple of hundred Swiss army soldiers in full uniform) walk down the entire course with skis on and stamp down the snow. It is then watered until it becomes rock hard, and finally the whole course is swept. Properly swept that is, with your average kept-in-the-kitchen-cupboard type of broom. Every loose bit of snow is a potential 'death cookie'. Hit one of those teeny-weeny bits of snow at 100 km/h and it's bye bye birdie.

The racers themselves must be a few bread cubes short of a fondue. Crashing at some point in their career is inevitable. There wouldn't be many racers who haven't broken a bone or two. Skiing is a dangerous sport, there's no doubt about that. In Switzerland alone, there had been 80 000 accidents the previous season. It's hard to find out how many people have actually died, though (it's not something a ski resort wants to advertise: *Come to Grindelwald—we only had*

fourteen deaths last year!). The mountain resort of Chamonix in France
(just one of literally hundreds of resorts) has an average of 105 deaths
a year (some of them involve mountaineering, but most of them are a
result of skiing accidents). And there are many ways to die too. You
could crash into a tree or a rock, a ski-lift pylon or even a snowboarder
(we can only hope!). You might be the best skier in the world and some
novice could crash into you. You could die horribly of frostbite or
hypothermia. Your cable car could get hit by a fighter plane (nah, that
couldn't possibly happen) and, finally, you will almost certainly die
when you see the price of a beer in a Swiss bar. Still, that doesn't stop
me and the 20 million other skiers who visit the European Alps every
winter from careering down a hill dodging people, trees and
hypothermia. And that's a lot of people looking absolutely ridiculous
walking around in oversized plastic boots.

I was sure Noddy was about to become accident number 80 001.
We were now on a narrow track and, even though it was the slowest part
of the course (well, slow to the racers but at 70 km/h, terrifyingly fast
for just about everyone else), it ran right next to a train track. Noddy
was skiing perilously close to the edge of the track. That train is the
Jungfrau train, which not only takes tourists to the highest railway
station in Europe, but transports skiers up to the slopes. Up until the
1930s this train was one of only a few in the Alps that were used as ski-
lifts. Everywhere else, skiing involved a ten-minute slog up a steep hill
and a ten-second schuss down again. Sod that! There are now over
14 000 ski lifts in the Alps (and 14 000 lift queues for Germans to push
into).

If I was worried about Noddy and the train track, there was much
worse ahead. We next had to ski through a five-metre wide brick tunnel
that went under the train track. 'Now take it easy, everyone,' I said, at the
top of the steep, narrow chute that led down to the tunnel's mouth. 'Try
to throw in a few tur ...' Noddy was already off. He looked like he was

having an epileptic fit on skis but, somehow, he managed to ski through unscathed.

It was Noddy's friend, Doddy, who caused havoc on the next section of the course. We were back on a crowded ski run again, and he bowled over a Ski Club of Great Britain ski guide. While lying sprawled out on the snow, the guide shouted something like, 'I say dear boy, that's frightfully jolly dangerous.' I'd bumped into (figuratively speaking) a few of the SCGB ski guides during the season (a new one would turn up every couple of weeks. They all had names like Jeremy Higginbottom-Smythe III, and they all said things like 'tally-ho', I even overheard one of them telling someone at lunch how he'd been 'poodling' down the hill. Then again, it was the snotty Brits who popularised skiing and held the first ski races in the 1920s. One of the first downhill ski races held in Wengen was won by Horatio Donald-Waghorn (and no, I didn't make that up). I don't think they've won a race since then. I do feel a little sorry for the Brits. Not only did they popularise skiing, they also were the pioneers and the original masters of soccer, tennis, cricket, rugby, golf and cycling. Sadly, the only game that the Brits pioneered and that they are any good at today is darts (oh wait a second, the newly crowned World Champion is Australian).

At the half-way mark there is a telephone box on the side of the run. I urged my clients to call home at this point. Just in case they needed to say their last goodbyes. The next section of the course, Hannegg Straight, was a 250-metre almost vertical drop. This is the fastest section of the race—the Lauberhorn boasts both the fastest and slowest sections of all the World Cup courses—and the skiers reach speeds of around 155 km/h. Mind you, that's nowhere near the speed skiing record (that is an event in itself. The racers there are a whole breadbasket short of a fondue—and could be missing the cheese as well). The highest speed recorded is 248.1 km/h by an Austrian fruitcake called Harry Egger. Let's just consider that for a minute. Think about doing 120 km/h on the freeway, then double it. That's how fast he went with nothing more than a couple of planks strapped to his feet.

Stupidly, that's exactly what I intended to do. With the course still in pristine condition for speed, this was my one and only opportunity to really go for it. But first I had to send my group down safely. 'If you want to go for a schuss,' I said, 'it's probably best to take it easy most of the way, then go for it after the third pole from the bottom.' There were ten poles on the side of the run spaced 25 metres apart. Naturally, Noddy went first. He got confused. He schussed from the third pole from the TOP! Within seconds he was doing at least 80 km/h. His skis began to shake like mad. So did he. Not long after that, he fell. Even though it looked terrible, it was hard not to be impressed. I'd never seen someone do fourteen somersaults before. It truly was an astounding sight. He tumbled off the track, knocked a pole and sent it flying, then did a final half-twist with a pike before collapsing into a heap.

He didn't move. Oh, shit! I was just about to bolt down when we heard laughter. It was Noddy. He was all right. 'If that had happened to anyone else,' his friend Doddy said, 'they would have been dead. It's lucky he takes all those drugs.'

Not surprisingly, the rest of the group went down rather tentatively. That left only me. I was going to go straight down from the very top. Speaking of which, in the old days of skiing, skiers had no choice but to go straight. When Sir Arnold Lunn was having a skiing lesson at Chamonix in 1898, one of his fellow students asked the instructor whether they could learn to turn, after skiing straight downhill all day. The instructor said that he had seen someone turn but added that he was unable to demonstrate how to do it himself. Noddy must have had the same instructor.

I immediately threw myself into tuck position and shot down the hill. And gee, did I shoot down the hill. It was the most exhilarating and, at the same time, most frightening feeling. I would have been travelling at over 100 km/h. If I fell, there was a very good chance I would break something. Or, even worse, die of embarrassment. I was at the bottom in seconds. Then came the hard part. Stopping. Any sudden turn of the ski and I could crash and burn Noddy style. I threw in a couple of sweeping turns and pulled up sharply in front of my group. 'You're a fuckin' nutter!' Noddy exclaimed wildly. This was coming from the man who put the nut into nutter.

The final section of the course was fenced off. What a pity. We wouldn't be able to finish the Downhill course. Noddy suggested we jump under the fence. I wasn't too keen on that idea. A few years back, in another resort, a fellow ducked underneath a closed off run and merrily skied down. Near the bottom of the run there was a length of wire stretched across the piste. He didn't see it. He ploughed into the wire and it clean chopped off his head. But wait, it gets worse. His now-headless body kept skiing down the hill and joined the normal run, scattering skiers, before crashing into a heap at the bottom of the run. I told my group this story and Noddy said, 'Cool!'

On closer inspection of the fence, I noticed there was a sign next to a small entrance. The sign had a large skull and crossbones on it with *ACHTUNG!* written in red underneath. It then had, in English, 'For Experienced Skiers Only' followed by a couple of lines of German. They're quite literal, the Swiss. It translated into something along the lines of 'If you are not a good skier, and you ski down here, you will die!' An arrow pointed off to the left and a safe route down to the bottom of the course. No one wanted to be a wuss and take 'the safe route'. They would rather die first.

The course took a couple of wide sweeping turns before the final drop to the finish line. We stopped at the edge. Below was a 20 metre sheer drop. It was so steep you couldn't see the top half of it. It was sheet ice. Not just icy snow, but clear shiny blue ice. This was the spot where the young Austrian skier split himself in half. To the left of us, some other skiers had opted for the 'clambering through the thick trees to get down rather than die' technique.

'There's only one way to go down,' I said, 'Go straight and don't turn. If you try to turn you will slip on the ice.' I went first to show how it was done. My heart skipped a couple of beats as I flew over the ice. There was no way on earth you could put in a turn on this ice. Even the best ski racers in the world would have had trouble. In fact, at the 1956 Winter Olympics in Cortina d'Ampezzo, the course was so icy that only seventeen out of the 75 starters crossed the finish line. The racers had no such problems here. They don't even touch the ice. They shoot off the edge and drop from the height of a three-storey building. Thirty metres after they land, the racers cross the finish line. That's the easy part. They then have only another 50 metres to come to a complete stop. Stopping, that is, while travelling at around 80 km/h.

I was not going quite as fast by the time I crossed the finish line. I'd already thrown in a few turns before then. But I still had to slam on the brakes to stop in time. In the race four days earlier William Besse (a Swiss fellow) won the race in 2 minutes 28.88 seconds. It took me about 20 minutes. The fellow who finished second in the race was only 0.002 of a second behind Besse. That's about ten centimetres of a ski length. Amazing. To race over four kilometres, with everyone taking a different line down the course, and end up separated by only 0.002 seconds. Over 40 racers completed the race and there were only seven seconds between first and last place. On the other hand, in the 1992 Olympics in Albertville, a skier was going so slow that another competitor overtook him. This fellow was from the Seychelles, which not only has a noticeable lack of mountains, but, more importantly, has no snow. The Moroccan guy who overtook him didn't even finish. He crashed into the post holding up the finish line. Not surprisingly, racers now have to reach a certain qualifying time before they can even enter the Olympics.

Even Doddy had a better skiing style than the fellow from the Seychelles. He did have something in common with the Moroccan, though. He skied smoothly down the ice, then crossed the finish line with way too much speed (he was waving his arms in the air as if he'd won the race—I did that, too) and crashed into the fence.

Noddy did exactly what I thought he would do. He tried to turn. He shot head first into the ice, and slid down face first to the bottom. Five minutes later, after he had collected his skis, he crossed the finish line. He had a huge big dumb grin on his face. A face, I might add, that was also covered in a horrible red graze.

At the top of the chairlift we stopped at a pub. Not the least of skiing's attractions is that it provides a great excuse for drinking. We stopped for two beers—I couldn't afford three without taking a week's advance on my wage. Noddy had four (the Ecstasy sales must have been going well). 'That was fuckin' brilliant, I'm comin' back next year and doin' that again,' Noddy announced. He didn't come back the next year. Doddy did, though. Noddy couldn't, because he was in jail for six months—Doddy wouldn't tell me what for. Noddy did, however, tell Doddy to tell me . . . that I skied like a cunt.

Toboggan

Mürren, Switzerland
February 1994

I've skied at around 100 km/h and not been afraid. I've jumped off cliffs on skis and not been afraid. But put me on a cute little wooden toboggan and send me down a scenic toboggan track and I'm a terrified wuss. I've seen nine-year-olds speeding down the track laughing and totally in control. What looks to them like a cute alpine barn by the side of the track brings me to sheer white-knuckled panic. I'm petrified I'll slam into it and be splattered while the nine-year-olds laugh merrily. Still, it's either hit the side of the barn or sail off a cliff into the middle of a busy ski run. I've tried both and can't recommend either.

One of my duties as a ski guide was to take the clients tobogganing every Wednesday afternoon (although I'm pretty damn sure I didn't see 'Daredevil Toboggan Guide' in my job description). I did this for 34 Wednesdays over two years, and every time that cute barn came into view, I'd curse the hell out of the Swiss for putting it there.

When the toboggan track was icy, it was at its scariest (or most exciting if you're into death-defying extreme sports—or if you are nine years old). It was on one of those icy days that I lost my toboggan, my nerve and ten years off my life.

That 'Toboggan Wednesday' had started nicely. Well, they all started nicely actually. The start didn't involve any tobogganing. I would meet the clients on top of the Almendhubel scenic lookout for a picnic lunch. The picnic lunch was 'cold meat' rolls (I was never sure what the meat was, but the cook told me that ham was too expensive and that this 'meat' was very cheap—I would suggest it was probably made from dead tobogganists). This was all washed down with a shot or two of Apfelkorn, a sweet and deceptively lethal apple schnapps. I always had at least four shots.

Joining me on this fateful day were eight clients who were looking forward to a lovely relaxed afternoon tootling down the hill. They had no idea what they were in for. Among them was an English fellow in his late forties who had been christened Daryl Deep Powder by Noddy and Doddy because he wore a pro skisuit with Deep Powder written across the back. He wasn't quite a pro skier though. In fact, the only deep powder he had seen would have been in his washing machine.

Noddy and Doddy didn't want to come tobogganing. 'Toboggans are for fuckin' sissy cunts,' Noddy told me.

Daryl Deep Powder was a strange one. He didn't ski with sunglasses on because he wanted a dark, even tan on his face. I explained to him that the sun was many times more powerful at altitude, and that it can burn the retina in your eyes and leave you blind. He just gave me a silly grin. He spent two weeks skiing with terribly bloodshot eyes that watered like mad. When we'd stop for lunch, he would leave us and go to a restaurant higher up the mountain so he could be 'closer to the sun'.

Noddy and Doddy teased him constantly. And not just about his tanning regime, either. At the final Friday night's fancy-dress party, Daryl Deep Powder came to the bar in his normal clothes. Noddy turned to him and said, 'What have you come as? A cunt?' That witty remark received the same silly grin. Daryl Deep Powder was a nice enough chap. He was just a few seats short of the full chairlift.

Our toboggans (or *schlitten* in German) were rather flash wooden ones. They were 'Davos' brand toboggans. The brochure for the 'Davos' claimed that they came with a *verstärkteraussenlatte* and included a *Kunststoff-rennbelag*. Now, my German is not perfect, but I don't know why the toboggan would come with a lace tablecloth and include an electric kettle.

You can buy a 'Davos Super', among another 121 different brands and models of toboggans, at the online Schlitten-Shop (www.schlitten.ch if you're interested in a bit of schlitten). Other big brands you could buy included Klappschlitten and Swingrodel. They're funny, those Germans. Imagine naming your toboggan companies after sexually transmitted diseases!

To ride a 'Davos Super' toboggan, you simply sit (or, if you are clinically insane or nine years old, lie face down) on top of the toboggan (it's raised about twenty centimetres off the ground) and rest your feet on the sled rails.

The first 500 metres of the 2.7 kilometre 'Bob Run' is so slow you almost have to get off and push your toboggan. I liked this part. The clients would always complain it was slow/easy/boring/fucked. It was when the toboggan run joined part of the ski run that it became interesting. This is where the turning part came in. To turn, you simply put, say, your left foot down onto the snow and the toboggan would veer to the right. No, left. No, sorry, right. Oh shit, I can never remember. This confusion on my part has led me (and quite a few of my clients) careering towards skiers and cliffs, causing great danger and embarrassment (I remember now, it's left . . . I think).

This part of the run would also be quite crowded with other tobogganists. The Swiss just love their toboggans. You wouldn't find many Swiss households without a Klappschlitten or a Swingrodel hanging in the shed. Indeed, tobogganing is so popular that there are over 150 fully-fledged toboggan clubs in Switzerland.

Yet, here's the most remarkable thing. The credit given for inventing the toboggan doesn't go to some yodelling mountain man. It goes to a polar bear—who was apparently a bit of a wiz with a circular saw and a lump of four-by-two. Actually, it's true (well, besides the circular saw bit). When a polar bear is faced with a steep snow covered slope, it just sits on its bum and slides down. The Canadian Indians observed the polar bears doing this and followed suit. Not long after that they were building toboggans out of wood. In fact, *toboggan* is a North American Indian word.

If my group of novice tobogganists managed to sort out my confusion and get the hang of turning, they would round the corner to find the run flattening off just in time for the entrance to the Bob Run proper. What made this next section so horrifyingly difficult was that the previous stretch of track was twenty metres wide and this section was about two metres wide.

Being the 'guide', I went first. Immediately I picked up speed. I'd never seen the track this icy. I couldn't turn around and tell the rest to turn back. I was too busy concentrating on trying to slow down. With every passing metre the sled went a little faster and became even more impossible to control. It bounced and buckled. I'd dig in my heels and they would just shudder uncontrollably, sending shock waves up my whole body.

I couldn't believe a young kid had gone down before me head first and lying down. He'd probably grow up to be one of those nutters who compete in the Olympic luge. The luge (which is actually French for toboggan) involves travelling down an even icier and steeper track, on a tiny toboggan, at speeds of up to 150 km/h. They do this lying down feet first and can't see where the hell they're going. To top it off, they do it wearing an indecently skin-tight, and dangerously thin, Superman suit. Then again, they seem totally sane compared to the certified nutters who compete in the skeleton. The skeleton is basically the same as luge except they go down face first. Try and tell me that's normal behaviour.

I was sure I was travelling at 150 km/h. Well, at least 120 km/h, anyway. OK, maybe 40. I dug in my toes and raked hard. It didn't seem to make any difference. Ahead of me loomed a sharp turn and the brick wall of the barn. Oh, shit. Which foot do I use to turn left again? I had a choice. Hit the wall or fly over a cliff. I went the cliff. Not that I had time to think rationally; I just thought, I don't want to hit that wall. At this point, I don't mind admitting that I was not exhibiting either icy calm or nerves of steel.

I flew through the air—rather impressively, too, I might add— and landed with a thud on the bottom of the embankment. I was lying immobile on the soft snow while my toboggan continued its journey, happily skidding along on its way to Italy.

I scrambled back up the embankment just in time to see Daryl Deep Powder plough into the barn wall with a terrible thump. I heard another bloodcurdling scream and I quickly ducked as another one of my clients sailed over my head and onto the ski run below. Further up the track I heard another almighty crash. Someone had miraculously managed to stop in the middle of the track, only to have someone else crash into the back of him. Another two slammed into them. Oh boy, was I going to have lots of fun filling out insurance claim forms. I first went to check if Daryl Deep Powder was still alive. Oh no, his eyes were very bloodshot and watering. Then I remembered. He always looked like that. Everyone else was a bit battered and bruised but OK. Except one. I didn't know if he was OK or not. He'd shot off down the ski run at around 150 km/h. He'd be in Italy by now—and possibly on the short list for their Olympic luge team.

At the end of the 'Bob Run' (or as one client called it, the 'Oh no, I've shat my pants run') we stopped at a *schnee* bar—a bar made from snow and ice, literally in the middle of a ski run. In Lindvallen in Sweden, they have a ski-thru McDonalds in the middle of a run. Imagine a McDonalds in the middle of a ski resort in one of the most expensive countries in the world: a Big Mac would be $125, and no, you wouldn't want an $80 apple pie with that.

Strangely enough, everyone was keen for a drink. This, I told my fellow tobogganists, is where a toboggan really comes into its own. As a seat. We all sat on our toboggans and sipped our $27 beers.

The last section of the 'toboggan run' was also a walking track. This involved a lot of weaving and dodging. Daryl Deep Powder got the weaving part down pretty well. He just couldn't get the dodging part, and had a head-on with a very large Swiss lady. If my understanding of her German was correct, she offered to shove his toboggan up his nose.

Oddly enough, no one wanted to do a second run. Most people only ever did it once. It was all right for them. I had to come back the next Wednesday and lose another five years off my life. Or my whole life. Whichever came first.

Donkey

Lindos, Greece
April 1994

'What's the donkey's name?' I asked. 'Dimitrios,' the donkey man mumbled. That's a funny name for a donkey. That's Jim in English. 'What is your name?' I asked in that stilted voice we all put on when we speak to small children and foreigners. He nodded twice and smiled. Right. So does that mean Dimitrios was his name or the donkey's? And, to make things even more confusing, Greeks shake their heads from side to side for yes (or was it up and down for no? I told you it's confusing). I knew my donkey was male because he was, well . . . hung like a donkey. A strapping fellow, to say the least. No wonder female donkeys have a glazed look in their eyes. A male donkey is called a Jack. So that is what I decided to call him. I didn't want to offend the donkey man by using his name for the donkey. Natalie had a female donkey. A Jenny. If you think that's silly, a male mule is called a John and a female mule is a Molly. A male zebra is a Simon and a female zebra is a Sharon. Actually, I made the zebra ones up, but it wouldn't surprise me.

Finding a donkey man wasn't easy. I'd talked Natalie into getting up at five to hike out to the point overlooking the village of Lindos to watch the sunrise (I'm a romantic at heart). Stumbling over the rocks in the darkness, we finally made it to the end of the peninsula. I produced a picnic breakfast and we sat down to watch the most glorious sunrise. On the way back to the village we passed a herd (or whatever silly collective noun is used) of donkeys lazily munching on rather unappetising looking dried-up grass (incidentally, two of my favourite collective nouns are a parliament of owls and a murder of crows).

'They're so cute,' Natalie cooed. They looked a bit sad and scrawny to me.

'Ee-aww!' a donkey blurted out from behind us. It sounded like a really bad impersonation of a donkey. Every single one of the eight donkeys was staring at us. We shuffled slowly passed them (it was a bit spooky, I have to say), dodging the piles of donkey shit we would have been stepping right in the middle of when we came this way earlier in the dark.

'Shall we do the donkey ride to the top of the Acropolis?' Natalie asked as we stepped into the main square of Lindos. The Plateia (square in Greek) was usually a maelstrom of noisy tourists, noisy mopeds, noisy souvenir hawkers and even noisier donkey owners trying to talk the tourists into taking a donkey ride. It was eerily quiet. There wasn't even a single postcard stand on the street. It probably had something to do with the fact that it was 7.30 in the morning. Everyone else was still asleep.

'*Kálimèra!*' I called out in front of the Donkey Terminus just off the square. *Kálimèra* is 'good morning' in Greek. It's one of the 40 things I know how to say in Greek. The other 39 are all swear words. The Greek kids at school only ever taught us swear words. I suppose it will come in handy if I ever have to ask a Greek person whether I can have anal sex with their goat.

Out of the shadows stepped a donkey man. He looked very surprised that someone was calling out for him instead of vice versa.

'Can you take us around the village before we go to the Acropolis?' I asked.

'Um ... well ...'

'We'll give you extra money.'

'Of course!' he said, with a beaming I'll-make-some-cash-out-of-these-tourists smile.

Lindos is the perfect cutesy Greek village. But that's the problem. Half a million tourists in floral shirts visit this tiny village every year. Most of them are daytrippers who are bussed in each day from the huge, cheap and ugly resorts that are peppered around Rhodes. Overlooking an idyllic bay, the dazzling white village of Lindos hugs a steep headland which is crowned with the magnificent 2000-year-old Acropolis. And, what keeps the village so perfect is that it's a site of national heritage. All houses must be built in traditional seventeenth century Lindian style (which is basically a concrete shack painted white with blue wooden shutters thrown on, but they still manage to maintain a simple elegance). Large hotel chains and major tour operators would be champing at the bit to slap an 87-room apartment block on the beach here. They would be salivating at the thought of all those tourists piling into Lindos everyday. The best those greedy bastards can do is take over a dozen scattered villas and rooms and call it Sunny Paradise Villas or some crap. It's so good to see they can't turn Lindos into yet another Housing-Commission-Flats-By-Sea.

Our donkey man lead Jack and Jenny out of the square and up one of the narrow pebble-paved alleys that wind their way in and out between the immaculately whitewashed houses. It was wonderfully quiet. Yesterday, all the large blue shutters were open revealing souvenir shops and ice-cream shops competing to see who could play the loudest Euro-pop song. Yesterday, we also would have been dodging the odd tourist. Not too many, though. Being only the first week of April, there weren't that many about. A lot of the restaurants and villas had only opened in the last week. Yesterday we'd just about had the beach to ourselves. The postcards in the souvenir shops showed the beach in midsummer, with barely a centimetre of sand to be seen between the sunning bodies.

'Mmmmmmm,' our donkey man groaned. 'Mmmmmmm, mmmmmm, mmmmm.' It sounded like he was having a rather pleasant sexual experience. He wasn't riding a donkey himself, but walking five metres or so in front of us. He would continue to 'Mmmmmmm' non-stop for the next hour. We came to an intersection and our donkey guide turned left. Jack tried to go straight ahead. 'MMMMMMMMMMMMMM!' our donkey man groaned in ecstasy. He'd just reached orgasm. Jack grunted and followed the donkey man. Now I get it. A continuous 'Mmmmm' means to follow while a big 'MMMMMMMM' tells the donkey it's stuffing up.

We came to a steep stairway and Jack gave an audible groan as he began his ascent. The stairs looked like they'd been painted yesterday. They were a sparkling white with lovely rose pink trims. Personally, I much prefer the ubiquitous white and blue paint scheme that's favoured by most Greek island villages. Apparently, the Greeks painted their villages in blue and white so it was reminiscent of the Greek flag. After 400 years of Turkish rule, this was their way of saying 'up yours' to passing Turkish ships (Rhodes was only given back to the Greeks in 1947).

As we rounded one of the countless twisting corners, we rode right through the middle of a sea of cats. There must have been at least a dozen of them. They weren't cute little fluffy things, they were scrawny, horrible looking brutes. They all jumped out of the way and scampered up stairs and cowered in doorways. You'll find cats all over the Greek islands, but they don't seem to belong to anyone. They all look skinny and dirty. The souvenir shops are full of postcards, books and calendars showing cats lounging about on pink walls and aqua pot plants. They all look beautifully coiffed and healthy, though (they must have brought over some well-fed German cats for the photography shoots).

Sitting in a restaurant on the island of Ios, I once threw a small piece of fried chicken to a mangy-looking cat that was hanging around. Within seconds two other cats appeared from nowhere. I threw another piece of chicken. 'How many cats do you think we could muster?' I said to my friend as I dropped a chicken bone on to the ground. Fifteen minutes later we had eighteen cats staring at us with glazed hungry eyes. It was actually quite scary. It looked like a scene from a Hitchcock film.

At the next corner Jack tried again to go the wrong way. 'MMMMMMMM!' the donkey man groaned angrily. Jack was not in the good books. While donkeys are treated like true beasts of burden in some countries, there's quite a few people who show an odd affection for them. In *Travels with a Donkey*, Robert Louis Stephenson described his donkey as 'patient, elegant in form, the colour of an ideal mouse, and intimately small'. When I did a search for 'donkeys' on the Internet, *hundreds* of websites dedicated to donkeys came up. Admittedly some of them were porn sites (hotasses.com was one, but I'm pretty sure they weren't referring to attractive donkeys). Actually, it doesn't matter what you search for on the Internet—you'll still get porn. Even if you do a search for the Mormon Tabernacle Choir you'll get hotchoirsex.com. I did a search on How to Crochet a Tea Cosy and got wobblyboobs.com.

Donkey.com was my favourite, and many other people's too, by the look of it. There had already been 366 675 hits! The site included a question page. Hundreds of people had written in asking questions of a donkey called Jordy! Here is an example:

Dear Jordy, Daisy, our very affectionate little girl donkey, has lately become somewhat irritable and aggressive. I think she is in love with my husband and is jealous of me. Please help me.

Frightening. I also discovered that zebras have been successfully crossbred with donkeys. They result is called a zonkey. I'm serious. If it's the other way round, it's called a zebrass. I've thought up a few more to add to the list. If you cross an ass with an anteater, you get an ass-eater. A hairy-nosed wombat and an ass becomes a hairy-ass. Or, you could always try and crossbreed a flying fox with a duck and make a flying fuck.

We passed a kaleidoscope of coloured doors. Each doorway was decorated with elaborate interlaced ropes. Inside the small rooms, you could see walls covered in ornate plates (the old Greek tradition of plate smashing wouldn't be too big here, I imagine). Now and again we'd catch a glimpse through an open doorway into a small courtyard decked out with pebbled black and white mosaics and pots of orchids and tulips. The Lindians obviously took great pride in their houses. Luckily they have escaped the peculiar tax laws and by-laws that make many houses in Greece look absolutely terrible. When they finish building a house in Greece, the owners have to pay a hefty tax bill. So, they leave it unfinished. Travelling through rural Greece you pass house after house with an ugly flat concrete roof and twisted iron supports poking up for the never-to-be-built second floor. This way they never have to pay the tax. Another law states that zoning orders can only be enforced if the offender is caught in the act. In strict zoning areas, whole floors, extensions and fences go up under cover of night. So, as you can imagine, the add-on pool room tends to turn out a tad shoddy.

We stopped at the doorway of one of the matching villas and were greeted by a man who had to be our donkey man's brother. He wore the same black Greek fishing cap, beige shirt and grey slacks as our donkey man. Then again, all middle-aged Greek men wore this ensemble. Just like all Greek men chain-smoked and all Greek men had a cousin in Melbourne. His name was Con (I at least got that one right). Yesterday, though, I was sure his name was Wanker. We had seen Con at the beach arguing with another man in grey slacks over how much space they could each have on the beach to put out deckchairs for rent. One would draw a line in the sand then the other would rub it out and draw another one two metres away. In between this (while we trying to have a nice relaxing day on the beach) they were shouting at each other. This went on for about an hour and every fourth or fifth word was *maláka* (literally 'masturbator' and one of the 39 useful Greek swear words I learnt at school). Con was a bit more subdued today. I didn't hear him say wanker once.

Jack was becoming impatient. He kept trying to move on. I was having trouble holding him back. I did a loud 'MMMMMM!'. Our donkey man gave me a short cold look. Only he could 'Mmmmmm'.

As we left Con, our donkey man told us what we had already guessed, that Con was his brother. He then went on to tell us he had twelve brothers and sisters. I'm pretty sure I saw one of his brothers that same evening at the Burnt Olive Tree restaurant (or whatever it was called). In fact, I'm pretty sure I saw about 40 or 50 of his brothers over the next week.

We struggled to fit past a Greek lady riding side-saddle on her donkey. She was wearing a black shawl, black dress, black cardigan, black tights and bright pink gumboots. She must have weighed a good 100 kilos. The donkey didn't look sad, more resigned to its fate.

Once we cleared the narrow streets of the village, a path led straight up to the headland and the Acropolis. To the right of the track rose steep and jagged cliffs. On the left was a sheer drop to the small bay which sparkled blindingly bright in the morning sun. Jack started to wander off the track and perilously close to the edge. 'MMMMMMMM!' our donkey man groaned. Jack just shook his ears as if to say, 'Yeah, yeah, I hear you!' and shuffled back on to the track. I'm not quite sure where Jack thought he was going. He ambled along slowly, head down, his small hooves holding firm on the steep and uneven path. Suddenly he veered towards the edge again. Our donkey man was having multiple orgasms now trying to keep him on the track. He stopped at one point and talked gently to Jack. It sounded like he was counselling him. I'm no donkey psychiatrist, but Jack seemed slightly, well ... suicidal. I think all those years (which was donkey's years!) of Mmmmm-ing had taken their toll and he had chosen today to throw himself off the highest cliff. And take me along with him.

I kept my eyes on Jack's feet. With only 40 metres or so to go, Jack stopped. He was staring over the cliff. He moved towards the edge, sending small rocks tumbling down the cliff face. 'Jack, don't do it,' I whispered. A donkey couldn't possibly have suicidal tendencies. Could it? 'Think about your family, your friends back at the stable,' I said. I'd hate to think what he'd do if he knew I'd eaten donkey salami. Meanwhile, our donkey man sounded like an out-of-control chainsaw. 'MMMMMMM!' 'MMMMMMM!' Jack moved closer to the edge. 'MMMMMMMMMM!' Suddenly Jack stopped pushing out with his hooves, stood still for a second then gave an audible sigh, and headed back onto the track.

I couldn't jump off quickly enough when we reached the top. I noticed a sign next to the medieval doorway leading up to the Acropolis. Handwritten on a thin piece of wood was 'Don't approach the edge of the Acropolis—DANGER—DEATH'. I contemplated writing underneath 'OR RIDE A DONKEY!'

We walked back down from the Acropolis (lots of old rocks and columns, but very impressive nonetheless). As we entered the village, marching up the steep steps towards me came our donkey man Mmmm-ing away, and Jack. Sitting on Jack was a German Frau the size of a beer hall. Jack was puffing and wheezing. He gave me a sorrowful look as if to say, 'I'm doing it this time. I really am.'

Motorcycle

Koh Samui, Thailand
May 1995

I have meccanophobia. A fear of motorcycles. Well, it's more like necrophobia (no, not the fear of wanting to have sex with a dead body, but a fear of death). The thing is, if you fall off a motorbike you're either going to break a lot of bones or you are going to die (a recent survey in the UK found that 98 per cent of motorcycle accidents result in some form of injury). Or, even worse, you are going to spend the rest of your life lying in a bed being fed pumpkin soup through a straw. I much prefer cars. If you crashed your car doing 60 km/h into a motorcycle, you would more than likely just end up walking away saying 'Oh, bother' with a rather nasty dent in your bonnet. The motorcyclist, on the other hand, would have a darn sight more than a grazed knee. There's a very good chance the rider's internal organs would end up like

Irish stew. If you really want to be turned off motorcycles, I recommend you look up www.rotten.com on the Internet, then scroll all the way down to 'motorcycle'. There is a photo of a guy who looks like he's had his head shoved into a mincer. It's enough to make you never want to go near a motorcycle again (or minced meat, for that matter). But I find the whole concept of riding in the rain perhaps even worse than horrible accidents. Now really, that can't be fun. I could go on. OK, I will. There's the constant noise and the fact that you have to walk around all day with helmet hair. Then there's those ridiculous biker's clothes—all that black leather makes you look like a death metal fan, or then there's the brightly colourful leather gear which makes you look like you've just stepped off a float at Mardi Gras.

Yet here I was riding a motorbike. It's just one of those things one does in exotic climes. Something in the air makes you want to get on a motorcycle without a helmet, wearing only a T-shirt and thongs (great for changing gears and using that life-saving death-defying brake) and ride on roads that look like Swiss cheese—all the while looking at the scenery and not at the oncoming traffic.

So there I was on a 125 cc Honda, dodging potholes the size of bathtubs on a sticky road out of Chaweng beach. I was attempting to discover the 'real' Koh Samui. Natalie had declined to join me on this occasion. Our last jaunt together had proved rather costly. Natalie had lost a lot of skin and I had lost a lot of money paying for repairs. I had dragged Natalie on one of my 'discovery' tours on the island of Rhodes in Greece and we'd spun out on a gravel road in the middle of a busy intersection. Natalie ended up in a messy pile on the footpath. I wasn't silly. I jumped off (Natalie was driving at the time) and managed to remain relatively unscathed.

As I left Natalie at the beach, she turned to me with a furrowed brow, 'Brian, *please* be careful. I know what you're like.'

'What am I like?' I mumbled.

'You're not a very good rider and you don't concentrate.'

'Hey, *you* were the one who crashed last time!' As soon as I said it I knew I shouldn't have.

'It was *your* bloody idea!' she said sharply.

The furrowed brow came back again. 'I know you want to play "famous explorer", but take it easy, OK?'

I was going to be careful all right. Very careful. My track record on motorbikes was shocking. The first time I ever rode a motorbike, I crashed after three minutes. I'd been asked by my friend's older brother whether I could ride a motorbike, so naturally (even though I'd never been on one before in my life), I said yes (I didn't want to look like a nerd in front of all his mates). I'd been watching them, so I had a rough idea how the gear things worked. I rode about 50 metres down a wide lane thinking, hey, I'm doing all right here. Then, when I went to turn around, I realised I had no idea how to change down and I crashed head on into a wall.

Still, a 'famous explorer' shouldn't let a complete lack of riding skills stop him. I wanted to see the real island. I wanted to find a beach where I wouldn't be asked every two minutes, 'You wan' massage?' Anyway, I was going to potter. I probably wouldn't even get into top gear. Forty km/h would be about as fast as I would go. Let me just put my pottering into perspective. The top speed recorded on a motorcycle is 519 km/h. I can't even imagine what it would be like being on a bike going that fast (I wouldn't know, anyway, I would have had my eyes closed). I hazard a guess that if you fell off, you'd have more than a grazed knee.

I had my day roughly planned out and, like all good famous explorers, I had a good map. It was a 50 kilometre loop around the island and there was lots to see. The first sight to see was the 'Twin coconut tree'. I thought I'd skip that, though. Later on, I would pass the 'Triple coconut tree'. I'd skip that too. I'd wait for the big one. On the north-east coast of the island was the 'Octuple tree'. Wow! Eight coconut trees.

It wasn't until I'd ridden about five kilometres away from Chaweng beach that I noticed I couldn't see any tourists any more. It was going to be difficult to keep away from tourists, though. Over half a million tourists visit this small island every year. Amazingly, if you came to Koh Samui in the early 1970s you would have been lucky to spot a tourist at all. Back then Koh Samui was an unspoilt island paradise, where no sound could be heard but the warm breeze whispering in the palm trees. Today the sounds of nightclubs, motorbikes and 'you wan' massage' are only drowned out by all the construction going on. In the last twenty years, over 200 hotels have been built on the island (since I was there seven years ago that number has doubled!).

I could already feel the hot engine against my legs (yeah, I know, it was my fault. I was wearing board shorts and thongs). If I had been riding one of the first motorcycles ever made, I would have had more than burnt legs. In 1869, the French Michaux brothers fitted a steam engine to a bicycle (I wonder if it had a whistle). It sold quite well. The only complaint was that riders said they got a bit hot. A bit hot! They were sitting on top of a boiler! You also had to keep stoking the boiler by adding small pieces of coke. Well, I suppose it kept their minds off the bumpy ride. The motorbike had wooden wheels.

With the state of the roads I was on, it felt like I had wooden wheels. Thankfully there wasn't much traffic. The guidebook had claimed that you 'should be prepared to be run off the road'. It also gave these pieces of advice: 'Make sure your horn is loud; When a tourist is involved in an accident in Thailand, he or she is at fault, regardless of whose fault the accident really was. Give way rules are regulated by size. The only thing below motorbikes are cyclists, buffaloes and chickens.'

By rights I probably shouldn't have been riding at all, but as I said earlier, nothing stops a famous explorer. Well, besides death.

I was doing my best to keep away from the 'touristy sights', but when I saw a sign for the Monkey Theatre I had to have a look. Maybe they'd be doing such classics as *Phantom of the Apera*, or my favourite *The Sound of Monkeys*. A dirt track weaved its way through a thick grove of coconut trees to a small clearing. There wasn't a soul about (the first show for the day wasn't for two hours). There was, however, about half a dozen monkeys chained to coconut trees. They looked miserable. A couple of them were trying unsuccessfully to break free of their chains. As I strolled over to a particularly sad-looking fellow, I decided I was going to let him go. It would be my good deed for the day. Just as I was leaning over to release my primate friend he gave an almighty squeal. People would have heard it at Chaweng beach. Then he kept on squealing. OK, if he didn't want to be set free then bad luck. He could spend the rest of his miserable life playing one of the Von Trapp children in *The Sound of Monkeys*.

Back on the bike, the road improved. Well, it was still bumpy, but it didn't have giant holes in it any more. One thing was certain: I wouldn't be trying to free the stars of the next two tourist attractions. Coming up there was a Snake Farm and Buffalo Fighting. I was, however, keen to see the somewhat dubious-sounding Fish Fighting. This was somewhere across the other side of the island. Now, that would be interesting (I wonder if the loser gets turned into a nice Thai red curry).

I must have taken a wrong turn. Was I in America? I was passing sign after sign to such resorts as Miami, Cocopalm, Waikiki, and even LA Resort. The road was now skirting the northern coastline. On the right there were beaches and resorts; the left was all coconut trees. In fact that's all I'd seen so far. Coconut trees. Mind you, that's not surprising. Up until twenty years ago, the main business of Samui was coconuts. Yet here's the remarkable thing: the eldest son of a coconut plantation owner would always inherit the whole plantation. The other offspring would have been given beachfront land, as it was of no value. Now those 'lesser' offspring own the lucrative resorts and are rolling in money.

I passed a pretty bay with no resorts in sight (it's probably got the Coco Palm Paradise Sunset Garden Island View Resort there now) and stopped at Mae Nam beach for a drink. A few ramshackle backpacker huts lay scattered about among the palm trees. The residents of Mae Nam were former pirates. They were offered this piece of land in the early 1970s by the King of Thailand in return for the cessation of their activities on the high seas (well, it was either that or get blown into little bits by the Thai navy). The pirates scored a great deal and had been living here happily ever since. I couldn't see any eye-patches or wooden legs about, though. They must have been inside their huts (probably making those pirate CDs that are in every second shop on Samui).

I rode past row upon row of coconut trees. It was your typical stickily hot day that Thailand is so good at, but the stiff breeze on the bike was keeping me cool. I was getting hungry. As part of my usual quest for authentic food, I wanted to wait till I got to the village of Hua Thanon. Apparently it was the only 'traditional village' on the island. I just had one major sight to see first, and I wasn't going to miss that.

There it was. The Octuple coconut tree. I have to say, it was very impressive. This one coconut tree had six stalks growing out of it into six full-blown coconut trees. Hey, wait a minute. Doesn't 'octuple' mean eight? There were only six. Maybe it was set up by the same mathematical genius who ran the 'Happy Hour' in the Green Mango bar on Chaweng beach that went from '6 to 9'.

Hua Thanon was worth the wait. There wasn't a neon sign in sight. Brightly coloured fishing boats bobbed noisily in the small harbour as they bumped against each other. I passed a couple of locals fixing a large net. They glanced up and smiled at me. I found a small, quiet restaurant near the harbour and ordered a green chicken curry and a 'mixed froot drink'. The waiter was incredibly friendly and attentive. Not because he wanted a big tip, he was just nice. As so many

Thai people are. Or maybe it was my Honda? In the early sixties their advertising strapline (which they used for many years) was 'You meet the nicest people on a Honda'. It must have worked. In 1950, Honda produced just over 2000 motorbikes. By the early sixties all the potential 'nice people' you could meet boosted sales to almost 600 000. Today, Honda is the biggest selling motorbike with over 30 million sales worldwide (gee, that's a lot of nice people to meet). Not bad for a company that came late onto the scene. The first commercially produced motorbike was in 1892. It was called the Hilderbrand and Wolfmueller. The bike had a bad reputation for skidding (as well as an unpronounceable name) so they went out of business. The next big manufacturer was Triumph from the UK in 1902. Harley Davidson followed in 1903. Long beards and bikie-sluts didn't catch on until a few years after that.

Now I don't mind a hot curry, but I lost the roof of my mouth on my first bite. The only way I could eat my green chicken curry was to cut off a tiny piece of chicken, put it in my mouth, then immediately shovel three spoonfuls of rice in, followed by a large gulp of my 'froot drink'. The waiter asked if it was OK. I couldn't speak and I couldn't taste any food for the next three days.

With a burning belly, I hit the road again. Not far out of Hua Thanon I passed a sign for the Phang Ka Snake Farm. Included in the list of attractions were 'Thai boxers fighting King cobras'. Maybe they could combine a couple of the local attractions as a unique potential crowd puller. They could have Thai boxers taking on the Fighting Fish. Or, the Fighting Buffaloes taking on the Octuple coconut tree. Now that would be interesting.

On the map I spotted a Mountain Lookout. It wasn't in my guidebook, so I thought it was worth a look. The dirt track was rutted with deep gashes from the monsoonal rains. It rose sharply and I had to use what little skill I had to navigate around the ruts. The track soon became incredibly steep. I'm no Steve McQueen, so I had to stop. I walked the last 150 metres to the top. It was certainly worth it. The view was spectacular. There were palm trees as far as I could see. Fringing the bright green of the palms there was a long strip of bleached white sand and, beyond that, the limpid aqua sea. The small islands dotted around the coast looked like giant green Christmas puddings. This was why I risked life and limb to be a 'famous explorer'. The view was intoxicating. I sat on a perfectly placed boulder and—I should say something like 'I took in the vista in all its glory'—but I actually dozed off to sleep. It was magically cool, and I was a bit knackered after my strenuous bike climb.

Riding down was not easy. It didn't help that I lacked the most basic of skills. I couldn't use the foot brake, because I had to use my feet to keep my balance. I had my hand tightly gripped around the handbrake as I crawled down the steep hill at a snail's pace. Suddenly, without any hint of a warning, the handbrake cable snapped. The bike and I hurtled down the track at full speed. How could I stop? In the split second that I had to make a decision, I pointed the bike towards the embankment. The bike tipped over and dragged me along the ground. I was still holding on (in hindsight, that was probably not a good idea). The bike stopped dead and I lay on the track dazed. I looked down at my leg. It was already totally covered in blood. A huge gash on my knee was gushing out more blood. The first thought I had was of Natalie saying, 'I told you so.'

How could I get down? There was no-one around. I was miles from anywhere. I tried to walk the bike, but I couldn't restrain the bike from careering down the hill. My heart was beating wildly, pumping more blood down my leg. My sandal was saturated. Sweat was stinging my eyes. I would have to ride the bike down and use the foot brake. For the first twenty metres the bike shot down the hill as I tried to get my foot on the brake. I pushed down hard and almost stacked again as the bike skidded. The bike slowed to a crawl again as I tentatively moved around the ruts. Twenty minutes later I was back on the main road. My T-shirt was dripping wet with nervous sweat.

I didn't even notice the dog at first. I heard the savage snarl at the back wheel. It could smell my warm and, I imagine, very tasty blood and wanted a spot of afternoon tea. This was just what I needed: rabies, cholera, black plague or whatever-the-hell disease a scrawny Thai dog could carry. I couldn't speed up. It was sheer agony to change up a gear and I was already going too fast for second gear. 'Fuck off you mutt!' I screamed hysterically.

I stopped at a shop on the side of the road and hobbled in, trying to look unperturbed by the fact that my entire left leg was covered in blood. I sneaked up to the counter without the lady seeing me. I plonked two large bottles of water and two rolls of toilet paper onto the counter.

I sat down away from the shop and tried to clean away the blood. My wound looked deep. Oh shit! A group of young Thai children gathered around to watch. 'There's a valuable lesson here, kids ...' I said. They didn't understand English, so I couldn't go on and tell them not to ride a motorbike if they were as rash and impractical as me. I made a rather dodgy toilet paper bandage and toddled back to my bike.

Part of the engine had a dent in it and something was dripping out. Oil? Fuel? It could blow up. Nah, it couldn't possibly get any worse. My leg was now totally stiff and throbbing and I had to stand up on the bike to change gears. I was having trouble sitting, let alone standing. I howled with pain as I bent my knee to change into second gear. It looked like I was going to travel the ten or so kilometres back to Chaweng in second gear.

My toilet paper bandage was already red all over when I turned into the main street of Chaweng. It wouldn't be too hard to find a doctor. Fixing up dumb tourists wounds was a thriving trade here.

Neon signs competed with each other to offer medical services. I went for DOCTOR—MOTORBIKE ACCIDENTS—24 HOURS. He had the best neon sign. Who says good advertising doesn't work?

I walked in trying not to limp. The doctor's name was Doctor Taweratphakdee (try saying that under a local anaesthetic). The reception looked clean. There was even (and I'm not joking) a two-year-old edition of *The Australian Women's Weekly* sitting among the magazines on the coffee table. I was led into the surgery by Miss Thailand in a nurse's uniform. The surgery was spotless as well.

Doctor Taweratphakdee came in wearing gloves. He sewed me up with a needle straight out of a sterile pack and applied a brand new bandage. Then, like every good doctor the world over, he charged me an arm and a leg.

I staggered back to my bike and walked it slowly back to the hire place. 'Look what you did to me!' I bawled, as I pointed to my heavily bandaged leg. 'The handbrake cable snapped and almost killed me!' The man looked over the bike. 'You must pay for brake and this,' he said, pointing to the dent in the engine. 'No!' I screamed. 'The handbrake snapped. It's not my fault.' He stepped behind the desk and brought out my contract. He pointed to a few lines of tiny writing at the bottom that said something like, 'Any damage to the bike will be paid for by the hiree. Even if it is our fault and the bike is dodgy. So there. Ha ha'. It was at this point that I lost it. 'You gave me a fuckin' dodgy bike. A bike with fuckin' dodgy brakes. You tried to fuckin' kill me and I still have to fuckin' pay!'

'Yes,' he said calmly, 'you pay me two thousand baht [about $110]'.

He had my passport. I couldn't do anything about it. I counted out the money and slammed it on the desk. 'I'm coming back tonight to torch the place,' I said, as I stormed out. Well, limped out, but with as much storming as I could muster.

When I reached our little bungalow on the beachfront, my leg was throbbing like a Harley Davidson. Natalie was lounging in a deckchair on the beach, reading a book. I hobbled up behind her and leant over to kiss her on the forehead. 'Hi baby, how you doin?' I said calmly.

'Oh, hello Famous Explorer. How was it?'

'Great. I saw heaps of stuff,' I said with false chirpiness.

'You look hot. Are you coming for a swim?'

'Um. No,' I said, as I limped around so she could see my leg looking like something from a mummy's tomb.

Natalie rolled her eyes. 'Oh Brian, what have you done?'

'Eight stitches!' I said proudly. I then went on to explain everything, from the octuple coconut tree and the green curry from hell to how the motorcycle hire people did their very best to try and kill me.

'Have you finally learnt a lesson then?' Natalie asked.

'Yeah,' I sulked, 'I'm never, ever riding a motorbike again.' Well, not until my next holiday, anyway!

Elephant

Chiang Mai, Thailand
June 1995

'Oh, de elefunt. Oh, de elefunt,' I sang. Well, did my best to sing. I was singing the Kamahl song 'The Elephant Song' but didn't know the melody (or the words for that matter). I was trying to teach the song to our *mahout* (elephant keeper, driver, trainer and handler all rolled into one). He'd just spent the last fifteen minutes trying to teach us a Thai elephant song. It went something like, 'Chang, chang, chang, chang . . . shing shong du blau du blau.' I remember that much because he made us repeat it over and over again for fifteen minutes until we got it right. 'There are much songs in Thailand about elephants,' he told us. 'Do you know much English songs about elephants?' Kamahl's elephant song was the only one I could think of and all I knew of it was the part where he sings, 'Oh, de elefunt.' Our mahout seemed to like it, though, and spent the next fifteen minutes singing 'Oh, de elefunt, Oh, de elefunt, Oh, de elefunt' over and over again.

Natalie and I were just half an hour into a four-hour elephant trek. We sat high above our elephant on a wooden platform that swayed gently from side to side as our oversized pachyderm friend strolled slowly down the wide path. Sitting on our cushions high above the jungle, I felt like the King of Siam. Dense jungle and bamboo forests pushed up over the track, forming a canopy that kept out the hot sun. The air was damp and still. In the distance, the high mountains covered in a thin mist looked like ghosts.

I had no idea where we were. Well, I knew we were somewhere near the Burmese border but that was about it. Two days earlier, we'd been driven two and a half hours north-west of Chiang Mai, then had been walking pretty much due north for the last two days. There were six of us and a guide. The other two couples were on elephants behind us. Our guide was nowhere to be seen, but hopefully on his way to the same place we were heading for.

We'd met our elephant and mahout in a large clearing in a field of poppies. I have to admit I was quite looking forward to our elephant trek. What wonderful and majestic looking beasties they are. Oh, and besides that, after walking for two days I was simply looking forward to having a sit down for a few hours.

We were introduced to our mahout, Chandra, who was affectionately patting and chatting to his elephant. He gave us a huge and genuinely friendly smile and then calmly walked to the front of the elephant, reached up, grabbed its ears and walked up the elephant's trunk, over its head, and plopped himself down on its neck. I hope he wasn't expecting us to do that. Thankfully, he pointed to a rickety wooden contraption. We simply had to climb up a ladder and then step onto the wooden platform.

Our elephant was an Asiatic elephant. The main differences between an Asiatic elephant and an African elephant are that the former has smaller ears and the female of the species is tuskless. Three hundred species of elephants have at one point or another roamed this earth. Now there are only two. At the rate we're going, by 2025 there will be only one. The African elephant will soon become extinct unless something is done about it. I rarely get on my high horse (or should I say my high elephant), but it's an absolute travesty. Between the years 1986 and 1989 alone, 300 000 elephants were killed in Africa (leaving about 600 000 in the whole of the continent). Most of them were killed illegally—slaughtered (often with machine guns) by poachers for their ivory. South Africa and Burundi are the biggest culprits. In a ten-year period (1976–86), Burundi wiped out its entire elephant population. All 200 000 of them. Naturally you need a market for all this ivory, and Hong Kong, Japan and Taiwan are the biggest culprits when it comes to buying the stuff (so they can make horrible carvings, or even worse, an aphrodisiac that is about as effective as shoving popcorn up your nose).

The Asiatic elephant isn't faring much better. Their problem is not ivory poachers, but the destruction of their habitat. The Thais have plundered their forests for timber and taken the elephants' home along with it. One hundred years ago there were 100 000 elephants in Thailand. Today there are barely 5000. It makes me mad. Well, I've said my piece. I'll get back off my high horse now and get back on my high elephant and back to the story.

Chandra sat below us with his legs tucked right under the elephant's ears, which every minute or so would flap about and slap his thighs. Chandra was quietly spoken and very polite—like just about every Thai person we met. As he spoke to us, he continually patted his elephant. He would stay with this elephant for all of its life.

Elephants are revered in Thailand (Thailand's flag from 1819–1917 was a white elephant on a red background). They have a profound spiritual significance. The Hindu god called Ganesh has an elephant's head and features in temples all over the country. Ganesh is the god of knowledge and the remover of obstacles. Which leads us onto its other capacity. The practical role of the elephant is almost as important as its symbolic importance. It is invaluable as a beast of burden. Not only have elephants been used to haul logs for centuries but they were also used in war. They were the forerunners of the tank. King Rama the First, who founded Bangkok in 1782, led an army spearheaded by men mounted on 300 trained elephants in an attack on Burma. Incidentally, the ensuing campaign involved climbing mountains so steep that the elephants had to ascend by coiling their trunks around trees and hauling their bodies forward. In the 1800s, King Rama the Sixth offered Abraham Lincoln a male and female elephant from which to breed a herd in the forests of America for use in the Civil War.

'Is the elephant a boy or a girl?' Natalie asked.

'Yes, a girl.' (I've since learnt that it's mostly females used to haul around people. Male elephants are too grumpy—the opposite of humans, then). 'Her name is Taraburritharemaya (or something very similar to that, anyway). You can call her Tara if you wish.'

'How old is Tara?' I asked.

'She is 27 years old,' Chandra replied proudly.

Tara was only a young'un then. The average elephant lives to around 60. The oldest recorded elephant lived to the ripe old age of 78. His name was Modoc. He was an Asiatic elephant like Tara. Born in 1898, he was shipped from Thailand to the US at the age of three. He spent 35 years in the circus, twenty years in the zoo and nine years co-starring in the television series *Daktari* (for which he had to wear large false ears to make him look like an African elephant). He died as a result of complications after surgery for an ingrown toenail. Mind you, in the wild most elephants die of starvation. When they finally lose their *sixth* set of teeth they can't chew food any more, so they simply starve to death.

'She loves me,' Chandra purred as he patted her tenderly on her head.

'How do you know?' I said.

'Because I love her.'

Elephants do fall in love like humans (but probably not in love *with* humans—sorry Chandra). Elephants are very much like us. Thai elephants start school at four years old and stay until they're ten. They will then work until they retire at around 50 (on full pension too, I might add). During the hot season every year they have a vacation— where they could very well fall in love (like humans, as I said before, but without the flower-giving and fights over the toilet seat). The female elephant gets five years maternity leave (after 22 months of pregnancy!) to bring up her calves. On *full* pay! (Calm down, girls, I know you're lucky to get a month.) A healthy elephant (who doesn't drink and smoke) can live to around 75, spending its twilight years in an elephant retirement sanctuary—most likely lounging about complaining that the young elephants of today just don't how lucky they are.

We stopped suddenly and Chandra yelled out something in Thai. A large branch had fallen across the track. Tara casually lifted it up with her trunk (a trunk, by the way, is made up of an elephant's nose and upper lip) and laid it carefully to one side. An elephant can learn up to 40 verbal commands, but can take at least ten years to learn them. Elephants may be slow on the uptake, but they can certainly learn some remarkable things. Bertram Mills's Circus has the 'Amazing Elephant Cricket Team'. An elephant, with cap and pads on, holds a bat with its trunk while from the opposite end of the pitch another elephant bowls the ball (no snide remarks here about Shane Warne). Five other elephants act as fieldsmen (or is that fieldselephants?). At the word of command, the bowler throws the ball down the pitch and the batsman (or is that batselephant?) takes a swipe at it. More often than not, the bat connects and when it does, the batselephant plods on down for a run. It gets better, though. Meanwhile, one of the fieldselephants stops the ball and throws it at the stumps. It takes years to train them, but in the end the elephants, 'play the game with enormous enthusiasm'. I suspect it's probably a darn sight more interesting to watch than a real test match, too.

There's even an elephant band. It is based in Thailand and its debut album came out last year. Ten elephants have been trained to play instruments including drums, mouth organs (not normal-sized ones, I guess) and xylophones. It can't be that good. Still, I bet it would have to be better than Britney Spears.

It was a horrible, sticky, warm day and we were going through our water very quickly (we also lost quite a bit over our shirts, because Tara's swaying made it hard to keep the bottle in your mouth). Chandra didn't have any water at all. He must have been hot with his legs under Tara's ears. Even Tara must have been thirsty. Elephants have to drink around 90 litres of water a day. That reminds me of a joke I found on the Internet (some sad bastard has set up a website entitled 'The world's biggest list of elephant jokes'—there are over 1000): Why do elephants drink so much?

To try and forget.

Actually, it's a myth that elephants remember things. They do forget. They can remember commands that have been drummed into them, but they can't remember what they did on their last vacation. Another myth is that elephants are afraid of mice. Not true. Elephants do, though, get scared out of their wits by dogs—even cute little puppies. Wusses.

'Are there any wild elephants in Thailand?' I asked Chandra.

'Maybe.'

Just as I was trying to figure out how there were *maybe* wild elephants in Thailand, what sounded like my dad's Victa mower came up behind us. A young Thai fellow pulled up next to us on a motorbike and shouted out something to Chandra. An argument ensued, with Chandra screaming and waving his arms in the air. He wasn't happy.

Chandra yelled a command to Tara and gave her a good whack with a stick that he produced out of nowhere. Tara began to gallop. That's right, gallop. We immediately began getting thrown around, crashing into each other. We had to hold onto the wooden rails of the platform with both hands or risk getting thrown off. Chandra gave Tara another whack with his stick (he can't love Tara all that much) and Tara stepped up another gear.

Chandra screamed out another order over the racket being made by our now stampeding elephant, and Tara ploughed into the jungle. I'm talking dense jungle here. We weren't even on the vaguest hint of a track. As we thundered through the dense gloom of the jungle, great fern leaves—three or four metres in height—stretched fan-like over our heads, making it darker, wetter and damn well uncomfortable. But that was by no means the worst of it. Every branch, every leaf, every vine and every tiny tendril of creeper was giving us an absolute hiding. I was trying to push the branches and ferns away from our faces with one hand, while doing my damnedest to hold on with the other. Chandra, who was sitting well below us, wasn't even getting touched. I do love the smell of the jungle, but not when it's literally shoved up my nose. My clothes were soaking wet and stuck to my skin. It was like a Finnish sauna—get yourself nice and sweaty, then whip yourself with a branch.

All of a sudden a cat landed on Natalie's shoulder. Wait a sec. What's a cat doing with eight legs? Arggghhhhh! It was a spider. A huge fuck-off spider. Natalie hadn't seen it yet. What should I do? I had to make an important decision. Brush the spider off my girlfriend's shoulder and possibly have the monster jump on me, or let it eat her. Hmmm? Shit! I closed my eyes and swiped it off, screaming as I did it. The spider was gigantic. It must have been one of those bird-eating spiders. This one would have snacked on ostriches.

'This is supposed to be fun,' I screamed, 'This is a bloody nightmare!' I don't think the King of Siam travelled like this. Chandra was in a hurry to get somewhere. We later discovered that he had another group to take. Normally they were very quiet and lucky to get a group once every few days, but today, for some reason, they had two. Our mahout had panicked and was rushing to get back and pick them up.

We were totally covered in scratches now, and they were already starting to sting in the heat. Another cat-spider plopped down at our feet. Natalie screamed. Without even thinking I stomped on it with my foot. It exploded like a water balloon. At least the spiders made us forget about the large black ants that were crawling all over us.

After fifteen minutes of getting horribly whipped, we turned off onto something that slightly resembled a track. We were now following a creek. Tara was noisily splashing her way through the shallow water. There were large trees on both sides of the creek bed. Tara was only missing them by centimetres (an elephant knows its own size and, even when travelling at great speeds, won't hit anything—not bad for a fat bastard).

Finally, thankfully, mercifully, we burst out of the foliage and into open space. We were now at a river and Tara leaped in and started galloping through the water. The water was knee-deep (I can say that, because the elephant is the only living thing—besides us humans—that has knees) and was soon splashing us with cool water. Aside from the getting-thrown-about-as-if-we-were-involved-in-a-horrendous-car-accident, and the being-totally-covered-in-scratches-and-ants, it was almost pleasant.

Suddenly Tara lurched to one side. Naturally, so did Natalie and I. We only just held on. Tara had stumbled on some rocks in the water and had almost fallen over. One thing is certain, if an elephant crashes down on you, the show is over. An elephant can weigh up to 5000 kilograms.

So you can imagine my delight when we slowed down to walk and then, only a minute later, stopped. Our four-hour trek had taken us just under two hours. Chandra turned around and—very politely and quietly—said, 'I am very sorry thank you. Can you please get off here thank you.' We were still in shock. He didn't even notice the fact that we looked as if we'd just stepped out of the eye of a hurricane. We hopped off onto the river bank. We were both unsteady on our feet and covered in sweat and bright red scratches.

I was just about to ask Chandra what the hell had happened when he yelled an order to Tara and she leaped back into the river again. They disappeared in a flurry of splashing water. I caught a glimpse of Tara's eye as she leaped into the water. It was an 'Oh well, better get got on with it then' type of look. I supposed she was used to it. She'd already been doing this job for around seventeen years and probably had another 23 to go. I hope she had good super and ended up in a nice retirement home. One with a large shaded verandah to lounge about on, and while away her twilight years.

Natalie and I, on the other hand, were beginning to worry we might while away the rest of our years in the middle of the Thai jungle. An hour later the other two elephants finally turned up. They'd taken a different short cut. One that didn't involve getting whipped by spiky ferns and being attacked by ostrich-eating spiders and giant blood-sucking ants. 'We had a lovely time,' the unscarred, unsweaty and unscathed passengers all chorused.

Sailing Ship

Yasawa Islands, Fiji
June 1997

It was the most romantic trip I'd ever been on. It was just a pity I was sharing a cosy room for two with a burly fireman from New Zealand called Phil who I'd only met that morning. There were nine other couples on this romantic trip of a lifetime. And us two lovebirds.

Actually, the trip couldn't have started more romantically (not to mention regally). I'd been sitting on the tiny beach of Beachcomber Island, when an American girl next to me screamed out, as only Americans can, 'Oh my Gaaaaard, look at that ship! It's beautiful!' I looked up to see a majestic white sailing ship anchored 500 metres offshore. A dinghy was chugging its way to our beach.

The beachful of people—mostly a backpacking crowd that frequented Beachcomber Island—watched on in utter amazement as I stood up, grabbed my backpack, and casually strolled down to the shore to be helped aboard the dinghy by a handsomely dressed Fijian man. I felt like royalty. This wondrous looking sailing ship had stopped just to pick up little ol' me.

I had booked this two-day sailing 'adventure' only the day before, and the lady in the booking office told me there was no need to head back to the mainland for the departure. The ship would be passing not far from Beachcomber and they would pick me up on the way. Frankly, I wasn't that surprised with this show of hospitality. In my first week in Fiji, I had encountered the friendliest and most hospitable people I'd met in all my travels through fifty-odd countries.

As soon as I stepped out of Nadi airport upon my arrival, a Fijian man asked me if I was OK and whether he could help me. More like help himself, I thought. Help himself to my wallet that is. Or, even worse, drag me to a novelty coconut sculpture shop. But, no. He'd seen that I looked a little lost (I spend most of my travelling life looking like this) and he just genuinely wanted to make sure I was OK. He even escorted me to the bus stop and put me on the right bus.

When I was caught stealing a hotel towel from the dorm room at Beachcomber (I'd forgotten mine. I always forget something when I travel—I once went to Morocco without any jocks and had to wear the same pair of Speedos for two weeks), I was sure I'd be in trouble. But I was wrong again. The staff member just smiled and winked at me as I stuffed it in my bag.

I was helped aboard the ship by a large, muscular Fijian man wearing a skirt. All my fellow 'adventurers' were on deck to greet me. Well, not necessarily to greet me, it was just that down below deck there was only a stuffy lounge area to sit in. We weren't sleeping on the boat. We would be staying on an uninhabited island somewhere in the Yasawa chain of islands to the west of the main island of Viti Levu.

The ship was just as I imagined and hoped it would be. It looked like a pirate ship—but without the cannons and scurvy. The *Ra Marama* was built from planked teak in 1950 for the then governor general of Fiji to host kings, princes, high-chiefs and heads of state. She was named after a war canoe that was capable of carrying 100 warriors. An important peace treaty was once signed between two warring tribes aboard that original war canoe. It turned out not to be worth the paper it was written on (or bark it was painted on), though. The two chiefs got into an argument and the visiting chief had his head hacked off with an axe.

The ship was a square-rigged brigantine. Well, according to Phil it was. Phil then went on to tell me all about rigging and mizzenmasts. My mind began to wander after 'square-rigged brigantine', but at least he wasn't talking about interior decorating and Doris Day films. I would have been a little worried then. 'Oh yeah,' I said, as if I knew what he was talking about.

I do know quite a few types of sailing ships. Well, I've seen a few on *Epic Theatre* at least. I can recognise a galley, a schooner, a sloop and a clipper—providing the people on board are wearing the right costumes. Mind you, there would be close to a hundred different types of sailing ships. Some of the names don't come up in conversation (or cheesy Italian historical movies) too often, though. Try these for size: there's a budgerow, a cog, a drifter, a flute, a packet, a snow, a pink and a xebec. Then again, I can't imagine a pirate yelling, 'Arrrr me hearties, let's get the "pink flute" ready for battle!'

Phil (who called himself Phul) was happy to see me climb aboard. He thought he was going to be the biggest gooseberry of all time. 'Two of the couples are on their honeymoon,' Phul told me, adding, 'We might get a chance to watch them have sex if we're lucky.'

The first best mate (or the first best man's mate, or the first something or other) introduced me to the rest of the seven crew. They were all dark, handsome, muscular men in skirts. Like all other Fijians I'd met, the crew made me feel like an honoured guest.

The weather was perfect. Too perfect. There was no wind to hoist the sails, so we motored slowly across the glassy sea as lunch was being served. It was a feast of grilled chicken accompanied by salads mixed with exotic fruits. The crew ate more than I do in a week.

After lunch, Phul and I scored the prime position for lying about and doing nothing. We were soon dozing off in the rope netting that was strung up from the bow of the ship. It could only hold two people and over the next two days it would become a hotly contested spot. There weren't that many places to go aboard the ship. The deck was only about 25 metres long and there wasn't too much room down below, either. It's absolutely amazing to think that a handful of countries in Europe (mostly Spain, Portugal, Holland and England) conquered over half of the world (including Fiji, which Captain Cook named Turtle Island) in sailing ships no bigger than the *Ra Marama*. And even more amazingly, they did all of this with men wearing tights.

We motored past a string of tiny islands through crystal-clear, vivid blue water. We were never far from land. The crew who weren't hoisting the poop (or whatever crew did) were fishing over the side. As the brochure-shot-like afternoon sun bathed the ship in a wonderful golden light, and as the nine couples shared that special couple moment on the deck of our grand sailing ship, Phul and I stood at the front of the ship drinking Fiji Bitter stubbies and trying not to look gay. All the couples were either holding hands or, in the case of the honeymoon couples, gazing lovingly into each other's eyes. While the couples talked softly and intimately to each other, Phul and I talked loudly about bloke things.

'The remake of, *Blue Lagoon* was shot on one of these islands,' I said, as I pointed to yet another idyllic looking island.

'Really!' Phul said.

We both stared at the island for a minute.

'I wouldn't have minded giving Brooke Shields one in that film,' Phul said.

'Yeah. It was a pity that her hair always managed to cover her tits.'

'Yeah, that was terrible.'

Wayasewa Island, our 'uninhabited island' home for the night, was bigger than I expected. We motored around a coastline of craggy mountains, thick with vegetation. We anchored offshore and were shuttled in the dinghy, eight at a time, to a tiny beach. Well, when I say beach, there were 100 metres of sharp rocks to clamber over before we actually stepped onto sand. Every ten seconds Phul would shout out, 'Ow!' He was walking across the rocks in bare feet. The Fijian crew on the other hand, also in bare feet, didn't even flinch as they jumped from sharp rock to sharp rock (they should be used to it. Firewalking is a popular hobby in Fiji).

I could see our *bures* (traditional Fijian huts) in amongst the trees. As the couples wandered off hand in hand to their little romantic retreats, Phul and I kept banging our heads together in our tiny *bure* as we tried to separate the double bed into two singles.

Dinner was put on. Well, more like put under. We were having a traditional *lovo*, where food is wrapped in banana leaves and placed on red hot rocks, covered in dirt and left to steam for four hours or so.

'Hey Phil, do you want to go for a hike?' I said. The couples were all holding hands again and I was feeling like a right gooseberry. We walked along the narrow beach and scrambled over the rocky headland to another even narrower beach. The sand was littered with coconuts. That beach came to a dead end so we turned inland and made a steep ascent through thick mangroves. After a few minutes of that, we realised we had no idea which way we had come from. 'We should be all right,' I said, 'we just have to head down when we want to head back.' There was not the slightest sound as we trudged higher and deeper into the jungle. After battling our way through a tangle of vines, bamboo and large ferns for half an hour, we gave up and turned back.

We slithered down over a final stretch of loose stones and found ourselves in a narrow valley. The sea was nowhere in sight. Oh, bother.

'Just head down, hey?' Phul grunted. We turned around to try and retrace our steps.

I didn't want to admit it, but we were pretty well lost. I was also getting very hungry. We'd found a grapefruit tree earlier, but the fruit had rind about three centimetres thick and the fruit itself was so sour that when we both tried it we looked like we were having a fit. I suppose if the worst came to the absolute worst, I could always just do what the locals had done for centuries. I could eat Phul. Just over a hundred years ago, Fiji was home to the fiercest cannibals in the South Pacific. To most Fijians cannibalism was a perfectly normal part of life (there's nothing like a good arm served with a mango and coconut sauce, I say).

Most of the victims were enemies taken in battle. Eating your enemy was the ultimate disgrace the victor could impose. Fijians were not without a sense of humour about it, either. They would often get a chuckle out of cutting off a piece of some unfortunate soul's tongue or finger, cooking it in front of them, saying how good it tasted and then offering a piece to the victim to eat.

I told Phul that he, being the burly man that he was, would make a good meal. I on the other hand, would be a bit stringy. 'Also,' I said, 'I could light a fire, because I've got some matches.' Phul said, 'Yeah, but I'm a fireman, so I can put it out when I've finished with it.'

Thankfully, we didn't have to do either as we found our way back to the beach and, eventually, just as it was turning dark, our camp. Dinner was worth waiting for. It was one of the most wonderful meals I'd ever had. There were large fillets of *walu* (a local fish a bit like tuna that the crew had caught earlier), chicken, yams and sweet potatoes, all of which had been cooked underground in the banana leaves. This was followed by fruit salad, which was made up of mangoes, papayas, bananas, pineapples and several other tasty things I couldn't recognise.

After dinner we sat cross-legged on mats around a community wooden bowl drinking *yaqona* (or *kava*). *Yaqona* is made from the pulverised root of the kava tree. Thankfully for us, they didn't make it using the traditional method. The kava root is normally chewed, mixed with saliva, then spat out into a bowl before the water is added. *Yaqona* looks like muddy water, tastes like muddy water and even after drinking nine bowls of it, *still* tastes like muddy water.

Yaqona is the local brew, and even though it is technically non-alcoholic, it gives one a bit of a fuzzy head. Some Fijians are kavaholics and drink up to six litres a day of the stuff. To drink it we had to follow the ancient ritual (or is it just an elaborate tourist set-up?). One would be offered a *bilo* (half a coconut shell), then you would clap once, take it in both hands, gulp it all down in one, return it to the server and clap three times in appreciation. Phul and I became quite good at this ritual.

Two of the Fijian men played guitar and sang (every Fijian man seems to able to play guitar and sing), while another strummed away on a ukulele. I was going to have a sing when I saw them bringing out the guitars, but after hearing them I didn't want to. Out of these beefy Fijian men came the sweetest, most harmonious singing voices you could ever imagine. Compared to them I would have sounded flat and out of tune. A bit like Bob Dylan.

I chatted to Waqa (pronounced Wacker), the best first mate's officer. He'd been a seaman for sixteen years. He had been at sea since he was twelve. When he told me he loved the job because he loved meeting people, I believed him. I hardly found out anything about his life (besides the fact that he had eight brothers and one sister) because he genuinely wanted to know all about mine. Usually I can bore people to sleep with my endless stories, but Waqa was actually interested. And awake.

The couples all went off to bed, leaving Phul and I to the endless supply of muddy water. A couple of the Fijians were looking a bit like the people in the TV room in *One Flew over the Cuckoo's Nest*—stupefied, with silly grins on their faces. I was feeling light-headed myself, but that probably had more to do with the fact that I'd drunk ten litres of muddy water. My lips were numb, too. It felt like I'd just been to the dentist.

I snuck off to bed and left Phul seeing if he could 'get really out of it'. A couple of hours later he stumbled into our *bure*. All he'd managed to do was get his lips and tongue so numb that he sounded like the Elephant Man when he spoke.

By eleven o'clock the next morning, I really felt like a pirate. The wind had picked up, so Phul and I asked to help put up the sails. We helped the crew hoist the yardarm and mizzen the mainsail. I had no idea what I was doing. I just pulled a lot of ropes and said 'Ahoy there' a lot.

I asked the captain if I could climb up to the crow's nest. 'We don't usually let people climb up there,' he said (maybe they were worried couples would fall off trying to join the mast-high club). 'But you have been helping the crew, so it is OK.' I'm not scared of heights at all, so I was quite cocky as I clambered up the rope rigging. Well, that was until I got halfway up. The ship was rocking from side to side and throwing me around like a rag doll. I could barely hold on.

When I finally made it to the crow's nest, I hung on to the railing so tight my knuckles went numb. But boy, was it worth it. The view was intoxicating (or maybe that was just the swaying). It was only the call for lunch that got me down.

Straight after lunch I got scared shitless again. Twice. We had anchored next to a reef ablaze with multicoloured coral and, as soon as we had finished our lunch, we all went snorkelling. My mum wouldn't have been happy with the crew. Don't they know you are supposed to wait an hour after you've eaten before you can go for a swim or you'll sink straight to the bottom?

I was scared shitless first of all when ET stuck his head out from some seaweed. I couldn't move with shock. ET wasn't just about to 'go hooome' either. He kept staring at me. Then he moved. He was a giant green turtle that had been hiding in the seaweed.

Then, only a few minutes later, I got *really* scared when I just about swam into a large and menacing shark. The crew had told us we might see a shark or two. They said we were 'not to worry' and that they 'wouldn't bother us because they get plenty of food in the sea.' I didn't believe that for a second. If I'm full and someone offers me a chocolate, I'll take it. And I would have looked particularly tasty in my fluoro orange board shorts. I didn't want to be the shark's after-dinner mint, so I swam away in such a hurry, and with so much thrashing about (very attractive to sharks, apparently) that I got cramp in my leg.

I was just getting used to our lovely old sailing ship when we dropped anchor off Beachcomber Island again. Waqa took me ashore in the dinghy and gave me a hug and a genuine 'it was very nice to meet you' farewell.

That night in the Bula Bar after a few Fiji Bitter stubbies, the American girl who'd been sitting next to me on the beach when *Ra Marama* arrived asked me who the ship belonged to. 'Oh, it's my parents', I said, 'they just drop me off now and again so I can have a break from them.'

'Oh, WOWWWWW!,' she exclaimed.

It's so easy. Americans will believe *anything*.

Truck

Townsville, Australia
September 2000

'How many gears has it got?' I asked. 'Eighteen,' Mick replied as he changed into yet another gear. I shifted uncomfortably in my seat. 'Eighteen! Which gear do you use to go around a corner?' Mick shrugged, 'Oh, anything from about four to ten.' 'Bloody hell!' I gasped. I have trouble choosing between five gears.

The one and only set of traffic lights on this side of Townsville turned red in front of us. Mick sighed. Mick didn't like traffic lights. He told me it takes a couple of kilometres and lots of clutch-pushing to get into top gear again. 'So how many wheels does it have?' 'Thirty-four,' Mick said proudly as he began the long process of working his way back up through the gears again. Mick's truck was long. Looking out the side mirror, I could barely make out the end of the last of the two trailers. Mind you, this was short compared to some trucks. Road trains, as they're called, can have up to six trailers. The back of them can be in another time zone.

'How many bananas you got?'

Mick counted in his head for a minute, 'One hundred and thirty-five thousand, give or take a few.'

'Minus six!' I smiled as I pointed to a small bunch sitting behind us.

'Nah, I friggin bought them!' Mick growled as he threw the truck into tenth or fourteenth gear.

'You're kidding, aren't you?'

'No, they're all green in the back.' *Very* green and *very* firm I discovered later. I also learnt that when they arrive at the central market in Sydney or Melbourne, they're put in a room and gassed for a couple of hours—the equivalent of four or five days ripening. 'Don't worry,' explained Mick, 'they frig around with everything we eat.' I suppose he's right.

I had met Mick a few years earlier when he worked as a coach-driver in Europe for the same tour company as me. We would meet up for a drink now and again when he was down in Melbourne. He would pull up in front of our little suburban house in his huge Kenworth (I always knew of his imminent arrival, you could hear the air brakes and engine roar four blocks away). Mick lived in Tully, north of Townsville, and carried bananas to Sydney and Melbourne. I'd always threatened to tag along for a ride one day, so when my brother moved to Townsville, I gave him a call.

I was due to meet Mick at five o'clock in the morning at a BP service station on the outskirts of Townsville. My brother Malcolm kindly got out of bed early to drop me off. 'This looks a bit suss. Are you sure it's not some sort of dodgy shipment of something illegal?' Malcolm said as we pulled into the gloomy, oversized carpark. In one shadowy corner, about ten trucks were neatly parked next to each other in a perfect line. It did, I have to admit, look a tiny bit suss. 'I don't know if you can have an illegal shipment of bananas,' I said, 'but then again you *can* get high on smoking banana skins.' The truck was easy to find. 'It's got NQX in big friggin' letters on the side of the trailers,' Mick had told me. Malcolm dropped me off and sped off in haste. ('Before the police arrive,' as he explained).

I knocked on Mick's cabin door, then knocked again harder to be heard over the loud hum of the huge refrigerator unit behind the cabin. Apparently green bananas have to be kept at fifteen degrees. Mick poked his head out of the open window rubbing his eyes. 'Oh, g'day,' Mick grunted as he opened the door. In a manoeuvre honed over the years, he spun out of the cabin and was down the steps in a flash. 'How are ya?' Mick asked as he grabbed my hand and gave me a big bone-crushing truckies' handshake. Mick didn't look like your stereotypical truckie. He wasn't wearing a blue singlet and he didn't have a big gut for a start. Mick was dressed in blue shorts and a matching blue-collared shirt. Amazingly, they didn't look too crumpled considering he'd worn them to bed the night before. 'We'll grab a quick cuppa here, then we'll drive down the road a couple of hours and stop for brekky,' he said as he brushed his fingers through his hair—his complete morning grooming ritual. 'This is not a normal truck stop,' Mick declared, 'it's too clean.'

Up in the truck, Mick sat miles away. The inside of the cabin was the size of your average family loungeroom. Directly underneath, in the gulf that lay between Mick and me, was the engine. Behind us was Mick's bedroom. A one-metre by two-and-a half-metre mattress.

The truck jumped into life and we pulled out of the truck park and onto the Bruce Highway with a deafening roar. If I was going to go on the great Aussie truck journey, then the Bruce Highway was the perfect place to start. The next best thing would be the Sheila Highway, but I don't think we've built that one yet. After only two kilometres I was already uncomfortable. Mick's seat had an elaborate suspension system. The passenger seat didn't. It felt like I was on a pogo stick and, with 2600 kilometres to go, Sydney seemed a long, long way off. 'Bloody hell, this is like an amusement park ride,' I shouted over the engine noise. Mick laughed, 'I drove a girl from Tully to Townsville once. Her tits were all over the shop. It was like two puppies fighting underneath a blanket. The next time I took a girl with me, I told her to wear a sports bra.'

The sun finally broke over the horizon and immediately warmed me up. The truck threw an incredibly long shadow over the bleached dry grass and low scrubland that stretched as far as the eye could see. Or, as it was written in my journal: 'dru gvoss aud law scirblaud.' With the bumpy ride, my journal ended up looking like the ravings of a lunatic.

I was not surprised to see Mick driving a Kenworth. Every time I saw him on the road in Europe he was wearing his Kenworth cap. In fact, I don't think I ever saw him without it. 'It's the biggest selling truck in the world,' Mick told me proudly, 'made in Australia, too.'

'Did you know in 1943 Kenworth produced the major components for the Flying Fortress bomber that dropped the atom bomb on Hiroshima?' I said. Mick looked impressed. Not because Kenworth were indirectly involved in killing thousands of people, but because I knew something about Kenworth trucks. 'And,' I continued, 'they built their first truck in 1915. Frederick Kent and Edgar Wentworth were bored motor mechanics who, in their *quiet* times at the workshop, built a truck from scraps lying around the yard.' Mick was now very impressed. I hasten to add that I don't normally retain such a wealth of truck trivia, it was just that I'd being doing my homework before I left.

Mick's Kenworth—well, the-company-he-worked-for's Kenworth —was four years old. It had already clocked up 1.43 million kilometres. That's the equivalent of driving around the entire globe 42 times. The average interstate truck driver who works for around 25 years does at least five million kilometres. That's 150 times around the earth, or up to the moon and back seven times. Australian trucks hauled stuff over twenty billion kilometres last year. That's to Pluto and back (but with a lot more roadhouses).

First stop was the Charters Towers Roadhouse. I was happy to get out of the amazing vibrating truck for a bit. It was only 7.30, but the sun was already quite warm. When I told Mick how warm I thought it was, he guffawed: 'In summer it's bloody 45 degrees here!' Inside the roadhouse, Mick walked straight up to the counter and ordered baked beans on toast. I laughed, 'It's such a cliché, truckies and baked beans.' Mick smiled, 'I normally don't have them but I reckon for your first ever truckies' meal you *have* to have baked beans.' The serves were huge. I struggled to put a dent in mine. Mick looked up from his nearly finished plate, 'What's wrong with ya, are you a poof? I'll put five kilos on ya before ya get home.' I'm not quite sure what one's sexual orientation has to do with your ability to eat large quantities of baked beans, but I only ate half.

Back in the oversized pogo stick, I grabbed the *Truckin Life* magazine I'd bought the day before. Stapled in the centre was a fold-out poster of 'Rig of the Month'. Mick kept glancing over. 'What is it?' he asked me. 'A Kenworth,' I said as I held it up for him to see. 'Nice!' Mick murmured. Truckies love their trucks. So much so, in fact, that back when the pull-out poster of 'Rig of the Month' had a girl in something like cut-off denim shorts and a boob tube draped over the front of the truck, truck drivers kept writing in and complaining. Because, wait for it, the girls were obscuring the view of the truck! So now 'Rig of the Month' posters have no girls. Just trucks.

I began reading out loud the stats on the 'Rig of the Month'. 'It's got a spring mattress and …' 'Jeez, spring mattress!' Mick's eyes lit up. '… and a microwave, flat-screen TV with Internet display, DVD and video player, percolated coffee machine and a fridge.' 'Wow, so it's got a spring mattress!' Mick said dreamily. He didn't care about Internet display or fresh coffee, he was more than happy with just a good night's kip. His mattress was foam. 'Can I have a quick look?' Mick asked. Mick went on to read every article in the magazine, front to back, while he was driving 100 km/h down a bumpy single-lane Queensland highway, only glancing up now and again to see if we were still on the road. At one point a truck came hurtling towards us. There was room for only one truck on the narrow road. I closed my eyes, expecting the worst. When I opened them we'd passed the other semi and Mick was engrossed in an article on the Bathurst Truck Show and Truckies' Ball.

Lunch stop was at a town called . . . Cou]udhl^ti>min (I couldn't for the life of me figure out what I'd written down). Ambling past the bain-marie inside the roadhouse I whispered to Mick, 'Is the food all right here?' The chicken pieces looked like they'd been there since 1983. 'Ah, you don't buy the chicken,' Mick whispered back, 'see that piece at the back, that's been there for two weeks, I'm sure it's the same piece.' The two ladies serving behind the counter looked like they'd been in the bain-marie since 1983 as well. According to Mick, the two ladies serving behind the counter serviced quite a few of the truckies for other needs besides dodgy-looking chickens and fuel. 'Harkers trucks pull in regularly for an overnight stop and get the full grease and oil change . . . if you know what I mean,' Mick said, giving me a wink.

'You find out what's good, then you stick to it,' Mick said, 'and here it's rissoles and gravy.' Mick then revealed to me some great truckie wisdom: 'Every good meal comes with gravy!' He once went to a roadhouse in Ingham, Queensland, and ordered rissoles and gravy. When they informed him they didn't have gravy, he walked out.

Back in the Mixmaster on wheels, I finally got my *Truckin Life* mag back. 'Hey Mick,' I yelled, 'it says here that long-distance truck drivers are prone to suicide, drug abuse and dying in road smashes.'

(The second would inevitably lead to the third, which would help to do the first.) 'And,' I added, 'how's this: 138 truckies committed suicide last year!' Mick looked pensive. 'Yeah,' Mick said sadly, 'probably got served too many meals without gravy.'

The scenery didn't change. Dry grass, low scrubland and a baby blue sky. It was flat, endlessly flat. Then suddenly, gum trees. 'Wow,' I said 'gum trees.' But before I even finished saying 'gum trees', it was back to dry grass, low scrubland and the baby blue sky.

The CB would burst into life now and again with other truckies waffling to each other over the static. As a truck thundered past us the truck driver buzzed Mick, 'Hey, look out mate, there's mermaids ahead.' Mick grabbed the mike and mumbled, 'Thanks, mate.' 'What's a mermaid?' I asked, pretty sure he wasn't about to tell me there were beautiful women with fish tails sitting on the side of the road up ahead. 'They're like truck police,' Mick snarled, 'they measure the length of the truck and carry portable scales to weigh it. There are big fines if you're caught.' 'Yeah, but why mermaids?' I asked innocently. 'Cos they're cunts with scales!' Mick grunted.

Apparently, the RTA (or whoever's responsible for the mermaids) hired a few Asian fellows to be mermaids. This turned out to be a problem. You see, quite a few truck drivers are Vietnam vets—something to do with not being able to face people, so they retreat to the solitude of the road. So when they were pulled up by Asian fellows in uniform, they would freak out and threaten to kill them. 'It's true!' Mick insisted, 'I haven't seen an Asian mermaid in months.'

The CB would intermittently break into incomprehensible babble, but when you *could* hear a full conversation, it went something like: 'Hey mate, there's cows on the road up ahead.'

'What's that mate?'

'Cows, mate.'

'Oh, thanks, mate.'

'No worries, mate.'

Certainly a far cry from the 10–4 days. When I was in high school in the 70s, CBs were the latest fad. I'd drop around to a mate's place (who had Rig of the Month posters on his wall—back when there were scantily dressed girls draped across the front of the truck), and watch as he waffled away in CB lingo. 'Roger, I've got a 10-29 on your breaker, over,' and other very strange sentences. I suspect it wasn't just me who had no idea what they were talking about. On top of this they even had their own alphabet and were quite proud of the fact that they knew Hotel, Tango, Foxtrot, Hippopotamus and Dishwasher (or something like that anyway). I would itch to have a go so I could take the piss. I'd last a couple of minutes saying something like, 'My 10–14 is on your 10–27 and my Charlie is Rogered . . . ' before the mike (or whatever) was snatched out of my hand. Or, to piss them off real bad, I'd just speak normal. The CBers hated that. The only rule now seems to be that you have to include the word 'mate' in every sentence.

When the CB burst into life half an hour later asking Mick for road conditions, I grabbed the mike and blurted out, '10-4 good buddy, let's go hunting bears.' Mick laughed nervously. The passing truckie probably got his rego and was already planning to serve him up with gravy the next time he saw him on the road.

Within what seemed like only a few minutes we were treated to a glorious sunset over the plains, turning the long, bleached white grass deep, deep orange. 'Not bad, eh?' Mick said with a big grin, 'I never get sick of those.' As we rounded a bend in the highway hundreds, and I mean hundreds, of emus stood perfectly still in silhouette against the burnt orange sky. It would have been perfect if it wasn't for the horrifying smell pervading the cabin. The barrel load of baked beans we'd eaten at brekky had taken their toll. It was sounding a bit like a 40-piece brass band tuning up. Luckily, before we both suffocated, we pulled up for dinner.

I was looking forward to dinner. We were stopping in the town of Roma, I was expecting a bustling little piazza with a quaint trattoria serving up a simple, yet tasty, homemade pasta. But sadly, no. It was the Roma BP Roadhouse full of men in blue singlets. We sat outside. The evening was warm and the verandah of the roadhouse was surrounded by vine-covered terraces. It almost felt like we were in Italy. Oh, besides the two large truckies next to us in blue singlets feasting on steaks the size of my head (drowned in gravy, of course, and talking in strong strine accents about clutch torques, stroke bores and the relative compression ratios of their gravy).

We ordered the grilled fish and gravy (as you do!). Mick eyed the two guys behind us. 'Grain!' Mick exclaimed.

'What?' I asked, a little confused.

'They're grain drivers.'

'How can you tell?'

'I can just tell,' Mick said with a knowing look on his face.

'What about those guys over there?' I motioned subtly with a nod—I didn't want to attract any unwanted attention; the arms on one of the truckies had a wider girth than my waist. 'They're cattle drivers,' Mick whispered (he too, didn't want to be beaten to a pulp). 'I can tell cos they're always dirty.' And boy, were they dirty. One looked like he hadn't had a bath since he had shared one with a rubber duckie and his little sister. 'Turd herders!' Mick declared.

'Sorry?'

'Turd herders. That's what we call cattle drivers.'

My meal was plopped down in front of me by a sweet old lady, old enough to be my grandma's grandma. The grilled fish was totally covered in a rich brown gravy. Exactly the sort of gravy you'd expect to get on roast beef. Amazingly, it tasted wonderful.

By this stage Mick's voice had turned into a Joe Cockeresque rasp. 'I'm not used to talking,' Mick croaked, 'I can go days without speaking to anyone.' Besides ordering his rissoles and gravy, of course. Gee, it must get lonely. The only company is other truckies, truck stop waitresses and the radio. Mick knew exactly where and when to pick up each radio station on his route. We must have listened to twenty different stations, and every single one of them boasted 'The Best Songs of all Time'. That's of course when they weren't playing ads for tractor equipment, a sale at Thommo's hardware or worming tablets for sheep. Back in the good ol' days, truckies may not have had 'The Best Songs of the 1870s, 80s and 90s', but at least they had someone to talk to. The first trucks were called steam vans and not only was there a driver to steer the truck, but he would be accompanied by a 'chauffeur' whose job was to keep the boiler stoked.

It was dark by the time we left Roma, and it seemed all the local wildlife were out to wave us on. In a space of only few kilometres we saw grey kangaroos, giant red roos, emus, assorted wallabies, bush turkeys, wombats, foxes, rabbits and a partridge in a pear tree. As we passed they all stopped and stared, their eyes lighting up like Christmas lights. 'Wow,' I exclaimed every time I saw a different species of animal, 'a bush turkey!' 'Did you see the cumquats?' Mick croaked. I peered into the gloom for any sign of small bright orange fruit in the trees. 'Where?' I said. I could only see murky eucalyptus trees. 'There . . . and there!' Mick pointed. It was the same eucalyptus trees. Then it clicked. 'Oh . . . you mean quokkas!' 'Yeah, yeah . . . same thing!' Mick grunted. I was just about to go into the difference between a furry mammal and a tasty little orange fruit when there was a huge thud on the front of the truck. This was followed quickly by a second even louder thud on the side of the truck. 'What was that?' I screamed. 'Friggin' roo,' Mick groaned. Mick hadn't even flinched. A big grey had leapt in front of the truck and bounced off just below the windscreen. Mind you, I suppose when you're driving a 63-tonne truck you can't just swerve to avoid cute furry creatures. Bizarrely, there were just as many dead animals on the side of the road as there were live ones. They were all in contorted poses and their guts glowed a vivid red under the bright truck headlights. 'Roos are *good* road kill,' Mick said matter of factly. 'They're solid. They just bounce off. Bloody sheep are the worst. They don't do much damage, but the buggers are full of blood, guts and gizzards. I hit one two weeks ago and there was blood and shit all up the back door of the truck twenty-five metres away from where I hit the friggin' thing. I pulled into a services, went to the loo, and came back to find every dog within fifty Ks sniffin' around the truck!' All of a sudden a few big drops of what looked like blood splattered onto the front windscreen. 'What's that?' I asked warily. Mick sighed. 'I dunno.' He hit the brakes just as another huge red splatter landed smack in the middle of the window.

'Jesus Christ!' I hissed. Mick laughed. Stuck in the bullbar at the front of the truck was a kangaroo's severed head. The poor bugger must have hit the truck head on (so to speak!), and got its head caught in the bullbar. Then its body had whipped around to the side of the truck (the second thump) and been ripped right off. Mick went back to grab some gloves while I stared at the kangaroo who was staring straight at me. As Mick struggled to pull the head out he said calmly, 'My record for one night is sixteen roos, two foxes, one emu and a handful of rabbits. There wasn't even a bit of damage. Then I hit one tiny friggin' bird and it cracked my windscreen!' Mick casually held the kangaroo head in his hand. 'See ya later,' he said to the head and unceremoniously tossed it into the shrub.

By the time we pulled over in the middle of absolutely nowhere after seventeen hours on the road (including fourteen hours driving), I was absolutely certain I could not do this job. Concentrate for fourteen hours of driving? I've got the attention span of a goldfish. I have trouble concentrating on the 40-minute drive to my parents' place. Mick drives up to 120 hours a week and sometimes goes days without a break. He'll get to Sydney, unload, pick up another load of something and head straight back to Townsville (reducing Australia's wildlife population along the way). The round trip only takes four days. Back in the 1930s, a round trip from Alice Springs to Sydney (with a few pick-ups and drop-offs along the way) could take up to six or even eight months. On one trip, the pregnant wife of truck driver came along for the ride. A month into the trip the baby was due, so the soon-to-be-truckie-dad dropped the expectant mother at Tennant Creek. He picked up his wife and new baby boy on his way back . . . five months later.

Mick very kindly bought along a tent. I wandered off into the bush trying to find a clearing and somewhere flat (and far enough away from the excruciatingly annoying hum of the trailer's refrigeration unit) to put down the fully erected tent I was carrying over my head. After stumbling around for a few minutes, struggling to hold the tent, a sleeping bag, a bed mat and a pillow (while also holding a torch between clenched teeth in a fairly futile attempt to see where I was going), I found a likely spot.

An orange glow lay across the horizon. Mick told me it was a bushfire. He said we would be safe. Nevertheless, I lay awake for a while wondering whether I'd be attacked by dingoes (apparently they have an attraction to people in tents) or burnt to death. Or both. The dingoes were probably waiting till I was slightly burnt on the outside and tender in the middle before they had me for their midnight snack. Then there were the strange noises. A brushing sound, followed by what sounded like panting. I'd never heard anything like it before. Maybe a wild cumquat perhaps? In any case, sheer exhaustion took over and I soon dozed off, dreaming of small orange fruit gathering outside my tent planning an attack.

Suddenly I jolted awake to the sound of unzipping. After a split second of pure terror, my brain pulled itself together. It's all right, I thought to myself, I don't think dingoes (or even wild cumquats, for that matter) can unzip a tent flap. Mick leaned in with beaming smile and a steaming hot mug of tea, 'No dingoes got ya then?' Back at the truck Mick opened a little compartment underneath the trailer to reveal a fine collection of breakfast cereals. It seemed bizarre standing in the middle of nowhere debating whether to have Weet-bix or Rice Bubbles.

It was with some dismay that I jumped aboard the jackhammer jalopy for another fifteen hours on the road. I'm a real 'have to have a shower in the morning' type of guy, and after two hours in the bouncing beast I was relieved to see a sign for Australia's Premier Truck Stop, the BP servo at Goondiwindi. 'The best showers around,' Mick promised me. This was a real milestone, too. We'd finally reached the border of Queensland and New South Wales. As we pulled up into the truck park, a Scania noisily drew up next to us. 'Girl's truck,' Mick grunted. Well, it was painted pink with red love hearts all over it. Oh, and THE POWER OF LOVE was emblazoned in large letters emblazoned across the front. The driver stepped out. He looked ready to audition for the Village People—and to be hired on the spot. He had tight black pants, a studded belt, a ponytail and a large droopy moustache. He bid us a good morning then headed towards the showers. I had a chat with him over a cup of tea in the café after my shower. His name was John and he'd been driving for 32 years. He'd also been married 32 years and reckoned he'd only seen his wife for about eight years of that.

By the time I finally dragged myself away from the refreshingly lovely hot shower, Mick had already filled up with fuel and was sipping a large mug of coffee. It cost Mick (well, his company) $698 to fill the tank with fuel. 'They give us a free cup of coffee,' Mick said brightly. 'Gee, for 700 bucks of fuel I'd expect a lobster dinner!' I moaned.

The scenery changed over the border. It was green for a start. We were in New England. However, this was nothing like England. There were endless blue skies and not once did I hear anyone whinge. I love the fact that in England you don't drive a truck, you drive a lorry. It sounds so camp. 'Oh, I drive a lorry!' It hasn't quite got the same manly ring to it as 'I drive a fuck'n truck, mate!' Incidentally, what does an articulated truck mean? Does it mean the truck is capable of eloquent speech?

As we were driving out of the town of Narrabri, I heard this classic as two truckies in front of us conversed on the CB: 'Hey mate, did you see that set of tits back there?' 'Nah, mate, missed them!' 'Oh, they were beauties, mate.'

Even though I felt guilty about it, I spent most of the afternoon napping in Mick's bed behind him. He said he didn't mind and that he was used to being by himself anyway. Mick wasn't planning on doing this driving thing forever. He was busily saving to take three years off and motorcycle around the world, visiting every continent (including slipping around the ice in Antarctica) and over 100 countries.

Murrurrundi was our final meal break before Sydney. I had a pie and the waitress asked if I wanted gravy on it. 'It's already got gravy in it!' I said. Truckies may love their trucks, but I think they love gravy more.

We finally pulled into the Sydney fruit and veg market at 10.30. Almost 30 hours of driving since we left Townsville the morning before.

Chris, another ex-tour company driver, was there to meet us. I was crashing at his place. Mick, Chris and I went out for a quick beer before Mick had to oversee the unloading of the bananas. As soon as we sat down, Mick and Chris started talking about engine bores, maximum torque and how to unplug a diagnostic steering column while you're eating a rissole covered in gravy. I didn't mind. I was more than happy to be sitting in a seat that didn't shake.

The Tube

London, England
September 2001

The Unedited Diary of an Underground Drunk
(except for the bits in italics which I've added later)

I'm not a huge drinker. I get drunk quite quickly. So boy, am I going to get rat-arsed!

I am about to attempt the Circle Line pub crawl. This entails drinking half a pint of beer in a pub at each and every one of the 27 stops on London Underground's Circle Line. That's thirteen and a half pints of beer in twelve hours. I'm normally well pissed after six pints. This should be very interesting—as should the diary I'm now starting. Just bear in mind that you may have to excuse my grammar and any sentences that make no sense at all—given what six pints does to my speech, I shudder to think what twice that will do to my writing.

1 *Tube*–**Bayswater** *Pub*–**Prince Alfred**
      Beer–**Carlsberg**

'Ladies and gentlemen, we apologise for the inconvenience. We're still trying to find a driver.' Find a driver? Where is he? Has he just popped off to the loo? Or are they still processing job applications? I just love the way the English will not only tell you the train is late, but also tell you why.

A few years back I heard this classic: 'We apologise for the late departure, the driver had his car wheel-clamped.' They will also tell you the train is late because there are leaves on the track, or the wrong type of rain (!) is falling.

This is not a good start. Particularly since I've just told Ira how wonderful the Tube is because trains come every couple of minutes. My fellow adventurers are Ira and Jacqui from Canada. I recruited them from the Hyde Park Hostel half an hour ago. Ira stepped off a plane only three hours ago. This is his first time in London and his first time on the Underground. He hasn't been to sleep for 22 hours.

Coincidentally, The Prince Alfred, the pub where we began our colossal task was the one in which I had my very first beer in London in 1987 when I had just stepped off a plane. The only difference was that on that occasion I attempted to drink thirteen and a half pints in just the one pub!

2 *Tube*–**Notting Hill Gate** *Pub*–**Windsor Castle**
      Beer–**Grolsch**

We've cheated already. We caught a District Line train. Even though it runs on the same tracks, it's not quite technically the Circle Line.

Some of my best swear words have been aimed at the Circle Line. I once had to wait while fourteen District Line trains went through before a Circle Line train showed up. My friend Phil announced after District train nine, 'If another fuckin' District Line train comes I'll throw myself onto the track.' By the twelfth, I had to physically restrain him.

We are having a meal at the Windsor Castle (the pub that is, not the Queen's residence). 'We better have something to soak up the beer,' I said. Plus the fact that I couldn't pass up the opportunity to have the bangers and mash. Mind you, the bangers and mash are a bit flash: 'Wild boar sausages on a bed of mash with rich onion gravy'.

'I had to go through a hidden door to go to the bathroom!' Ira exclaimed. 'This country is crazy.'

3   *Tube*–**High Street Kensington**   *Pub*–**Prince of Wales** ***Beer*–Kronenbourg 1664**

A Circle Line train takes almost exactly one hour to do a full loop. In 1884, when the Circle Line first opened (the first section was opened in 1863, making it the oldest underground railway in the world) it took the same amount of time. Not bad, considering the trains were hauled by steam engines. Just one of the Circle Line trains travels the distance from London to Sydney seven times a year (I'm getting all my trivia stuff out of the way early before I get too pissed—I don't just know this stuff off the top of my head, by the way. I'm lugging around a pile of trivia notes with me).

4   *Tube*–**Gloucester Road**   *Pub*–**The Rat and Parrot** ***Beer*–Fosters**

I'd only just been telling Ira and Jacqui how I'd been on the Tube hundreds of times when I got caught in the ticket machine. The station attendant chap has to let me out. I am so embarrassed. Not as embarrassed though as I was at Earls Court station a few years back, while I was waiting for the last train. A Danish girl and I were snogging and groping each other on the platform (as you do!). We were both a little pissed. While we were going for it, an announcement blurted out around the whole station, 'Could that couple on platform number five please control themselves? Thank you!'

Even though the train is almost full, I can't see (or hear) any English people in the carriage. It is full of tourists. Half the train seems to be studying Tube maps. I can hear smatterings of Spanish, German, Dutch and something that sounds like Jabba the Hut.

'What pub is next?' Ira has just asked. 'The Fish and Hippopotamus?' I think he's getting the hang of silly English pub names.

'This is easy', Ira says, as we step off the train, 'It doesn't matter how drunk we get, we just have to remember to get off at the next stop.'

5   *Tube–***South Kensington**   *Pub–***The Hoop and Toy**
   *Beer–***Becks**

'We're always going east, remember that', I say as we try to figure out which platform to head for.

'But it's a *Circle* Line,' Ira retorts, 'so at some point we must have to travel north, south and west.'

Fuck. I thought I was being clever.

The Hoop and Toy is the first and only pub I ever worked at. I worked here for two months. They didn't have an electronic till then, so we had to add up in our heads. Too many years of sitting at the back of Maths class drawing rude pictures hadn't stood me in good stead for this. If someone bought more than three drinks, I'd just make up a figure in my head. I got away with it, though. Luckily, drunk people will pay any figure you throw at them.

6   *Tube–***Sloane Square**   *Pub–***The Rose and Crown**
   *Beer–***Becks**

'Hello, how are you today?' Someone is speaking to me! No one speaks on the tube. No one even makes eye contact.

'Oh! I'm good thank you,' I say. People are already looking at us, thinking: 'Are those two strangers (and strange foreigners) *talking*?'

'What's your name?' he asks. He is American.

It isn't until after I've told him my name and where I am that I notice his name tag: Elder Cas Thomas, Mormon Church.

'So, what are you doing in London?'

I don't want a lecture on why I shouldn't be getting rat-arsed in 27 London pubs, so I tell him I am in London to do some publicity for my first book.

'Oh, I have a book here you might be interested in,' says Elder Cas.

He hands me *The Book of Mormon*. I wish I could give him a copy of my first book, *Rule No.5: No sex on the bus*. I bet he'd find the rampant sex and debauchery in that interesting.

'I have to get off here,' I say as I stand up. ' I've got another twenty pubs to drink at today.'

7   *Tube*–**Victoria**   *Pub*–**The Plumber's Arms**
    Beer–**XXXX**

Ira: 'I feel all right. I reckon I could still drive a truck.'

Me: 'Do you drive a truck?'

Ira: 'Nup, but I reckon I could still drive one.'

It's peak hour. Thousands of people are swarming about. We are the only ones smiling. Victoria is the busiest station on the London Underground. In peak hour, over 34 000 non-smiling people pass through the station every hour. Just over 76 million passengers pass through it every year. Over 20 million individual passengers ride the Tube each year—that's more than the entire population of Australia.

8   *Tube*–**St James Park**   *Pub*–**The Old Star**
    Beer–**Heinekin**

A delay. And they won't tell us why.

'Someone's probably chucked themselves on the track,' I say. *I later learned that I could have been close to the truth. Victoria Tube station has the record for the most suicides on the Underground.* It's not something they'd announce, 'I'm sorry ladies and gentlemen, but a man has thrown himself onto the track and we're just waiting for someone to come along and pick up all the limbs and guts.' I actually met the guy who picks up the limbs and guts. He was on call 24 hours a day. If there were any suicides, he would be paged to come and clean up. What a horrible job. It's almost as bad as being a Mormon Elder.

9   *Tube*–**Westminster**   *Pub*–**Lord Moon of the Mall**
     Beer–**Becks??**

Me: 'Blow your nose.'

Ira: 'What?'

Me: 'Just blow your nose.'

Ira blew his nose.

Ira: 'Oh, my God!' There was black soot in his hankie. 'What the hell's that?'

Me: 'It's from all the soot in the Underground.'

When I worked in London a few years back, I would come home from work every night and blow out a pile of black soot. Travelling on the Tube for twenty minutes is the equivalent of smoking a cigarette. I don't see the Underground having to put up warnings like 'Waiting for a train KILLS', though.

Ira: 'Hey, Isn't that Big Ben?'

Me: 'Nah, that's just a clock tower. Big Ben's heaps bigger than that.'

Ira: 'Oh.'

This pub is a haunt of politicians. Jacqui and Ira have just accosted the Under Secretary of State for the Defence Minister's Secretary (or something like that) at the bar and said, 'Gee, you must be happy about the war in Afghanistan then. It gives you something to do!'

It's lucky the Police Minister isn't here as well. Jacqui just stole three empty pint glasses as souvenirs from the bar, and they're poking out the top of her bag.

10 *Tube–*Embankment   *Pub–*Halfway to Heaven
*Beer–*Grolsch

'Mind the gap. Mind the gap.' The recorded announcement tells us.

Ira: 'How do you mind it? Does that mean you have to look after it?' I know I must be getting a wee bit merry because I laughed for about five minutes when Ira said that. The London Underground recently experimented with someone mimicking Marilyn Monroe for the warnings to 'Mind the gap'. I think someone mimicking Elvis would have been better. 'Ah ... mind, mind thuh' gap, honey. Thank yoo, thank yoo very much!'

Boy, we stink. I was doing my best not to breathe my boozy breath into the face of the guy squashed up against me. It's six o'clock now and the Tube is packed. At least Ira isn't offending anyone. He has his face squashed up against the window of the door.

Jacqui: 'Did you notice anything strange about the pub we were in?'

Me and Ira: 'No.'

Jacqui: 'Nothing?'

Me and Ira: 'No.'

Jacqui: 'It was a gay pub. The whole pub was full of men holding hands. Two of them were kissing in the corner.' *To be fair though, we were having trouble noticing anything at all at this point.*

Ira: 'Do you think they thought Brian and I were gay?'

Jacqui: 'No, you aren't dressed neatly enough.'

11 *Tube*–**Temple**   *Pub*–**The Wellington**
Beer–**I don't know, but it was brown**

Supposed to be the Seven Stars pub. Can't for the life of us find it. Have walked into nearest pub.

Jacqui: 'I was groped on the train.'

Ira: 'No, you weren't. You fell on that guy and he put out his hand to stop you bowling him over.'

12 *Tube*–*Blackfriars*   *Pub*–**The Black Friar**
Beer–**Yes, that's correct**

A beggar sitting in the middle of the stairs has just asked us for some spare change.

Me: 'No, sorry, I haven't got any.'

Beggar: 'That's all right, I take credit cards, cheques, drugs, anything!'

13 *Tube*–**Mansion House**   *Pub*–**Slug & Lettuce**
Beer–**Fosters**

Five minutes to find Tube. We have to lift our game. We're running out of time.

Jacqui: 'People said I slept with Jarrod but I didn't.'

Ira is swinging from the handle things.

Ira: 'What was the name of the last pub we went to?'

Me: 'The Aardvark and Turnip?'

Ira: 'Oh, that's right.'

14 *Tube*–**Monument**   *Pub*–**Ye olde Cock Tavern**
Beer–**Hmmmm?**

Yeah yeah. Ye olde Cock Tavern. Ha ha ha ha ha. *Sitting in the Ye olde Cock Tavern we come up with our own names for pubs:*
The Jocks & Socks

The Muff & Tit
The Banana & ????? *I couldn't read my writing here*
The Steaming Asparagus
The Bearded Clam
We laughed all the way to the next pub.

15   *Tube–***Tower Hill**   *Pub–***Chesire Cheese**
*Beer–***Carling Black label**

Jacqui has got three Englishmen in suits doing aerobics near the bar. While Ira was doing star jumps, he told me he could still drive a truck.

My navigational skills have diminished somewhat. It's taken fifteen minutes to find the Godforsaken bloody damn Tube stop.

16   *Tube–***Aldgate**   *Pub–***Hoops & Grapes**
*Beer–***Yes indeed**

Ira has fallen asleep on the platform. When I say on the platform, I mean *on* the platform. He is sprawled out like he's dead.

A man: 'Is he all right?'
Me: 'Yeah, he's a Canadian.'
I shake Ira awake when the train is pulling in.
Ira: 'I could drive a truck . . . but I probably shouldn't.'

17   *Tube–***Liverpool Street**   *Pub–***Slurpin Toad**
*Beer–***Bloody Fosters again**

It's ten o'clock. We're not going to make it. The pubs close at eleven.
Ira: 'We have to make it. Let's skol our beers.'
We run to the Tube. Not a good idea. I hope I don't chuck.
Ira: 'I'm good.'
Jacqui: 'I feel like shit.'
Ira: 'You look good!'
Jacqui: 'Fuck off. I look like shit.'

18   *Tube*–**Moorgate**   *Pub*–**Old Dr. Butlers head**
    Beer–**A very quick one**

We wait seven minutes for a train.

Jacqui: 'I could have a baby in seven minutes.'

Ira: 'We could try and make one in two.'

Ira's head is bobbing up and down on the window.

Jacqui: 'We're on the pink line.'

Ira: 'It's the gay line.'

Jacqui: 'No it's not. It's the metropolis line.' *We were actually on the Metropolitan Line, but she was close.*

A couple are snogging at the other end of the carriage. He is trying to eat her. That reminds me. We forgot to eat dinner. Oh, well.

19   *Tube*–**Farringdon**   *Pub*–**The Mitre**
    Beer–**XXXX (shit, I remembered!)** *But not how to spell.*

We missed a stop. I want to finish at the Mitre pub. It was built in 14 something. I used to drink there years ago when I worked around here.

We walk the wrong way. Some local garbos kindly gave us a lift in the back of their truck. *There's another mode of transport, at least!*

Ladies and gentlemen, time please. We're last to leave pub. We didn't make it. Not that I'm pissed. Not at all. Train to ???? *I can't read this word. It looks like ... Deewa head.*

20   *Tube*–**Edgeware Road**   *Pub*–**They're all closed**
    Beer–**I've had enough**

I'm writing this in my bed. We caught the last Tube. They threw us out of the pub. Men in bright orange overalls were on the train holding the biggest spanners I'd ever seen. 'Protection Master' was written on their shirt. Their faces were covered in black soot. They were also holding bits of wood that measure stuff. *I think I meant a spirit level.* They told me they measure the track to see if it's straight and if it's not they fix it. Ira told them they weren't doing a very good job. 'The train's rocking all over the place'.

Jacqui stole all these ads from above the seats. One said, 'Happiness is . . . letting people off first.'

The Morning After

Well, we almost made it. Still, twenty pubs and ten pints of beer is not a bad effort.

I only have vague recollections of the last few pubs and Tube rides. I was mightily impressed with my writing under the circumstances, though, (what I could understand of it, anyway).

What I didn't write about was being chased out of the station by a staff member of the London Underground at Edgeware Road. Ira had tried to outdo Jacqui. He stole a huge 'Slippery When Wet' poster (just what you need!) and I seem to remember a rather large chap in a suit chasing us up the stairs with Ira giggling like a madman. Jacqui ended up with six different pint glasses. I just ended up with a sore head, an empty wallet—and another chapter!

Bicycle

Beijing, China
November 2001

There are eleven million bicycles in Beijing. Amazingly, they all seemed to be on the streets at once and I was riding smack in the middle of them all. I didn't quite blend in with the masses, though. Well, for a start I wasn't Chinese. But more importantly, I was riding into a swarm of very perplexed-looking cyclists travelling in the opposite direction. Oddly enough, no one abused me or even said a word. They just rang their bells. So much so, in fact, that it sounded like Christmas.

I did have one thing in common with the rest of my fellow cyclists. I had the same sort of bike. A black clunky thing called a Flying Pigeon. Most of the cyclists were riding Flying Pigeons (one of Deng Xiaoping's campaign promises when he rose to power in the late 1970s was that there would be a 'Flying Pigeon in every household').

I didn't expect my hire bike to be too flash. Not for 60 cents a day. However, it would have been nice if the front wheel didn't wobble like one of those rogue ones that send supermarket trolleys crashing from one side of the aisle to the other. It might also have alleviated my trepidation about riding in a city of twelve million people if the brakes worked when I wanted them to. I hoped I didn't have to stop in a hurry. Or at all, actually.

This was my first day in Beijing. I'd arrived the night before. In the morning, when I'd spotted bicycles for hire outside the hotel, I thought I'd do as the Beijingites do. Risk life, limb and lungs in the Beijing traffic.

The morning was hazy. The sun was a sickly dull glow behind a blanket of thick pollution. The road ran beside an oily, brown river. It looked like a sewage outlet (I later discovered it was Beijing's main river). I rode through the bell-ringing locals while trying to avoid a head-on collision for ten minutes before I decided to do one of the most daring and dangerous things I'd ever done in my life. I attempted to cross the road. I hesitantly followed another cyclist into a tiny gap in the traffic. We didn't get very far and ended up marooned in the middle of the road as cars flew by us at a dizzying pace. One zipped centimetres past my back wheel. The other chap pulled out in front of a truck, nonchalantly squeezed his brakes and veered out of his way, with only millimetres to spare. I closed my eyes and followed. Riding a bicycle in Beijing is not for the faint-hearted. Apparently, 30 000 cyclists die on Chinese roads each year. Most of them of heart attacks, I imagine.

I was now on the correct side of the road. Even though the bicycle lane was quite wide, the bikes were still handlebar-to-handlebar. Ten abreast at least. I love riding and I ride a lot, but none of the cycling skills I've honed over the years prepared me to dodge a bicycle laden with ten piglets or a rider towing a massive trailer piled high with what looked like everything he owned. Including his wife.

And nothing, and I mean nothing, could prepare me for trying to dodge the spitting. Giant globules of gob were flying around like very large raindrops. A few people somehow managed to produce gobs as big as my head.

What I saw next, however, made me concentrate even more on my riding skills. Two cyclists, who had bumped into each other were partaking in a spot of bicycle road rage. An old fellow got off his bike and started swinging punches at the other man. I rode by just as the old fellow, who must have been in his seventies, picked up a brick. I wanted to watch some more, but I had to negotiate my way around a smoky bus that had jumped onto the bike lane in front of me. I followed the rest of the cyclists as they rode around it and into oncoming traffic. Not one of them even flinched. I closed my eyes again.

I hadn't had any breakfast yet and I was hungry, but everything in the hotel restaurant had been written in Chinese (funny that) and I wasn't keen on accidentally ordering dog's spleen as my first meal in China. Not for breakfast at least.

My first 'tourist attraction' I stopped at was the Temple of Heaven. The bicycle-park was full with at least five thousand bikes that all looked identical. I parked my bike next to the only bike that wasn't black. That should make my bike easier to find, I thought—provided the flamboyant rebel with the dingy brown bike didn't leave before I got back.

The Temple of Heaven park was a quiet oasis in the middle of a very noisy Beijing. The only sound was the sound of thousands of cameras going off immediately after shouts of, what I could only imagine is, Chinese for 'say cheese!'. The park was full of temples. As temples go, they were very impressive. I got the most excited, though, when I found some food I could recognise. I had a sausage on a stick. Or a bull's penis. Whatever—all I know is that it tasted spicy and delicious.

Back at the bike park, the only bike that wasn't black had gone (surprise, surprise). I was very pleased with myself, though. I found my bike after only a minute of searching.

I reached into the basket at the front of the bike for my map of

Beijing and . . . it was gone. It must have fallen out. OK, now what do I do? I stood there for a minute, shrugged my shoulders, said 'what the hell?' and jumped on my bike. It would be all right. I had studied the map of Beijing the night before. Beijing's main streets all form a north-south and east-west grid. All I had to do was to take note of which way I was riding. I knew I had to go back the way I came, turn right up the 'main' street and I'd hit Tiananmen Square and the Forbidden City. From there, I'd ride around the walls of the Forbidden City and a large park, then head down to the river. From the river I *should* be able to find the hotel. As long as I kept going straight, I'd be fine. If I had been riding one of the first bicycles, which appeared around 1790, I wouldn't have had any problem with that. They could only go in a straight line. They also didn't have any pedals (they worked *à la* Fred Flintstone, by sheer unimproved foot power). They were reasonably popular in Paris (must have been a *lot* of straight roads). To turn, first you had to stop (there were no brakes either, so you just had to slow down), get off, physically lift the bike and point it in the direction you wanted to go, get back on, then . . . yabba-dabba-do!

The 'main' street was a chaotic mess of bikes, taxis, buses, cars and people. Lots of people. The colours, noise and smells enveloped me. It was madness and I loved it. There was so much going on I didn't know where to look.

I passed huge restaurants, each trying to outdo the others with elaborate neon signs that would put Disneyland to shame. I passed a shop selling shoddily made, shiny polyester pants next to a shop selling Georgio Armani suits. In front of the Armani shop, an old lady had spread a blanket on the footpath and laid out the six pumpkins she had for sale.

Every twenty metres the smell changed. Smoke, fruit, sewage, noodles, polyester pants, car fumes, strange spices and, now and again, the most delicious smell of something exotic cooking. I stopped every ten minutes or so and wandered into a shop (the Chinese must send their best shoddy clothes overseas, because most of the stuff on sale in Beijing looked like it had been stitched together in Art and Craft time at the local kindergarten). I stopped at one point to eye-off a gorgeous Chinese girl. She was dressed exquisitely and had the most radiantly beautiful and flawless skin. She was chatting to a friend, then suddenly turned her head and . . . spat the biggest gob I'd ever seen in my life onto the footpath in front of me.

Accordingly then, I stopped for a quick snack. I wandered down a side street full of food stalls where all sorts of things were being fried, grilled, sizzled and sozzled. I passed a man happily munching fried grasshoppers on a stick. There was quite a choice of snacks, though. There was whole roasted sparrow on a stick, whole octopus on a stick and deep fried scorpions on a stick. I was totally amazed. Do the Chinese serve every meal on a stick? Eventually, I found a man who wasn't cooking strange beasties on a stick. I had beef on a stick (I think). The Chinese don't mind the odd culinary oddity. They are known to dine on bear paws, tiger's testicles, owl soup, thousand-year-old eggs, pork's uterus, drunken shrimp (live shrimp swimming around in a bowl of rice wine that you have to capture with your chopsticks) and bull's penis and testicles on a stick (my friend San ate this one time in China. He said it tasted like brains. He has also eaten deep-fried cockroaches—which he said tastes like popcorn—and roasted caterpillars, which look exactly, but taste nothing like, Cheezels). I found the information about tiger's testicles and the pork's uterus on a website entitled 'Weird and Disgusting Food'. The Australian section included Vegemite and beetroot.

I ate my beef on a stick like the locals did. Standing in the middle of the footpath, dribbling the sauce all over my shirt.

The only problem with all this stopping was that I had to park my bike in a bike park every time (if you don't park your bike in a designated bike park, you get your bike towed. Really!). At least it didn't cost me a fortune. The parking fee was about 4 cents. In one of the bike parks, I spotted a brand new mountain bike. It was a Peugeot. Wow, that would cost the average Chinese person about seventeen years wages. Mind you, it would cost me about six months wages.

Peugeot make a nice bike. Quite a few car manufacturers make bicycles. Actually, most of them were making bikes long before they started manufacturing cars. You can also buy a Ferrari, Lotus, Mercedes Benz, Aston Martin, Porsche, BMW and even Kawasaki bicycle. Yet here's the remarkable thing: Ferrari or Porsche don't make the most expensive bike. That claim to fame (and busting your bank balance) belongs to a British bike called Stif. And I tell you, I'd feel well stiffed paying for one. Their top-of-the-range bike, The Flipper, sells for, wait for it . . . just under $21 000. The Flipper weighs a mere nine pounds (that's $2333 a pound!). The brakes, gears and pedals are made in Japan. The frame is made in the USA, the handlebars are made in England, and the saddle is made in Italy. For $21 000, you'd hope the tyres were handmade by blind Tibetan monks.

The tyres on my Flying Pigeon looked a bit the worse for wear. At least if I got a puncture I would be OK. On just about every corner was a mobile bike repairman set up on the footpath. Getting a flat tyre fixed would set you back about 6 cents. They all seemed to be busy.

The Chinese do love their bikes. Their fascination with bikes began in the late nineteenth century, when two Americans pedalled from Constantinople to Peking. Crowds greeted them in village after village, describing the strange vehicle as 'a little mule that you drive by the ears and kick in the sides to make him go'. Today, the bicycle is the most popular form of transport (besides trusty old feet, of course) in China—and the rest of the world. In fact, there are three times as many bikes made each year than cars. Amazingly, China has almost a third of the world's 900 million bicycles.

I needed a respite from the 300 million bicycles and stopped at the biggest neon-signed restaurant in the street (it must have used half of

Beijing's electricity supply). Two pretty hostesses met me at the door and escorted me to my seat. The inside of the restaurant was cavernous. However, only one other table was occupied. Three businessmen in the far corner were loudly slurping soup (owl soup?). Four waiting staff handed me the menu. It was in Chinese. When they all came back again to take my order I did a rather good impersonation of a chicken. It took me a lot longer to order some rice. It's not easy to imitate rice!

While eating my chicken dish (which was just lovely, by the way), I looked up and counted sixteen waiting staff standing against the wall. That's four waiters per customer. Not bad for a $4 plate of chicken.

When I remounted my bike I let out an involuntary groan. The Flying Pigeon bike seat sure wasn't built for comfort. I tried to get some speed up, but the bike was in danger of shaking itself to bits. There wasn't much danger of breaking speed records on this old rattler. Incidentally, the highest speed recorded on a bicycle (on the flat, too) is 268 km/h. Mind you, I bet that bloke didn't have traffic lights and bicycles overflowing with sacks of chickens in front of him.

The 'main street' suddenly opened up and I was riding into Tiananmen Square. Even the eight-lane road that ringed the square looked tiny in comparison to the vast space in the middle. There was hardly any traffic, but a car still managed to almost hit me. He had eight lanes to choose from and he was weaving across all of them. It looked like he'd fallen asleep at the wheel. I was so busy being totally flabbergasted by the size of Tiananmen Square, I almost ran over an old fellow on a bike that looked older than he did (it did have pedals and steering, though).

I tried to ride into the square itself but a guard who was wearing his little brother's uniform screamed at me and pushed me away. I see, they won't let bikes in the square, but tanks are OK.

I parked and strolled into the square. There must have been 100 000 Chinese people in there, and all of them were taking photos of each other. Oh, besides the little girl I saw squatting to have a wizz in the middle of it all. Wee flowed under people's shoes. Her own political statement perhaps?

I tried to park my bike near the entrance to the Forbidden City, but I was yelled at again. It is forbidden to park your bike at the entrance to the Forbidden City, but it's not forbidden to spit all over it.

Once inside, as I expected in the middle of China, James Bond told me all about the Ming Dynasty. I had hired a tape player and headphones, which you listened to at marked spots for historical spiels, and Roger Moore was the narrator. He would say things like 'Why don't we go for a stroll round the courtyard together?' and 'Your time is up, Blofeld'.

I spent three hours roaming around the impressively large (and largely impressive) grounds. I was dragged into a small art gallery by an art teacher and, once he realised there wasn't a chance in hell that I was going to buy anything, we had a nice chat. Well, it was more like him asking me how much things cost in Australia (house, car, food, clothes and prostitutes), then converting it into *yuan* on his calculator. When I told him my how much my bike at home cost me (about $800), it was as if I told him I was sleeping with his sister. And his mum.

I rode around the outskirts of the Forbidden City (looking at my map that morning, I figured it would take about half an hour to ride around the walls—it took *two and a half* hours). When I finally got to the edge of the park, I turned left. If my calculations were correct, the road would lead straight down to the river. I couldn't believe I was traipsing around one of the biggest cities on earth without a map. My sense of direction is normally more like senseless direction. Once, I took a group of people on a bike ride in Interlaken, Switzerland, and led them quite astray. It started when the bike track we were riding on totally disappeared under a blanket of snow. Not only did the snow make it almost impossible to manoeuvre, I couldn't find the track. Moments later we were lost. I then led them along what was formerly just the wrong track, but had now turned into a trench filled with six inches of smelly mud; then across a field full of smellier cows; and finally through a minefield of even smellier steaming poo. Well, at least it helped them forget about their hands being frozen onto the handlebars.

I was already hungry again (you know what they say about Chinese food), and ready for dinner. I wanted Peking Duck. I couldn't go to Beijing and not have Peking Duck. I asked a pedi-cab (a rickshaw with a bicycle) driver where I might find a restaurant that served a good Peking Duck. 'Ah, quack, quack,' he said. He jumped on his bike and motioned me to follow him. Every ten seconds for the five-minute ride down the street he turned around, said 'quack, quack', and laughed.

I propped my bike outside Quanjude restaurant and staggered inside. My bottom was killing me. My manly bits had taken a beating too. Riding a bicycle is actually not too good for a man's bits and pieces. Particularly a mountain bike. According to a paper by Ferdinand Frauscher entitled 'Subclinical microtraumatisation of the scrotal contents in mountain biking', mountain bikers have a high frequency of extratesticular and testicular disorders. On a scrotal ultrasonography the frequency of scrotal abnormalities in mountain bikers (who rode a minimum of two hours day, six days a week) was 96 per cent. My God. That means, most diehard mountain bikers have battered balls.

Mind you, you can now buy specially designed bike saddles with holes in them. The men's saddle has one long skinny hole straight down the middle. The one on my bike at home claimed it was 'Designed to reduce cycling-related genital numbness and the risk of erectile dysfunction'. The women's saddle has a small round hole in the middle, but is a little coy and polite when it comes to describing its medicinal benefits; 'Designed to reduce cycling-related discomfort'. But then again, 'Designed to reduce cycling-related clitoral numbness and the risk of vaginal dysfunction' somehow sounds a little crass.

I soon forgot my sore bottom and probable scrotal abnormality when I tasted my Peking Duck (or Peking *Dark* as it was written on the menu). The restaurant was perfect, even though I wasn't sure if it was a duck restaurant to begin with—there were large tanks in the foyer filled with lobsters, eels, cute turtles and sea slugs, all waiting to be cooked. When I walked into the massive dining room, I knew I was in the right place. There were a hundred tables, all full of locals eating various duck parts. A bevy of cooks, decked out in the tallest cook's hats I'd ever seen, were pushing around silver trolleys with large roast ducks perched on top.

I couldn't finish my dinner. I was given enough duck and pancakes to make about twenty large serves. This was followed by a massive bowl of duck soup (all the bits that aren't used, including the beak, are used to make the soup).

I waddled out of the restaurant and groaned again as I remounted my bike. I was already knackered, and I'd only ridden twenty kilometres or so. I was pretty pathetic. Even more so when you compare my little jaunt to the world's longest ride. A German chap called Walter Stolle cycled 646 960 kilometres and visited 211 countries (and boy, would he have major extratesticular and testicular disorders—that's if he had any left at all).

It was dark when I left the restaurant. Beijing's power supply was running on overtime. The whole street looked like a Chinese version of Las Vegas. The road I was travelling on took a curve to the right. Oh shit! The roads are supposed to go straight. Now I was confused. Particularly when the road veered to the left, then to the right again, before stopping at a large intersection. There were six roads leading off the intersection. Using logistical mathematics and the direction of the wind, I determined which road to take. Well, OK, I took a punt.

The road stopped at the river. I looked in both directions trying to figure out which way to go, and there, to the left of me, was the massive edifice that was my hotel. I couldn't believe it. I'd found my way around Beijing without a map. All I had to do now was to find my room. Damn, I knew I should have drawn a map.

Horse

Outer Mongolia
October 2001

Simon looked like a giant frog. Simon was tall and the stirrups on his horse were short. His knees were poking out at right angles. What am I saying? We all looked like frogs. The stirrups on all Mongolian horses are short. The Mongolians may have invented stirrups, but they seem to have opted for the rather unconventional 'frog mount'. This not only makes you look silly, it's damn well uncomfortable. I'd only been on my horse for ten minutes and I was discovering new (and painful) muscles in my thighs. Thank God we had leather saddles. Mongolians, on the other hand, use wooden saddles. One false move on hardwood, and there goes any chance of having children. Genghis Khan (or Chinggis Khaan as he's known locally) and his Mongol hordes rode for days on end sitting on wooden saddles as they conquered their way across Asia and Europe building the largest empire the world has ever known. I must admit, though, after a day in one of those saddles I'd be ready to sack and pillage too. No wonder they tore out people's eyes.

Our guide's name was (now, no sniggering please) Oddcock. 'Is it bent or bright green or something?' I asked him (it's OK, he didn't understand English). Oddcock was heavily suntanned. It looked like he'd fallen asleep in the solarium. His face was orange. It matched the orange sash that was beautifully wrapped around his large purple overcoat (it's called a *del*, and makes him and many other Mongolians look like they're wandering around in their dressing gowns). He also had on the knee-high black riding boots that you see worn everywhere—including by little old ladies on the checkout counter at the supermarket.

As I said, Oddcock spoke no English, but he was very impressed by my Mongolian. I knew how to say giddy-up in Mongolian. '*Chu*' would be heard many times over the next two days. Simon ended up saying it so many times he sounded like a train.

I'd talked Simon and Anouk (two Sydneysiders I'd met on the Trans-Mongolian train) to join me on a two-day horse trek up in the Mongolian steppe. We'd hired a jeep and driver and bumped our way 100 km north-east of Ulaanbaatar to Terelj national park. This was where we met our horse guide, Oddcock.

I tried to find out my horse's name. 'Me, Brian,' then I'd point to my horse, 'horse …?' I did this five times before I found out my horse's name was Mori.

Mori had his work cut out for him. We'd only been in the saddle for ten minutes and he had to ford the fast-moving Tuul Gol river. Amazingly, Mori never faltered or fell. The river current was strong and the river bed was made up of large uneven rocks. I thought he (and I) was going to get washed away. Mori, like all Mongolian horses, was rather short in stature. A warning: don't in any way call a Mongolian horse a short-arse in front of a Mongolian. They will be terribly offended. And if Ghenghis Khan is any indication, that's not a good idea at all. When someone offended him, he would pour hot metal into their eyes. And to think, Ghengis rode from the Mongolian steppes to the castle walls of Europe on one of those cute ponies you get at your local school fete (please don't tell the Mongolians I said that).

Mongolians are very proud of their vertically challenged horsies. The horse is the country's symbol. You can find them frolicking through grassy fields on nearly all of Mongolia's banknotes. As well as stamps, postcards and even bottled water labels. Mongolia's biggest day is based around a horse race. It's like the Kentucky Derby only dustier, longer and with riders even shorter than jockeys. Riders must be between the ages of seven and twelve. Over 1000 horses compete in a 35 km cross-country race.

They are also particularly proud of their Takhi horse. It is the only true wild horse left on the planet. Tragically, by the mid-seventies they had almost vanished. There were only about a dozen left in zoos around the world. A few were introduced back onto the Mongolian steppes 25 years ago. There are now over 1500 of them romping happily in the hills.

The first wild horses actually appeared in North America over a million years ago. Eight thousand years ago, after they'd spread across Asia, South America and Europe, they became extinct in North America. They didn't show up again until the Spanish stormed through the Americas on horseback over seven thousand years later. The local Indian tribes originally thought they were one creature —man and horse.

Mori and I were like one. He did what I wanted him to do. When I pulled the rein to stop, magically he did. Just to test out his obedience I made him do a 360. He did it without hesitation (Oddcock was a little baffled, though). I'd never experienced anything like this before. Every horse ride I'd ever been on, the horse would simply follow the lead horse or a well-trodden track. Even though you felt you had control, you had about as much control as the captain of the Titanic. The horse just wouldn't change course.

Then again, I suppose it does help to know what you're doing. On my first ever horse trek fifteen years ago, I wanted to ride like the man from Snowy River. 'Hands up those who have riding experience,' asked our guide, before the start of a two-day trek up in the Victorian high country. My hand shot up straight away. I'd been told if you can ride, you get to canter at high speeds, jump logs, ford turbulent rivers and generally do things a lot less dull than rolling through the countryside slower than you could walk. Never mind the fact I'd only ridden once before. When I was twelve. I spent most of the next two days hugging my horse's neck in sheer panic as it flew over logs and screaming in pain at any one of the 967 times my balls took a battering.

We entered a forest, dense with moss-laden larch trees, and it immediately became cold. When I say cold, it was probably about ten degrees. That's nothing. In two months' time it would be a balmy minus 50. It's so cold that horses often die, frozen to the spot, still standing up. They can stay like this for months. The whole country becomes just one big freezer, with frozen rump steaks ready to be sliced off dotted around the countryside, all ready to throw on to the barby. The steppes and mountains of Mongolia are among the world's least hospitable environments. That would probably help to explain why Mongolia is the size of western Europe, yet has the population only slightly larger than Adelaide's. And why the Mongolian hordes rode far and wide to find a place where they could walk around in shorts.

Simon was already lagging behind. I didn't have to turn around to see where he was. I could hear him 'Chu-ing' in the distance. His horse was not at all interested in a walk today. We were soon out of the forest and onto a wide plain. It was flanked by stunted mountains covered in trees in twelve shades of gold. The sky was a crisp deep blue. The only sound was the soft plodding of Mori.

Oddcock was beautiful to watch. Easy and nonchalant in the saddle. Well, what I could see of him anyway. He was soon far ahead of me. Anouk was 50 metres or so behind. I couldn't even see Simon. I could only just hear a faint, '*Chu*, damn it, *chu!*'

I trotted up to Oddcock. It took me a minute or two to get the rhythm thing happening (in the process I only lost the use of one testicle for a few weeks). Suddenly, from behind me, came the sound of thundering hooves (I was guessing it wasn't Simon and his stubborn horse). A boy of about nine galloped past with a long pole in one hand (used to lasso livestock) and casually munching on a apple with the other. He didn't even have hold of the reins. It's not surprising, really, when you consider that most Mongolian kids learn to ride before they can walk. In fact, just about everyone in Mongolia can ride a horse. They've had plenty of practice, too. It was the Mongolians who first jumped on the back of a horse 4000 years ago. Funnily enough, it actually started as a teenage prank. My teenage pranks weren't quite as successful. Even though unplugging the whole outside speaker system of my high school, so no-one could hear the morning bell to start class, was a brilliant idea, it didn't really change the world (we did miss the first ten minutes of maths though!).

The Mongolian boy chatted to Oddcock for a minute, then disappeared as quickly as he arrived. It was not long after that that Oddcock disappeared. I couldn't see him anywhere. And what really made my task of spotting him difficult was that we were no longer on a track. We were riding through broad grassy plains surrounded by rolling hills. Oddcock could have been anywhere. I couldn't even ask Simon and Anouk. They were miles back. Then, to my utter surprise, Mori saved me. He neighed. Straight away, Oddcock's horse neighed in return. A horse will neigh to find out, by listening for an answering neigh, if there are horses nearby. I looked up to where the neigh was coming from. Up on the hill above me I caught a flash of purple, red and yellow. I gave Mori a quick poke with my heel and a couple of *chus* and he immediately scrambled up the grassy slope.

'*Chu, chu* ... FUCKING *CHU*!' Simon screamed. He was still stuck at the bottom of the hill. Anouk had already joined Oddcock and me at the top. Oddcock beckoned us to follow him and we charged back down the hill. We would go around the hill instead of over it.

As we passed around a bizarre rock formation, two giant black vultures rose from the half-munched carcass of a cow in front of us and flew to a nearby rocky outcrop. They looked downright nasty as they stared us down. 'Watch it,' I said to Simon. 'You're going so slow they'll be after you next!'

Oddcock had galloped off ahead. His legs were like steel springs. Mine, on the other hand, felt more like a slinky. Not only that, I had forgotten to bring my stockings. And no, it wasn't because we were planning a drag night in the middle of the Gobi, but to stop me losing all the hair of my legs. Wearing stockings under your pants stops the constant rubbing. Oh, and it also makes you feel like breaking into show tunes.

It was time for a bit of a gallop. I held the rein in one hand, while with the other I grabbed the long lead rope around Mori's neck, and whacked his flank. He was off in a shot. There may be a Mongolian word for giddy-up, but I soon discovered there isn't a Mongolian word for 'Whoa!'. Only a strong tug of the rein and a slightly shrill 'for God's sake ... STOP!' made Mori slow down.

Up ahead, two *gers* stood out bright white, like toadstools, amongst the burnt orange and yellow gold landscape. The *ger* (a circular, wooden-framed tent, insulated with homemade wool felt) is the traditional home of the Mongolian people. Their nomadic lifestyle has, for the most part, remained unchanged for millennia. This family were goat herders. They, like the sheep, cattle, yak and camel herders of Mongolia, would follow the seasons and pastures around. A ger can be dismantled (it all folds up like an accordion) and packed onto the back of a camel in a couple of hours (what a great way to deter your in-laws from popping in). Fortunately for us, they weren't just about to move and, more importantly, under nomadic tradition it is a duty to welcome any visitor. Mind you, we certainly weren't welcomed by the family mutt. The scraggy looking thing approached Oddcock with bared teeth, growling angrily. The horse didn't even flinch when the dog attached itself to his tail. The dog was swinging around having a grand old time. Oddcock shouted something in Mongolian and a man jumped out from a ger (in his dressing gown of course) and grabbed the dog by *its* tail and swung it around some more. Oddcock had said 'Can I come in?' which translates literally into 'Please hold the dogs!' And no, I don't understand Mongolian, it's a common greeting. I found it in my Mongolian phrase book. It also recommends we open a conversation with 'I hope your animals are fattening up nicely'. I hoped I had no need for some of the other phrases like 'Where is the cow-dung box?' and 'I have terrible constipation'. I actually hoped I didn't have to say anything at all. The Mongolian language is a collection of impossible tongue twisters. I tried a hundred times to say 'thank you' in Mongolian but it just ended up sounding like I was pissed off my head. I couldn't even pronounce Mongolia's main unit of currency. It's called a *Tögrög*. Even a simple word like road becomes '*örgönchöloo*'. And if you're in Mongolia, whatever you do, don't get lost. You won't be able to tell anyone that you are. It's '*bi töörchikhlöö*'.

This family was very la-di-da. They had a two gers. As well as milk, meat and skin for clothes, their goats produced lucrative cashmere. A horse was tethered to a pole near the front door. This was their family car. There were other horses nearby, but there was always one on standby in case someone wanted to pop out to the 7-Eleven.

The inside of the ger looked like a set from *Playschool*. The furniture was kindergarten sized. A set of tiny stools sat around a low table in the middle of the ger next to a pot-belly stove which had a metal chimney that poked out through a hole in the roof. Four small beds were squashed up against the wall. On the back wall was a dresser. It was covered in old photos, including a large shot of the ger's owner posing stiffly, but proudly, in Red Square, Moscow (Mongolia was basically a Russian state until only ten years ago). The whole room was very snug.

The family came in to greet us. There were three of them and they all had bright red rosy cheeks and the biggest and friendliest smiles I'd ever seen. The father's name was Tulga, his twenty-something year old son was Badrakh and mum was (I had to get Badrakh to write it down and I couldn't, for the life of me, pronounce it) Gnhtsetseg. Mum and dad were both in the traditional matching dressing gowns (mum had a rather fancy silk one on). Both Tulga and Badrakh, like Oddcock, were bow-legged from spending half their lives in the saddle. Gnhtsetseg gestured for us to sit down at the kiddie table, then stepped outside. I was expecting her to return with a tiny tea set and some fairy bread but she plopped a large white bucket on the table in front of us. It was full of a white substance like jelly. 'Yogurt,' Badrakh, who spoke a smattering of English, told us. I was tentative at first, but if you don't at least try anything that is offered to you in Mongolia it is considered extremely rude. I was taken quite aback— the yogurt was sweet and delicious. The best I'd ever had, in fact. This was followed by things that looked a bit like doughnuts. *Bordzig*, I was told. They were served with yak's-milk cream. Again, they were delicious. Even if they were cooked in mutton fat, and the cream was so fattening that you could feel your waistline growing with every bite you took. There is no word, or equivalent word, in Mongolian for cholesterol. That's clever, that is. If you don't have a word for it, then it doesn't exist. It must work. I didn't see one fat Mongolian. On the contrary, I saw quite a few Mongolian women with the most wonderful bodies. And, when I say I saw their *bodies*, I mean I saw their *bodies*. I went to your average sort of nightclub in Ulaanbaatar and every half an hour the dance floor would clear and two girls would come out, dance about and get their kit off. What a wonderful country.

There were two things I knew I wouldn't be having for dinner. A Mongolian BBQ and vegetables. Mongolian BBQs are a western invention and don't exist in Mongolia at all. The closest thing they have is a traditional dish called *boodog*. A goat is gutted, then all the guts and intestines and shit are put back in with spices and hot rocks, then thrown whole onto a fire. Nowadays though, the locals prefer to use a blow torch!

Dinner was meat dumplings. 'What sort of meat is it?' I asked Badrakh.

'Yes, meat.'

'Um, what type of meat?'

'Meat!'

OK, it was more than likely one of two things. It was probably either mutton, which is the Mongolian staple, or, because they had goats, goat. Then there was the slight chance it could have been one of the other meats the Mongolians eat: they include mice, rats, dogs, marmots and—a Mongolian favourite—boiled sheep's intestines. There were no vegetables. Just meat. In fact, a lot of the population don't eat vegetables at all. They don't even have a word for vegetable in their language. The closest word they have is the word for grass. According to Mongolians, only animals eat vegetables (did you hear that, vegetarians?).

The dumplings were nice. Even with the generous helpings of fat. To a Mongolian, meat without fat is unappetising and inadequate. A solid piece of fat is a delicacy. When I told Badrakh we don't eat fat, he asked me, 'what do you do with this?' I told him we throw it out. He repeated what I said in Mongolian and there was an audible gasp of shock from the Mongolians.

'Where you from?' Badrakh asked us.

'Australia,' I said.

'Ah, Bee Gees!'

That was the fourth time a Mongolian had said that when they found out where I was from. It certainly made a change. Whenever you tell foreigners you're from Australia they usually say, 'Ah, kang-ar-oo!'

'Bee Gees very good. You have brumby too.' Badrakh said with a beaming smile.

The Mongolians certainly love their horses. Out of the 150 or so breeds, Badrakh knew the Australian one. On matters equine I am no expert but I could only think of a couple. I can think of the Arab, draught and ... that's about it. I looked up a horse book when I returned home and even the ones the book said were very popular I hadn't heard of. There was the Tennessee Walking Horse, the Suffolk Punch, the French trotter and the Bosnian half-breed. There were also ones I couldn't even pronounce like Døle and Wielkopolski.

Badrakh had started riding when he was three. By seven he was hunting with a bow and arrow ... while riding. 'I do it with gun now,' he said, pointing to the wolf pelts that covered half the wall.

Tulga poured me a drink from a large metal jug into a ceramic bowl. It looked like a Fluffy Duck (the cocktail that is, not the bird). It was *airag*. Fermented mare's milk. It was bubbly and fresh (so fresh in fact, there was horsehair floating on the top). Tulga motioned for me to skol it. I grimaced as I downed it in one. It tasted a bit like sour milk. Mongolians get drunk on it. Badrakh patted his stomach, 'People not from Mongolia have many time on the toilet.' Great. I wished he'd told me that before I downed half a litre of the stuff.

Next came the Mongolian vodka. Chinggis Khaan brand vodka. Chinggis Khaan tortured and slaughtered the entire population of some cities. Now, not only is there a vodka named after him, but also a beer, chocolate, Ulaanbaatar's most expensive hotel and even

Mongolia's favourite rock band. We drank the vodka with 7-Up. Badrakh got quite merry. We found out, through Badrakh's interpreting, that Oddcock was a cattle herder and sometimes took people on horse trips. He also told us the Mongolians have a problem with drunk people riding home and falling off their horses. I suppose it would be a bit hard to take their keys off them.

We were all in bed by nine o'clock. Gnhtsetseg piled blanket upon blanket on top of me. It was warm *in* the ger now but it would get cold later. The room smelt heavily of mutton fat and cooked yak dung (it's dried out to use as fuel for the fire). In the nearby woods, wolves howled. They sounded hungry (Badrakh had told us jokingly, 'they would like you for a nice dinner.' He also told us the woods had wild bears, wild dogs and maybe even a snow leopard). The wolves were howling all around us—including in the ger. No, actually it was Oddcock snoring but he did a very good impression of a howling wolf. Amazingly, I drifted off to sleep after only a few minutes.

I had to have a pee (or, as the Mongolians say, 'I'm going to see a horse'). I had to go outside. I didn't know what time it was but the room already had a slight chill in the air. Badrakh had left a torch on the table for any nocturnal toilet visits. I quietly stepped outside. Well, after putting on most of my clothes and then stumbling head first into the door. A wooden fence surrounded the two gers. I wasn't quite sure of its purpose. Even the most cretinous of wolfs could crawl underneath it. I left the gate open in case I had to make a run for it back to the ger. A couple of wolves were still howling in the distance. There was no way I was going to use the outhouse. It was over a hundred metres away, near the edge of the forest. I opted for the less daunting middle of the field. Howling wolves tend to give one stage fright, so I couldn't pee. Meanwhile, I was sure the howls were getting closer. Finally, after quite a while, I managed to pee. Bloody hell I thought, stop making so much noise. My wee, cascading on the hard ground, sounded like a waterfall.

I was so scared I didn't even shake properly when I finished, in my rush to get back to the ger.

It must have got cold during the night. When I awoke, my water bottle, which was next to my bed, was frozen solid. Happily, I was still snuggly warm in my bed. I felt like a lazy sod while I watched Gnhtsetseg start the fire with some yak dung, but she motioned for us to stay in bed. By the time I crawled out of bed the ger was nice and warm. When I say crawled out of bed, that's exactly what I did. I couldn't feel my bottom. I walked like I had a ger pole shoved up my arse.

I washed my face with a mug of warm water. Boy, I could have done with a hot spa (and a massage, and a couple of soft cushions to sit on). During the winter, Mongolians don't wash at all. They don't wash themselves or their clothes. A lot of Australian taxidrivers must be Mongolian.

Breakfast was more doughnut things, yak's-milk cream and *suteytsai*. This is warmed mare's-milk tea with salt and rancid yak's-milk butter added. As long as you dodged the horse's hairs it wasn't too bad. The Mongolian staples of mutton fat and rancid yak's-milk butter may sound unappetising, but at least the country doesn't have a McDonalds. I was so excited when I found out they didn't have one. Badrakh had never even heard of them. What a wonderful country. Please, please, please, please don't let them into your country. A McRancid yak's-milk butter burger may sound very tempting, but a drive-thru ger in the middle of the Gobi would just look dreadful.

There was lots of grunting and groaning as we mounted our horses. 'I'm gonna make my horse go today,' Simon exclaimed, 'I'm going to show him who's boss!' Ten minutes later he was already lagging behind. We crunched our way over frozen streams as we were led up and down steep, forested slopes and across boggy marshes. We rode through the middle of a few wild yaks, who glanced up nonchalantly from their quiet grazing as we shuffled past.

Lunch was steamed bread and left-over cold dumplings. The fat had congealed nicely. I really didn't want to get back on Mori. I could not only not feel my bottom any more, I couldn't feel my thighs either.

After twenty minutes, Simon finally gave up. He dismounted and started walking. 'My knees are rooted!' he moaned. He'd only walked twenty metres when Oddcock turned back and started shouting something. 'What's he saying?' Anouk asked. 'I think he's saying . . . get back on, you wuss!' I said, laughing. Oddcock was motioning him to get back on. Simon grumbled something about a horse Nazi and remounted his stubborn steed.

I went to reach for my camera and couldn't find it. I'd dropped it somewhere. Oddcock had taken a photo of me maybe fifteen minutes before, so I must have dropped it after that. I wasn't that worried about the camera, but I wanted my photos. You can't replace them (I've always said that if my house was on fire, the first thing I would grab would be my photo albums. Oh, and then probably my wife). I turned Mori around and headed back. Oddcock was already out of sight. I passed Simon and Anouk and told them to wait there. I shuffled along slowly scanning the ground. After about ten minutes I came to a large patch of long grass. I couldn't see through the thick grass so I jumped off. Mori took this as a good opportunity to nick off. He bolted and stopped abruptly thirty metres away. Oh, good! I took a step towards him. Mori took a step back. We played this little game for five minutes until Mori got bored and trotted away. OK, now what could I do? Oddcock would have to come looking for me. Wouldn't he?

Oddcock was surprised (to say the least) to find me standing in a field without my horse, and a few kilometres away from where I was supposed to be. Oddcock charged off and was back with Mori in tow in under three minutes. Oddcock looked genuinely troubled when I told him (well, after five minutes of charades anyway) that I had dropped my camera. We marched back up to the top of the hill where Oddcock had earlier taken my photo. We'd already lost almost two hours and I was happy to give up the search, but Oddcock was determined to find it.

In the distance I could hear a galloping horse and Anouk's voice. I couldn't figure out what she was saying. She was screaming something. I just hoped Simon hadn't been eaten by the vultures. 'Simon's found your camera!' she was screaming. Good old Simon. And, more importantly, bless his little lumbering horse. He'd shuffled ever so slowly back along the track and Simon had spotted it in the grass.

Just when I thought (and prayed for my legs' sake) that we couldn't be far from Oddcock's ger, we rounded a corner to find a whole new valley. I still had quite a bit more pain in my bottom to go yet. It was slowly getting dark. In the shadows formed by the nearby mountains, it was already getting noticeably cold. It had been probably twenty degrees for most of the day. Suddenly, it was around five degrees. My lips were parched from the dry mountain air. I'd left my lip balm back at Oddcock's ger but I wasn't too keen to use the Mongolian cure for dry lips. They rub their own urine on their lips—in Mongolia they take 'suck more piss' literally.

After about an hour, Oddcock indicated that we should gallop. One quick 'chu' and Mori was off. It was such an exhilarating feeling thundering through a landscape with no fences, no telephone poles, no buildings and no people. Just us, mountains and a few wild yaks. It would have been perfect, if not for the fact that every stride made my thighs feel like they were getting torn apart and I could feel my internal organs shaking loose. Even Simon had his horse in a gallop, of sorts.

It was dark when we crawled into Oddcock's camp. I clumsily dismounted Mori and collapsed on the ground. I looked like a tortoise on its back. My legs were stuck in the 'frog mount' position. I couldn't move them. Simon was the same. We both broke into uncontrollable laughter. I kept laughing even when I noticed my elbow was poking into an impressively large pile of cow shit.

Later that evening (lying in bed because I couldn't move) I was flicking through my Mongolian phrase book when I came across the word 'mori'. It was Mongolian for horse. I'd spent two days calling my horse 'horse'.

Train

Beijing to Moscow
October, 2001

Km 7685 – I found a dead Chinese guy in my compartment. Wait a sec, he moved! The train was still twenty minutes away from departure and this Chinese fellow was already fast asleep in the top bunk. I left him snoring away and went for a wander to see if there were any live people on the train. I found Barnaby, from Sydney, squashed into a compartment with three tiny Chinese people and their impressively large collection of cardboard boxes. This was Barnaby's second attempt to catch the Trans-Mongolian train. He'd got pissed, slept in and missed the earlier train (he'd been celebrating the fact he was leaving!). That was a week ago.

I went back to my compartment and found Simon and Anouk sitting quietly on the bed below the sleeping Chinese fellow. Out on the platform our carriage attendant (*fuwuyuen* in Chinese) stood to attention next to the door looking quite dapper in his crisp uniform and hat. Even if it *was* too tight for him. The buttons were straining to stay done up.

Km 7680 – Only 7680 kilometres to go! There is a signpost *every* kilometre counting down the kilometres from Beijing to Moscow. This epic train journey (known as the Trans-Mongolian) takes seven days and crosses seven different time zones (and three countries—China, Mongolia and Russia). It's the equivalent of travelling from New York to San Francisco. And back again. I was breaking up my journey by getting off in Ulaanbaator, the capital of Mongolia, and then Irkutsk in Siberia for a few days. (I can't go too long without a shower so I have to break up any long trip). Those who are looking for a real marathon effort can catch a series of trains from Vila Real de Santo Antonio in Portugal to Ho Chi Minh City in Vietnam. The total distance is 17 852 kilometres. Fifteen days on trains—now that's a long time without a shower.

In the cabin next-door a Mongolian girl was playing Britney singing 'Oh Baby Baby' on a state-of-the-art CD player. The Chinese guy was now snoring louder than the rumbling of the train. It sounded a lot better than Britney.

Km 7638 – The suburbs stretched on forever (as I suppose they have to when the population is 12 million!). There was apartment block after apartment block, surrounded by people either riding a bike or squatting by the side of the road (the Chinese are very good at this. That and spitting).

Km 7622 – Apparently you could see the Great Wall here. I ran from the compartment to the corridor and back again, but somehow managed to miss the whole damn thing. I did get a rather nice photo of the back of someone's head, though. When I opened the window in our compartment to take another photo, a mighty cold wind blew in. Straight into the face of the sleeping Chinese fellow. He didn't move. The wind was blowing his hair around like mad, but still he didn't move. It took two of us five minutes to get the window closed again. The Chinese guy didn't even flinch when I screamed out 'FUCK!' after jamming my finger.

Km 7492 – The ghastly haze that hung over Beijing like a dirty blanket had been replaced by clear blue skies. We passed through fields of wheat and lines of poplar trees. Majestic snow-capped mountains lay in the distance. The view out the window was like a moving postcard. That was all very well, but I needed a crap (courtesy of some dodgy Chinese dumplings I'd eaten the day before). We'd only been on the train for three hours and the toilet at the end of the carriage already stank. The horrific smell was creeping up the corridor. I must admit, though, that I'd contributed to that smell somewhat. I'd been for a wee an hour before and, as the train suddenly lurched around a corner, I'd pissed all over the window.

Km 7461 – 'Just another shitty town,' Barnaby moaned as we pulled into our first stop. The whole city was grey. Grey roads, grey houses, grey factories, grey cars, grey bikes and even grey people. Nails must be expensive there. The roofs on most of the houses were being held down with rocks.

The Fat Controller (for that is what I christened the attendant) didn't let us out until he'd finished polishing the door handles(!). I rushed to the station toilet. Inside was a long concrete ditch. A neat line of Chinese men squatted over the ditch casually pooing away. Their buttocks were virtually touching each other. One chap was sipping on a large mug of tea and smoking a pipe. A man who looked to be at least a hundred shuffled over to let me in. I stood there for a minute. There was no way I could squat like that. The Chinese have the ability to squat with their feet flat. I know if I attempted it I'd fall in the ditch. I apologised (I'm not quite sure why) and scuttled out.

Then again, it could have been worse. A friend of mine had a rather strange experience in an outhouse toilet in northern Thailand. For a start the outhouse itself was odd, because there was a foot-high gap between the floor and the wall. When he squatted down over the hole in the ground he noticed something else: there was a large, well-worn stick propped up against the wall next to him. He thought nothing of it and went about his business. Halfway through, he felt what seemed like something nibbling on his bum. He looked down to see a pig eating his poo as it was coming out. The pig was trying to get its snout right up his bottom. That is what the stick was for. It was to beat away the pigs.

I shouldn't complain then, I only had a somewhat smelly loo to face.

Km 7401 to 7338 – That's about how long it took Barnaby and I to walk the length of the train to the dining car. We opened and closed 28 doors along the way. We passed the posh people in the 'flash' compartments. They were in first class (or 'soft class'). We were in second class (or 'hard class'). There were only two beds in a first-class compartment (as opposed to our four) but, besides being a bit more spacious, the only real difference was that they had a couple of nice paintings on the wall and a rather ornate table lamp. Back in 1901, people in first class on the Trans-Siberian didn't just have large compartments with a separate lounge area and adjoining shower and toilet. They also had access to a library, piano bar, hot bath, gym, barber and pharmacy, and at night one of the toilets was converted to a dark room for the benefit of any photographers on board.

Km 7334 – I had 'Crispy chicken and ruce' for lunch. There was a huge 'No Smoking' sign above the door inside the dining car. Well, the English version said no smoking, but I think the Chinese above it must have said 'Please smoke with abandon'. *Everyone* was smoking, including the cook, attendants, waitress and security guard (whose gun, I noticed when he walked past, was just about to fall out of its holster).

In between attempts to dissect my stringy chicken, I caught glimpses of the Great Wall out the window. At the base of the distant barren mountains the wall snaked its way up and over ridges for the next 50 kilometres. Barnaby wisely opted for a liquid lunch of beer. My rice was very nice, though. The Chinese do a good rice (and ruce, too).

Km 7326 – The Chinese guy was still asleep. His snoring sounded like he was choking to death. His mouth was open wide enough to fit a pillow (it was *very* tempting!).

Km 7321 – Where was everyone? There are 1.2 billion people in this country and I hadn't seen a single soul for over an hour.

Km 7314 – Ah, there they all are. The city of Detong. Another dirty, grey, depressing city. The platform was full. Hardly any of the crowd were passengers, however. There were ladies selling noodles and beer and the most dirty-looking children I'd ever seen. The Fat Controller emptied a large bag of rubbish into a bin and the children dived in before he'd even finished. They were after food scraps. One of them gave a smaller boy a good whack in the face to get what looked like my left-over chicken carcass.

Barnaby bought some noodles from the Hunchback of Detong. Barnaby had eaten only packet noodles for the last two weeks (he told me he was on a tight budget). Two other Australians from first class were also buying noodles. 'What are you guys doing here?' Barnaby asked. 'Don't you have room service?'

Km 7253 – I tried to have a little nap but was woken by 'Oh Baby Baby' coming from next door. Barnaby came back from the now very smelly toilet. 'I just walked past the Mongolian girl from next door,' he said with a big grin on his face. 'She's in her underwear! She's got huge tits'. I went for a wee look, but she was dressed and listening to 'Oh Baby Baby' again. I walked past the Fat Controller's tiny compartment ('den') on the way to the loo. Six of his fellow attendants were squeezed in with him smoking and eating large bowls of noodles at the same time (that's nothing, two days before I'd seen a Chinese guy smoking while he cleaned his teeth).

Km 7234 – I stood in the corridor staring out the window. A lot of people seemed to be doing this. A Chinese man who was standing next to me asked me if I liked Chinese food. 'Yes, I love it,' I said (besides dodgy dumplings of course). He was very surprised when I told him that a Chinese restaurant in Melbourne, The Flower Drum, had been voted best restaurant for the last four years. He almost fell over when I told him how much it cost per head—about $150. 'That is one month pay for many Chinese peoples,' he said. No wonder he almost fell over. That's the equivalent of the average Australian spending $3000 on a meal (and forget shouting your girlfriend).

Km 7222 – The dead Chinese guy finally woke up (probably had something to do with the Mongolian kid who burst into our compartment with a toy ray-gun and proceeded to make loud electronic whizzes and beeps into his ear). He grunted, then rolled over and went back to sleep. I was close to calling the Fat Controller before that. He honestly did look dead.

Km 7185 – The four of us trekked down to the dining car for a beer to celebrate the first 500 kilometres. By the time we got there, we'd reached 514.

A Chinese guy at the table next to us blew his nose on the pretty lace curtains. We stayed for dinner (I suggested that by the time we walked back to our compartment it would be dinner time, anyway). The dinner menu was the same as lunch. There was a choice of Crispy chicken, Crispy pork or Crispy mushrooms. As we sat and admired a glorious sunset, the Chinese fellow next to us was having another good go at the lace curtains.

Km 7130ish – Even though it was dark I knew we were in the Gobi desert. I could taste it in my mouth and feel it achingly in my eyes. The whole carriage was under a brown gritty cloud of dust. The gale outside rushed round the crawling train with an eerie moan. Everything in the compartment became thick with dust. I just hoped it was getting into the electronics of the Mongolian girl's CD player next door.

The sleeping Chinese man was gone. He (or someone) had taken his bags too. It only took Barnaby five minutes to move into his spot.

Km 6857 – 'Bloody hell,' Barnaby said as he stormed into the compartment.

'What's happened?' I said with concern.

'The Mongolian girl's in her knickers and bending over her bed!'

I went for a look (for a bit of cultural enlightenment only of course), but she was dressed again. I think Barnaby was making it up.

Km 6843 – 'Gee, it's cold,' Anouk said with a shiver. 'This is nothing,' I said, as we scampered up the platform of the last Chinese town before the Mongolian border. 'Ulaanbaator is the coldest capital city in the world. In winter it regularly gets to minus 40.' 'I'm glad I bought a hat then,' Barnaby quipped.

We were stuck at the station for two hours while the train went off to the 'bogie-changing shed'. The Russians (being a paranoid lot at times) built all their railway tracks three inches wider than the rest of the world's so other countries couldn't invade their country by train (as you would of course!). Giant hydraulic lifts raise the carriages and the bogies are replaced with Russian ones.

'Is there a shortage of toilet paper in Mongolia?' I asked no-one in particular. While we waited at the station, Mongolian ladies rushed outside to the shops and returned with huge packages of toilet paper and boxes of grapes. They sat in the waiting room laughing and getting merry on Mongolian beer. We were surrounded by The Great Wall of Toilet Paper.

Km 6838 – We only moved a few kilometres then stopped. We were at the actual border now. An hour passed. I needed a piss. Because we were at a station, the toilet had been locked by the Fat Controller (so people wouldn't wee on the station). I pleaded with him to let me use it, but he just shook his head. I motioned that I would piss out the window. He motioned that he would chop my dick off if I tried.

Km 6364 – Ahhhhhhh! Finally, a piss. The Fat Controller let me use the toilet even though we'd stopped at a station. We were in Mongolia. I couldn't piss on a Chinese station, but it was all right to piss on a Mongolian one.

Madam Lash was not happy with Barnaby. He peeked his head out of the compartment and she angrily waved him back in. Madam Lash was the Mongolian border guard. She was slowly moving down the carriage checking passports. Barnaby called her Madam Lash because he said she looked as if she was on her way home from an S&M party. 'Look out everyone,' Barnaby said, 'Here comes Madam Lash. I think she's got a whip!' When she finally got to our door and grunted for our passports, I burst into hysterical laughter. She wore long black suede boots, a green mini-skirt, a nasty looking jacket covered in buttons and badges, bright red lippy, a shaved head and a tall menacing looking hat. She looked very angry. I was hysterical. It was two o'clock in the morning and I was tired. All four of us started laughing. Madam Lash screamed at us. She took stamping passports very seriously. I was sure her whip was about to come out. I tried desperately not to laugh, but Barnaby was sniggering under his blanket. After a story I heard from an American guy I met in Beijing, I was risking the chance of getting hauled off the train, but I still couldn't stop. He'd been travelling with a young English guy for a month, and when they got to the Mongolian border, the English guy was grilled as to why he only had a Mongolian visa for ten days and he'd been there for eighteen. They wanted US$5000 to let him go. 'I don't have it!' he said. 'OK . . . US$250, then,' the border guard told him. He didn't have that, either. He borrowed $40 from the American. The last the American guy saw of him he was surrounded by guards on the platform as the train pulled out. He didn't even get to say goodbye. He never heard from him again. 'He's still got my forty bucks, too,' he said.

Km ? – I went to the toilet in the middle of the night (the rocking of the train shakes your bladder around and makes you want to go all the bloody time) and bumped into the Fat Controller in his long johns polishing door handles in the corridor. He stood to attention. I had to squeeze past him. I just fitted passed his stomach. I turned around to see him furiously polishing the door handle I'd just touched. If only he'd showed such cleaning devotion to the toilet.

Km 6473 – We awoke in the middle of the Gobi desert. Looking out the window as I lay in bed, I could see vast undulating plains covered in short straw-coloured grass. The sky was a deep blue. We were in 'the land of the big blue sky' or, as Mongolia's also known, 'the land of no fences'. Maybe they should change that to 'the land of many power poles'. They crisscrossed the desert as far as the eye could see. Power poles ran along next to the track as well. Perched on just about every second power pole was a buzzard. They're smart bastards those buzzards. They knew that when the train went by, mice would scurry out of their burrows. Thousands of them would scatter in all directions. The buzzard would then have a smorgasbord of critters to choose from. They looked really cocky about it, too.

Km 6417 – 'I'm in Mongolia,' I said, as I stood on the platform of Choyr train station. I never in my wildest dreams thought I'd be saying that in my lifetime. An icy wind blew up from the Gobi desert and blew sand up my pants. Locals were getting off the train with their packages of toilet paper and grapes. Packs of what looked like rabid dogs ran up and down the platform. There was no one selling food here. Just a little old man selling Mongolian vodka. He looked as if he'd sampled quite a bit of it himself over the years. Simon bought a large bottle for two dollars. 'A good price, hey?' Simon said. I tasted it. It tasted the way I imagine battery acid might.

Km 6144 – We pulled into Ulaanbaator to the accompaniment of guess who. 'Oh Baby Baby'. The suburbs of Ulaanbaator were made up of neat fenced-off-yards. In the middle of each yard was a ger. It looked like the whole city was on a camping holiday.

The Mongolian women on the train were greeted by their husbands. They ran along the platform as the train pulled into the station frantically searching for their smuggling spouse. As soon as the train came to a halt, the men jumped aboard and began hastily unloading the toilet paper. Either there was an incredible demand for toilet paper in Mongolia, or the men were really hanging out for a crap.

Km 6144 – (4 days later) The *provodnitsa* (Russian for 'attendant') ushered me onto the train. She scared the hell out of me. I scurried aboard. She only had two white teeth at the very front. The rest were stainless steel. She looked like Jaws from the James Bond films (but not as good looking).

A rather robust English fellow struggled into the compartment. He had the biggest bag I'd ever seen. 'What's in that?' I asked jokingly, 'Your rock collection?'

'Nah. A dead fox,' he said sincerely.

He smelt terribly of BO (or was that the dead fox?). Bloody hell, he's not going to smell any better after two nights. Two German girls squeezed their way into the compartment while Steve (the robust Englishman) tried unsuccessfully to put his bag away, all the while puffing and panting. He had to leave it between the seats. It wouldn't fit anywhere else. He himself was going to have trouble fitting in his bed.

I opened the window to let in some fresh air. One and a half minutes later Jaws stormed into the compartment screaming at us. I wasn't going to mess with Jaws. She looked like she could bite through metal.

Km 6000 – (I'm guessing here. It's dark outside) Steve wouldn't shut up. He'd been everywhere (apparently). Every time you said something he would top it (in his own estimation at least) with a better story or superior opinion. He asked what CD I was listening too. Travis, I said. 'Oh, there's a lot better Scottish bands than them,' he said. Who, I thought? The Bay City Rollers?

'I'll get really sick of these packet noodles,' I said (there was no dining car on this leg, so it was BYO food).

'Noodles!' Steve guffawed, 'I had to eat bats' testicles in Botswana for three days.'

Jaws came in and dumped our sheets on the bed. The sheets looked and felt as if they were made of tea towels. 'These are comfortable!' Steve exclaimed. 'In Laos I had to sleep under maggot-infested blankets.'

I was going to go for a wander up the carriage to get away from Steve, but in the end I was glad I didn't. The two German girls did a full strip (Germans are never shy) before getting into their PJs. I tried not to look. Honest.

Km 5950ish – We'd only been going for a couple of hours, but I was going to have to kill Steve. He told me *his* horse-riding trek in Mongolia was better than mine because he rode on an authentic Mongolian wooden saddle and not a wussy leather one. It was time to get out the Walkman. I didn't think my batteries would last the 36 hours to Irkutsk, though.

Km 5900ish – I finally dozed off to Travis (who are nowhere near as good as the Bay City Rollers, apparently!).

Km ? – Steve got out of his bunk noisily in the middle of the night and crashed out the door. We heard him throw up down the corridor (must have been the bat's testicles). At least he attempted to clean it up. Well, if he hadn't, Jaws would have probably bitten his head off. When he returned to bed, I was tempted to say, 'That's not a vomit! When I was in Budapest ...'

Km 5735 – The train had stopped sometime in the middle of the night. We were at the Mongolian/Russian border. Jaws was patrolling the corridor. She'd changed out of her uniform and was wearing bright green tracky pants and a floral T-shirt. She still looked scary.

'Gee, we've been here a while,' I said (about three hours, I figured).

'This is nothing,' Steve bellowed from the top bunk. 'I was stuck at the Moldovan border for nine days!'

That was it. I was going to kill him.

I started speaking (in my clumsy way) in German to Sylvia and Antje, so Steve wouldn't keep saying something like, 'Ah, you think the border here is tough. I once had a full rectal probe with twelve inches of garden hose.'

Km 5735 – (still) What a miserable place. Out the window I could see a grey station, dilapidated antique train carriages and grey soldiers standing in the cold rain.

Km 5735 – (yes, still) While I was filling out my *seventh* form, I said to the guard, 'This is ridiculous!'. He just stared at me. Steve grunted, 'This is not ridiculous. On the Sudanese border, I had to fill out 97 forms.'

We were the only carriage left on the track. God knows where the other ones had gone. I had to laugh. Not too hard, though. I needed a piss.

Km 5735 – (OK, now it's getting silly) Christ. How long does it take to stamp a passport? I was trapped. I couldn't go to the toilet and Steve's BO was doing my head in. Jaws was smiling happily.

Km 5735 – We moved at last. Six hours and ten minutes after we stopped.

Km 5733 – We stopped. We'd moved two kilometres. Well, at least we were in Russia.

Km 5733 – It was 'groundhog' day. The same Russian guards had asked us for our passports three times. They would disappear for fifteen minutes, come back and ask the same questions, then snigger when they read my surname from my passport 'Tack . . . her' (must mean something funny in Russian).

Km 5733 – It was snowing. We'd been here so long it had turned into winter. We'd been here two hours. I was reading *Harry Potter* (trying to take my mind of needing a piss) and I was jealous. Harry was on the Hogwarts Express and it was moving.

I begged Jaws to let me go the toilet. She finally opened the door when I mimed pissing my pants.

Km 5717 – It was bleak outside. But it looked beautiful. It looked beautiful because we were moving. Eight hours it took to stamp a couple of passports. An icy wind swept across a desolate ('This isn't desolate, you should see the Sudan') landscape of stunted trees and snow-covered hills. We passed a station where everyone was wearing huge coats and fur hats. One guy would have put the guards at Buckingham Palace to shame. He looked like he had a whole black bear on his head.

Km 5688 – It was dark already. Meanwhile, we'd spent most of the day at the border. Music suddenly burst out of a speaker in our room. Well, if you want to call it music. It was like a Russian version of Dire Straits. I tried to turn the volume down but the knob wouldn't budge. Gee, a Swiss army knife comes in handy sometimes. Not only does it have a bottle opener and toothpick, it also has a 'Russian train speaker fucker-upperer'. But alas there was another speaker right outside our door as well. We had a choice. Close the door and suffocate under Steve's BO or leave it open and listen to Direski Straitski. Thank God for the Walkman.

Km 5656 – We had quite a long stop at the town of Ude Ude (this is where the Trans-Mongolian joins onto the Trans-Siberian line). While the two German girls and I were having a beer at the Ude Ude train station bar, Jaws came bolting up the platform towards us. 'Train ... go!' she yelled when she saw us. Bless her big woollen socks, she was worried we'd miss the train. She gave us a big steely grin when we hopped back on board. She wasn't going to lose any of her flock.

Km 5025 – I awoke with a fright. Jaws was leaning over me and all I could see was a mouth full of silver teeth. She was shouting, 'Irkutsk, Irkutsk!' I pulled up the blinds. We were in Siberia. The menacing grey clouds and driving rain and snow from yesterday had given way to glorious clear blue skies. We were passing through a village straight out of a Hans Christian Andersen tale. Tiny wooden houses with intricate window frames of green and blue were covered in fresh snow and wispy smoke trickled out of the even tinier chimneys. Behind the small village was a thick forest of white birch trees already stripped bare for the winter.

Km 5020 – Irkutsk station was packed with ugly Russians wearing fur hats. As we slowly pulled into the station, I noticed there was not a single person smiling. Then, among a sea of grey and black, I saw a sign with BRIAN THACKER on it. I could not believe it. I was even more surprised when I saw who was holding the sign. It was Anna Kournikova (well, a girl who looked vaguely like her). I'd booked a tour to Lake Baikal before I'd left Australia. I was expecting a busload of people but it was just me and Anna Kournikova. My own personal guide. Even a rather fresh temperature of minus five degrees couldn't wipe the smile off my face as I stepped down from the train.

Km 5000 – (two days later) I walked the length of the train trying to find someone to have a '5000 kilometres to go' beer with. I could only see Russians. There were now only two of us in our compartment. Akihiro (from Japan) and I seemed to be the only non-Russians on the whole train (in 1930 a travel writer was surprised to meet a Russian in the dining car. The whole train was full of foreigners).

This would be the longest stretch for me. Four days and three nights. Boy, was the toilet going to smell after that! I wouldn't smell much better, either.

Km 4995 – Our new attendant looked like your run-of-the-mill roly-poly hospital matron. She had orange lipstick on. She came into our compartment and vacuumed the carpet. We'd only been going for 25 kilometres.

Km 4919 – I had dozed off in the warm sun that streamed through the window, but was woken up by a gigantic sweaty Russian with a trolley of beer and chips. He looked like a mad scientist. He was wearing a lab coat and thick round glasses, and tufts of wild hair stuck out of his balding head. He gave me huge friendly smile. '*Sprechen ze Deutsch*?' he said. '*Ja, ein bischen*,' I said with surprise. He didn't speak any English and greeted every foreigner with, 'Do you speak German?' He asked me where I came from, then asked if I had any Australian coins for his collection. I gave him a few I found at the bottom of my bag. He then invited Akihiro and me to the dining car after dinner to see his entire collection. When he'd left Akihiro said, 'You speak Russian very well.' He looked quite puzzled when I told him we were speaking German.

Km 4748 – We were treated to a delightful sunset as Akihiro and I sat down in the empty dining car. Hopefully the restaurant wasn't run by the local Buryats people. Apparently they don't like doing the dishes. Neither do I, but I wouldn't quite go as far as they do to get out of it. Dinner implements are not washed, they are *licked* clean then put back in the cupboard. Unwashed plates, spoons and forks are often passed from family member to family member to have a lick until they're clean.

The dining car was very flash. The nicest one so far. The tables had lace tablecloths and linen napkins. There was even a large array of meals on the menu. That was until we started pointing at things and the waitress kept saying *Nyet*. By the time we'd finished pointing there were four things left available (well, ten if you count the six different brands of cigarettes—which were listed in the middle of entree and main course). When in Russia, do as the Russians do, so I ordered *borscht*. It seemed like a good idea but, no matter where you are, and whichever way you look at it, *borscht* is still beetroot and onion soup. This was nothing like the Trans-Siberian in 1908. Passengers in the dining car could feast on caviar, French champagne, roast partridge with sugared cranberries, and fresh sturgeon (the chef had a tank of live fish in his kitchen).

Km 4670ish – Vadim the mad coin collector joined us after dinner. Under one arm he was carrying a huge pile of coin books. In the other he had a large bottle of vodka. To the accompaniment of the Russian version of the Partridge Family piping through the hard-to-escape speakers, Vadim very proudly showed us all the coins in his collection. All 3500 of them. It was the only the large glasses of vodka (that he kept topping up) that kept me from dozing off. Akihiro got pissed off his head and was trying to sing along with The Partridgski Family.

Km ? – I stumbled to the toilet at 3 a.m. to find Akihiro asleep on the floor. He was cuddling the toilet bowl. As you will have gathered from my earlier descriptions, the toilet is not pleasant. Unlike the dining car, the toilet had not been upgraded during the journey. Nor had it been licked clean by the Buryats. It would be three more days until Akihiro could have a shower. I tried not to touch the wet bits on his clothes as I carried him back to our compartment.

Km 3877 – It was nine o'clock (I think). Or maybe it was ten. But the sun had only just risen, so it must be eight. I spent the next half-hour trying to figure out the time. Do I put my watch back an hour or two? Or not at all? Now I was really confused. I'd already lost track of what day it was.

I pulled back the curtains to see we were in Austria. It looked like Austria. Pine forests blanketed in snow covered the surrounding hills. Next to the track a giant hamster was riding a horse-drawn sleigh. Actually it was a large man wearing so many layers of fur that he looked like a giant hamster.

Km 3852 – A greasy fry-up is good for a hangover. But this was just grease without the fry-up. There was a fried egg somewhere hidden in all that grease. Probably not a good idea to get tanked up on the first night. I felt like shite, and a shower was still two-and-a-half days away.

Km 3842.5 – The halfway point between Beijing and Moscow. I'd planned to have a celebratory drink at this point but, beside the fact I was feeling a bit how's-your-father, it was only 10.30 a.m. (or maybe 9.30?). I celebrated instead by raiding my cherished Cherry Ripe supplies.

What is the Russian obsession with the band Smokie? I must have heard 'Oh Carol' fifteen times so far in Russia. They were playing it on the train again. I suppose it was marginally better than the Russian version of Britney Spears that was playing earlier.

Km 3670 – I tried to use the toilet at the train station we were stopped at. It was closed. On the way back to my carriage I checked out the station kiosk. They sold beer, cigarettes, chewing gum and brass door-handles (you never know when you will need a brass door-handle on the Trans-Siberian).

I explained to the Matron that the station toilet was closed, so she kindly unlocked the train's toilet for me. 'No poo poo,' she said as I stepped in. When I had finished, I stepped out onto the platform again. Behind me I heard the toilet flush. The wind caught the piss and sprayed it onto the platform. I just got out of the way in time. A huge 'poo poo' followed.

Speaking of which, one of the funniest things I've seen in my life involved a train and pissing. When I was fifteen I was catching a train home from an Australian Rules football final at the MCG. There had been 98 000 people at the game, and most of them looked like they were on the platform. It was packed. Even after hundreds of us had squeezed onto the train, the platform remained full. As the train slowly pulled out of the station, a drunk bloke next to me forced opened the door, pulled out his old fellow and casually started pissing. By the time we'd reached the end of the platform, he would have pissed on two hundred very shocked people. I almost wet myself laughing.

I jumped back aboard to see Akihiro stepping out of the toilet. I told him he better keep away from the Matron. She wouldn't be happy with him 'poo pooing'.

Km 3567 – I walked the length of the train. I passed the Matron busily scrubbing the toilets (and what a wonderful job she did. It was spotless. Well, until I pissed all over the window again, anyway). I wandered into third class. It was basically just one big carriage piled high with triple bunks full of extras from a bad 1970s spy film. Jaws's whole family was here. There was enough stainless steel here to build a hundred kitchen sinks. The smell was terrible. Steve would have got some funny looks if he was here. He would have smelt too nice. Squashed into one corner was the Russian weightlifting team. I am not joking. One was wearing his Russian national team weightlifting tights! (Just the thing to wear on a train. I'll have to remember to bring mine next time.)

Back in 1900, this carriage would have been luxury. Back then there was a fifth class. There were no beds. In fact there weren't even any seats. On the outside was a sign that read 'To carry 12 horses or 43 men' (or '4 Steves and his bags').

Km 3546 – Siberia: Beautiful one minute, God-awful the next. This could be their tourism slogan. In between the Hans Christian Andersen fairytale villages and Austrianesque landscapes were huge grey industrial cities. Rows and rows of drab apartment blocks that looked like they were made of papier-mâché were surrounded by rubbish. There was rubbish everywhere. It was piled high in the streets, in parks and in people's yards. Most of it seemed to consist of Coke cans.

Km 3539 – I stepped off the train for some fresh air. Well, I hoped it was fresh air. On the 6 April 1993, a radioactive waste reprocessing plant in this area blew up, contaminating an area of 120 km^2. As I stepped onto the platform, I was rushed by old stooped-over ladies dragging ingenious carts made of wooden crates, string and old scooter wheels. They were selling beer, bread, yogurt, buns, dried fish and whole roast ducks. I didn't want to develop a second head, so I didn't buy anything. Akihiro bought a dried fish. I tried to explain the second head he would develop, but he didn't understand. Either that or he wanted a second head.

Km 3439 – I had tried all the meals on the menu now. As well as the *borscht* there were frankfurters, steak (I don't think it was beef, probably yak) and roast chicken. Each meal came with sixteen chips, twelve peas and two slices of fluorescent green pickle (here comes my extra head!). The Russian beer was surprisingly tasty, though.

It was loud in the dining car. Smokie and Suzie Quatro were blasting out 'Stumblin' in' and there were two tables of drunk Russians. They weren't eating. They were just drinking vodka.

Km 3414 – Well, I wanted a bit of excitement on the train. I certainly got it. On the way back from the dining car, I passed through one of the small corridors that are at the end of each carriage. People congregate there to smoke, and I was confronted by two drunk Russians. They were both in their early twenties and both were pissed out of their heads. One of them asked me a question in Russian. His eyes were rolling around in his head. He was way out of it. I said I didn't understand, so he started shouting at me, grabbing my arm so I couldn't get away. He reached into his jacket and brought out a gun. A gun? It took a second for my brain to register that he was holding a real-life handgun. As he was bringing the gun up to my head, his friend screamed out 'NYET! Nyet!' and grabbed his arm. The gun fell to the floor. They both dived to the ground and a struggle to get the gun ensued. It took me another few seconds for my brain to figure out that it was probably a good idea to get the hell out of there. I opened the door and bolted down two carriages to my compartment and locked the door. My heart was racing like mad. Who said this train trip would be boring?

Km 3402 – There was a knock on the door. As soon as I'd got back to the safety of the compartment, I'd locked the door. My heart skipped a few beats. The door opened. How were they getting in? The door was locked. It was only the Matron (she had a key). She proceeded to vacuum the floor.

Km 3335 – I thought I was going to have a heart attack. It was eleven o'clock and I was snuggled up in bed, when there was another loud knock on the door. 'Hello,' I said, with a whimper. A man answered in Russian. Oh well, this was it. I'd had a good life. I couldn't complain. He knocked again. I opened the door waiting for the mad gunman to casually finish me off. Two giant Russian lads stepped in. One was wearing a tight singlet. He was built like Arnold Schwarzenegger. I could go on and say they beat Akihiro and myself to a pulp, but they couldn't have been nicer fellows. They'd just got on the train at Novosibirsk and were staying in our compartment. I was lying in bed in my underwear but it didn't stop Dima producing two large bottles of beer. He was so thrilled that there was an Australian and a Japanese guy in his compartment. We sat up for three hours drinking beer and eating peanuts (all the while I was still lying in bed in my underwear).

Dima and Oleg had been to Train University together. And no, I'm not making that up. Oleg showed me a brochure. The place was huge. There were lots of pictures of the scariest looking teachers I've ever seen. They would give you nightmares. There were also photos of students standing around on train tracks in blizzards (that looked like fun!). Dima was now a train carriage designer and Oleg was a lecturer at the Train University. The Train University was in Irkutsk. 'It's very famous in Russia,' Oleg told me.

Km 2466 – I awoke to a dull and freezing day. Snow lashed the streaky windows. The train trundled past frozen salt lakes and soggy fields of wet snow. Oh, and birch trees. There were always birch trees. I woke a couple of times during the night (wondering where the mad Russian gunman was), but went back to sleep feeling safe. I had my own personal beefy Russian bodyguards in my room. 'Don't worry. I will kill him,' Dima assured me.

Km 2409 – Dima, Oleg, Akihiro and I put together an absolute breakfast feast. And, what a feast it was. Dima's mum's homemade hamburgers and boiled eggs, Oleg's uncle's homemade cheese and a huge loaf of crusty bread, Akihiro's Russian sausage and Japanese Teriyaki tuna, and my contribution of tomatoes, bananas and hot chocolate from Australia. Possibly the best breakfast I'd ever had. All the while watching Siberia pass by the window.

Km 2144 – The town of Tyumen was another huge industrial city (the largest in Siberia). It was another Godforsaken place. I couldn't imagine living here. Siberia is frozen solid for eight months of the year and a mosquito ridden swamp for the rest.

Dima was just about jumping up and down with excitement as we stood on the platform. A train went past pulling a goods carriage he had helped design.

I rushed up to the front of our train to get a photo of the locomotive. All but 300-odd kilometres of the Trans-Siberian route are electrified. That in itself is an amazing achievement. Let alone laying a few thousand kilometres of train tracks through some of the most inhospitable landscape on this planet.

For the train spotters among you it was a Czech Skoda ChS2 (and no, you might ask, it wasn't the ChS4T!). Trainspotting is quintessentially an English pastime. The first anoraks appeared in the 1950s. There are some 500 000 trainspotters in England. Now, I'm not going to say straight out that they're sad bastards, but here are some quotes from the memoirs of a 1950s trainspotter. John Rowe starts out by saying that 'My days spent trainspotting were the best of my life'. Among the many gems were 'the 15-inch gauge line was really something to be seen and never failed to fascinate me' and 'What a fantastic place Bristol Temple Meads was. This was always an exciting day out. You just didn't know what was going to happen next. I saw a 7F there once. It was absolutely marvellous'.

Microsoft even have a 'Trainspotter Log' program. You can 'keep detailed records of all the trains you've seen, including even what you were doing when you saw it' (that could be a bit of a worry. I'm picturing grown men in anoraks with their hands down their pants).

Trainspotting is very new in Russia. It has only caught on in the last few years. Before that, if you were seen taking photos or notes of trains you were sent to Siberia (you'd need a good anorak there). Russian trainspotters back then had secret clubs and would meet in the basements of abandoned buildings.

Km 1816 – I was going to change my clothes but, sod it, I thought. I could never smell as bad as the Russians. I hadn't taken my T-shirt and underpants off for three days (or was it four days? I don't know. I'd lost track of time).

Km 1777 – We passed the obelisk to mark that we were leaving Asia behind and entering Europe. To celebrate, the Matron came into our compartment and vacuumed again. We must have the cleanest carpet on the train.

Km 1431 – I very tentatively made my way to the dining car. I hadn't been there since the Mad Drunk Russian Gunman incident. I didn't even have my bodyguards any more. They'd got off at the last stop. I was the only person in the restaurant. There must have been at least 500 people on this train and nobody ate in the dining car. They all ate in their compartments. The combined smell of BO and dodgy Russian sausages down the carriages was overwhelming.

Sombre organ music was playing as I sat down. The waitress left the carriage almost immediately. There was only me. The music sounded decidedly ominous. It had to be a set-up. They were waiting for me, I was sure of it. The Mad Drunk Russian Gunman was going to burst in any second now and blow me away.

The thing is, I had a lovely time. There was something new on the menu. An almost tasty pork schnitzel (with nine extra chips!) and the most stunning scenery of tall pencil pines frosted with snow. It looked like Christmas (I even asked the waitress if she had Jingle Bells, but she just grunted—Russians are good at that).

Km 600ish – OK. I give up. I've got no idea what the time was. My watch said nine o'clock, but it was pitch black outside. I lay in bed daydreaming about hot showers, clean clothes and a meal that didn't involve peas and pickles.

Last night we passed through the towns of Bum and Perm. I searched the map for their twin towns: Tits and Mullet.

Km 500 – Yee-ha! Only 500 kilometres to go. Akihiro and I celebrated by having a beer that I'd bought at some unpronounceable train station the night before. I didn't know if it was too early to have a beer. I had no idea what the time was.

Km 487– I finally figured out what the time was. It was 9.30 (Moscow time). So my calculations were wrong. The way I'd figured it out, it was 10.30 and we'd been on the train for seventeen days, when in fact it was only four days. Maybe it *was* a little too early for a beer. Or not early enough.

Km 356 – The time had changed again. It was now . . . oh, I give up.

Km 342 – Another Godforsaken town. Black smoke seemed to envelop the whole city. Black soot covered everything. The ubiquitous rows of apartment blocks looked like they were built on top of a rubbish dump. I suppose you don't need a rubbish dump when the whole town is one.

A local train slowly crawled by us. It looked like everyone in the train was off to the Ugliest Person in the World competition. And gee, would the judges have trouble picking a winner!

Km 187 – The Matron came in for one final vacuum. She was humming 'Oh Carol'.

Km 99 – Double figures! I started clapping I was that excited. The train was pottering along. I'd figured out the day before that the train was averaging about 60 km/h (it took me a while to figure it out but, hey, there's a lot of time to fill). If the train had been a French TGV train it would have taken just over a day to do this journey. The TGV travels at an average speed of 300 km/h. The highest speed recorded for a train was on the 18 May, 1990. It was a TGV and it reached 515.3 km/h. If the Trans-Mongolian went that fast, it would take fifteen hours to go from Beijing to Moscow. It took us 132.

Km 94 – After 4000 kilometres of birch and pines, we were treated to a kaleidoscope of autumn colours. The ground was totally covered in a carpet of orange and yellow leaves. Amazing. Russia can be so beautiful one minute and the most horrible hellhole on earth the next.

Km 62 – It only took me 7623 kilometres to be able to go to the toilet without holding onto the rail. And not once did I piss on the window.

Km 49 – The whole carriage smelt of perfume, aftershave and deodorant. The Russians had decided, with 49 kilometres to go, that they wanted to smell nice.

Km 0 – Fittingly, as we crawled into Yaroslavski station in Moscow, Smokie and Suzi were belting out 'Stumblin' in'. I tumbled out of the train feeling like shite. I looked (and smelt) like a Russian. I was dishevelled, unshaven, had greasy hair and I smelt of BO, stale vodka and *borscht*. As I stood on the platform getting my bearings, a drunk Muscovite staggered towards me and threw up on my boots.

Trams, Tuk Tuks & Submarines

There's another book in the modes of transport I'm *yet* to try—or yet to make an exciting journey on (not much happens on the No. 96 tram). Someday, somewhere you'll probably spot me waiting impatiently in the queue for (or haggling for a better deal on) a canoe, hot-air balloon, dog sleigh, barge, pedicab, ice skates, jeepney, submarine, becak, golf cart, song-thaew, paddle steamer, rickshaw, skidoo, bemo, jetski, bamboo-raft, parasail, outrigger, canal boat, tractor, cyclo, tram, rollerblades, horse drawn sleigh, tuk tuk, yak, mule, llama or ostrich ...

I'd like to take this opportunity to thank a few people. First of all, my lovely wife Natalie, who supported me every inch of the way and never once complained about the countless weekends I spent typing away in the study. James Richardson not only added sparkle to my manuscript, but gave me no end of encouragement. My agent, Anthony Williams, who believed in me in the first place. But you still wouldn't have a book in your hands if not for the gang at Allen & Unwin, including Andrea McNamara, April Murdoch, Jemma Birrell, Polly from Perth and the lovely Sophie Cunningham, possibly the best publisher in the world.

If you have any funny transport yarns you'd like to share with my other readers, you can post them on my website at brianthacker.tv. You will also find links to help you buy a helicopter, find out if your plane is going to fall out of the sky, see the aftermath of a motorcycle accident, or post a question on the donkey agony aunt page. Or just drop me a line—you could end up on the opening pages of my next book!